To

Ken Haddix

To a good friend, I hope you
enjoy these annual trips to
Spruce Creek.

Chris Meek

The
HATCHES
MADE SIMPLE

CHARLES R. MECK

The Countryman Press

Woodstock, Vermont

Library of Congress Cataloging-in-Publication Data:
Meck, Charles R.
    The hatches made simple / Charles R. Meck.—1st ed.
       p. cm.
    ISBN 0-88150-558-7
       1. Fly tying. 2. Aquatic insects. I. Title.
    SH451 .M43 2002
    688.7'9124—dc21
                                    2001058357

Cover and interior design by Carol Jessop, Black Trout Design
Cover photographs by David Klausmeyer
Black and white photos by Charles R. Meck
Color photographs of insects by Charles R. Meck
Color photographs of flies by David Klausmeyer
Line illustrations on pages 25, 37, 39, and 41 by Christopher Bell
Maps on pages 151, 228, and 229 by Paul Woodward, © 2002 The Countryman
    Press

Published by The Countryman Press, P.O. Box 748, Woodstock, Vermont 05091

Distributed by W. W. Norton & Company, Inc., 500 Fifth Avenue, New York, NY 10110

Printed in the United States of America

10 9 8 7 6 5 4 3 2 1

CONTENTS

ACKNOWLEDGMENTS

S everal years ago the Cleveland Museum of Natural History Trout Club made me an honorary member. Just recently my son, Bryan Meck, and I gave a talk at the club. At that meeting I was discussing the hatches when it suddenly came to me—in the middle of this talk—why not write a book on this aspect? The very next day I began writing *The Hatches Made Simple*.

Thanks are due to Bryan for his help on the Michigan hex hatch. Bryan traveled several hundred miles (from Rochester, New York) to experience the hex hatch and all of its craziness. He wrote the article on the hex hatch in chapter 6.

I said this in *How to Catch More Trout* and I mean it even more now: Over the past couple of years much of what I've included in this book has been presented at various conferences, workshops, and conclaves. As a result of those talks and encouragement from the audience for more information, I wrote this book. Thanks to Chuck Furimsky and Barry Serviente, who conduct fly-fishing shows in Marlboro, Massachusetts; Somerset, New Jersey; Denver, Colorado; Seattle, Washington; Charlotte, North Carolina; and College Park, Maryland. For nine years they have been kind enough to include me in their great programs.

I've been a frequent contributor to *Pennsylvania Angler and Boating* magazine for more than five years. That publication, issued by the Pennsylvania Fish and Boat Commission, is possibly one of the top publications of its kind in the United States. A lot of the credit for the prestige of that magazine goes to its editor, Art Michaels. Thanks to Art for allowing me to write about the hatches of Pennsylvania many times.

I am also a writer for *Mid Atlantic Fly Fishing Guide* out of Allenwood, Pennsylvania (if you'd like to subscribe, write to Box 144, Allenwood, PA 17810-0144). Mike O'Brien and Jerry Stercho are the editors of this fine periodical. You're missing out if you've not read this great fly-fishing magazine. It has frequent articles on the streams and hatches of Pennsylvania, Connecticut, New York, Maryland, New Jersey, Delaware, and Virginia. Thanks to both men for allowing me to write about many of the hatches in the Northeast.

Thanks also to Gary Hitterman, Shaun Hitterman, and Chip Hidinger, all from Arizona. We get together weekly throughout the winter in Arizona to tie flies and talk. I learn a lot at those fly-tying sessions.

Thanks also to Paul Weamer, a good friend and fellow fly fisher. Paul is one of the finest young fly-tyers I've ever seen. Paul tied all the special spinner and dun patterns for this book. He ties commercially and works for a fly shop near the West Branch of the Delaware River.

Thanks to Craig Josephson for his help with the brown drake on the Yellow Breeches in south-central Pennsylvania. One evening Craig and I, with big butterfly nets, walked around a lighted convenience store in Boiling Springs, Pennsylvania, searching for brown drake spinners. We found some. Craig also was the first to give me the idea for this book. For years he's talked about the gray mayflies of spring. I just expanded on that.

Other people like Jake and Donna McDonald and Jack and Lorraine Cooper have helped tremendously. Jake and Donna operate the Upper Canyon Lodge near Alder, Montana. They have invited me back to their lodge several times. I'll never forget that trip to Labrador. Jack and Lorraine made that trip memorable and an important part of this book. Their camps on the Minipi River produce great memories that last for years and years. Thanks also to Steve McDonald of Doylestown, Pennsylvania, for helping tremendously with the section on Labrador fishing.

Thanks also to Roland Smith, a professional photographer from Philipsburg, Pennsylvania, who is always willing to help.

INTRODUCTION

Those memorable fishing trips—I remember many of them even after 20 years have passed. I still remember that great late-June morning on Henry's Fork in Idaho when I matched a hatch of western green drakes. Trout fed for hours on these large mayflies, and a size 12 pattern matching that hatch caught plenty of fish. What about that early-July float trip on the Kootenai River in northwestern Montana? That unforgettable trip too occurred because we matched a hatch of pale morning duns on a nasty cold, overcast, drizzly day. How about that most memorable of trips on Penns Creek in central Pennsylvania on July 4? That day I caught more than 60 trout by matching a blue-winged olive hatch.

And then there are those fly-fishing trips I'd like to forget. One of those occurred on Pine Creek in north-central Pennsylvania when a brown drake appeared on the surface. It was the first time I'd seen that hatch, and I had nothing that even vaguely copied the natural. For years that hatch and that trip haunted me.

What do all of these fly-fishing trips have in common—both the good and the bad? What do the majority of my noteworthy trips have in common? They center on a hatch of insects on the water, trout rising to them, and a good imitation that matches that hatch. Matching the hatches while trout rose to feed on them made those days memorable.

Predicting when a hatch will appear is always a problem. If you're fishing in the morning in summer, what hatch can you expect to see? What about a summer evening—what can you expect to see at that time? How about a fall afternoon? With a bit of knowledge about the hatches you too can meet and fish them—at any time of year. That was exactly the premise of my first book, *Meeting and Fishing the Hatches*.

But even after myriad books on the hatches have been published, fishing them is still complicated. *The Hatches Made Simple* should help you in several important ways. First, it should help you tremendously with pattern selection by showing you what mayfly colors predominate at the different times of the day and season. Second, it will limit the number of patterns you'll need to match many of the major hatches to a manageable few. Third, it will show you where and when to see many of the more important hatches. Finally, *The Hatches Made Simple* will give you a better understanding of the hatches and how they can help you in your final goal—catching trout.

Before we look into simplifying the hatches, it's important to know just what a hatch is and why it's important. (See chapter 2 for much more information on what constitutes a hatch and why fishing hatches is important.) Have you ever seen trout feed in a rearing pond or hatchery? Have you watched how they feed? Trout are opportunists. When food is available, they gorge themselves. Compare a hatch, or the appearance on the surface of insects, to feeding time at a trout hatchery. The insects that create a hatch can be mayflies, stoneflies, caddisflies, or other aquatic insects—or they can be landborne bugs that have been blown or wandered onto the surface. When a hatch appears, trout also feed voraciously, often continuing until the hatch has ended. During these spurts of feeding activity, trout lose their timidity. They become more aggressive and will readily take a fly pattern that copies the insect or natural on the surface. Of course, the more angling pressure a river or stream receives, the more selective these feeding trout become.

So matching the hatch can work when insects are on the surface and trout are feeding—but it can also work when there is no hatch. For example, if trout are feeding on Hendricksons for an hour or two in the afternoon, a pattern matching that mayfly might be a good choice in the evening or the following morning. Even after a hatch has ended for the season, a pattern matching it might be a good selection. If that's the case, then knowing which mayfly hatches when will help you catch trout.

COLOR OF THE HATCHES

But knowing each hatch can be extremely complicated. There are hundreds of hatches (presently 569 and 680 species in the United States and Canada, respectively) across North America. That's the bad news. The good news is that you don't have to know the hatches—you just have to understand what mayfly colors are common at certain times of year. Look at the streams and rivers of the East, Midwest, or West. In early spring you'll see little blue-winged olives, western March browns, quill Gordons, blue quills, black quills, speckle-winged duns, and Hendricksons. What do these early-season hatches have in common? All the insects have dark gray or dark brown backs.

Why does this happen? Why do mayflies that appear in early spring have dark-colored backs? Look at the surroundings. Once they appear, most of these mayflies rest on stones, rocks, or branches of trees—and in early spring, rocks and trees are generally dark gray or brown. A bright-colored mayfly would stand out and be easy prey for other insects or birds. This is protective coloration at its finest. Another theory is suggested by Fred Arbona Jr. in *Mayflies, the Angler, and the Trout*. He feels that the color of mayflies has a lot to do with absorption of the sun's energy. In spring, when mayflies most need warmth, they're all dark in color. Whichever theory (coloration or sun energy) is correct, the fact is that early-spring mayflies—in all areas of the United States (and for that matter, in other countries also)—are dark brown to gray.

Table I.1 should help you separate the colors of mayflies at different times of

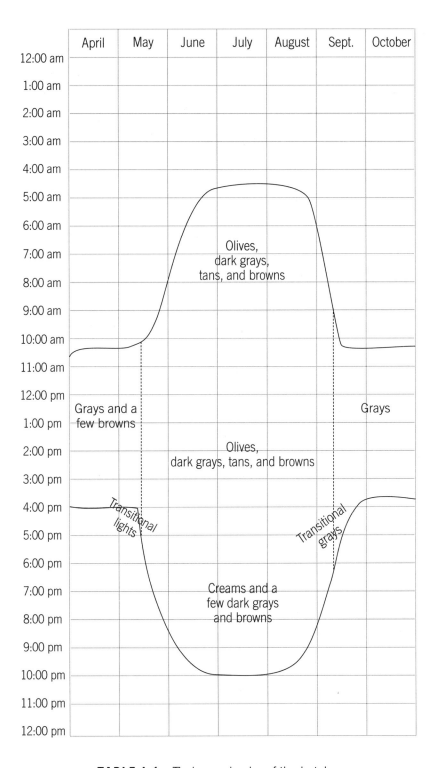

TABLE I.1: Timing and color of the hatches

the year. You'll see two listings in that table—"Transitional Lights" in spring and "Transitional Grays" in fall—that you might not understand. Around the middle of May, sulphurs begin emerging. For the first couple of days, these mayflies usually emerge in the afternoon, just like the grays of early spring. After two or three days of such daytime emerging, however, sulphurs begin appearing just at dusk. In fall slate drakes that had been appearing in the evening begin appearing in the late afternoon.

What about the summer mayfly colors? When do most of the light-colored mayflies appear? Because of their light color, mayflies like the sulphur, light Cahill, yellow drake, and pink lady usually emerge near dusk. *Those insects most visible to predators such as birds and larger insects seem to wait until near dusk to appear.* (In Labrador, however, bird predation doesn't seem to be a problem, and some green drakes emerge in the morning.) From mid-May through August bright colors predominate in vegetation, and light-colored mayflies don't stand out the way they would in early April. You will find a few dark brown and dark gray mayflies—like the brown drake, slate drake, hex (*Hexagenia limbata,* which can be classified as light or dark), and giant slate drake (*Hexagenia atrocaudata*)—emerging on summer evenings, but the majority will be cream or yellow.

Tailwater sections of rivers produce the most exceptions to the premise that cream mayflies emerge in the evening. In these cooler waters some cream mayflies commonly appear in the afternoon. Look at the West Branch of the Delaware (a tailwater) and the Beaverkill (not a tailwater), both in New York State. Paul Weamer says that on the West Branch, the hatch of assorted sulphur duns (*Heptagenia* and other closely related species) is heaviest in the heat of the afternoon in July and August. On the Beaverkill, however, the same hatches appear in the evening, and are less heavy.

With the exceptions noted, some mayflies normally appear on summer mornings and afternoons. What colors predominate then? Those mayflies that appear in midsummer in the morning and afternoon are usually dark in color. Mayflies with gray, dark olive, and dark brown bodies rule the daylight hours at that time of year. These colors are less easy for predators to see. There are very few exceptions. One outstanding exception is the pale morning dun of the West—but not all pale morning duns are pale yellow. I have seen this species (*Ephemerella inermis*) vary in color from dark tan to olive to yellow. Furthermore, I have witnessed many hatches of this species in the evening.

What about fall hatches? When will these appear, and what colors can you expect to see? In fall most mayflies are again dark gray, and many appear in the afternoon.

Let's take this hypothesis one step farther—to Labrador, Canada—and see how the hatches there agree or disagree. Only one major cream hatch, the green drake, appears on the Minipi River system in Labrador. Guess when that one cream hatch appears? You got it—in the evening. The river has plenty of brown, gray, and olive hatches—but most, if not all, of these emerge during the day. The cream mayfly that does emerge in Labrador in the evening has selected the week (hatches begin about July 25) with the warmest temperatures to emerge. Why? If the duns appeared when evening temperatures were cooler, they wouldn't be able to take flight. I experienced such a hatch one evening: Millions of duns were unable to take flight because of temperatures in the 40s.

Can it be any simpler? Dark flies appear in early spring. Cream flies (and a few brown, tan, and gray) appear most often on summer evenings. Olive, gray, and dark brown flies emerge in the morning and afternoon in summer. And finally, as in early spring, fall hatches are mostly gray. That's it—it's that elementary.

Do you need further proof about the colors of mayflies? Look at tables I.2 and I.3. These have been copied directly from *Meeting and Fishing the Hatches,* first published in 1977—they have not been changed in any manner. These tables vividly reveal the color of mayflies at different times of day. Look at the dominant patterns I recommended for the morning and afternoon: Most are dark brown, gray, or olive. And look at the preponderance of light-colored mayflies listed on both tables for summer evenings.

What time of day can you expect see most hatches? Most often, they occur at the most comfortable time of day. What does that mean? In chilly April the "most comfortable time" would be the afternoon; in summer it would be evening or early morning. In fall the most comfortable time of day is again the afternoon. The quill Gordon is a good example. That particular hatch begins appearing on a small north-central Pennsylvania stream, Sixmile Run, in mid-April. I have witnessed fishable quill Gordon hatches there as late as mid-June. In April the hatch most often appears from 1 to 2 PM. In mid-June I've seen the heaviest hatch after 5 PM—the same hatch but different emergence hours because of weather conditions. The spinner of the same species again exemplifies this "most comfortable time" theory. In April the spinner appears over the water to lay eggs shortly after noon. In June I've seen spinners of this same species lay their eggs around 7:30 PM. Tailwaters again mess up this hypothesis. These bottom-release situations mask the real air temperature, and mayflies sometimes appear in the heat of the day.

Study also the brown drake hatch in the United States versus the same hatch in Labrador. In the States the hatch appears near dusk; in Labrador it comes off in the afternoon. (See chapter 8.)

TABLE I.2: Patterns Recommended for Western Rivers.

MORNING	AFTERNOON	EVENING
April		
	Western March Brown—14 Little Blue-Winged Olive Dun—20	
May		
Blue Dun—18 Dark Red Quill—16 Light Rusty Spinner—18 Dark Rusty Spinner—18	Blue Dun—18 Salmon Fly—6 Dark Red Quill—16 Western March Brown—14	Brown Drake—12 Salmon Fly—6 Light Rusty Spinner—18 Dark Rusty Spinner—18
June		

Quill Gordon—12
Western Green Drake—12
Speckle-Winged Dun and
   Spinner—14 or 16
Blue-Winged Olive Dun—14
Pale Morning Dun—16 or 18
Salmon Fly—6
Blue Dun—18
Dark Brown Dun—20
Dark Brown Spinner—20
Dark Blue Quill—16 or 18
Dark Brown Spinner—16 or 18
Pale Olive Dun—20
Pale Morning Spinner—16 or 18
Dark Red Quill—16
	Quill Gordon—12
	Western Green Drake—12
	Speckle-Winged Dun and
	   Spinner—14 or 16
	Pale Morning Dun—16 or 18
	Salmon Fly—6
	Blue Dun—18
	Dark Brown Dun—20
	Dark Brown Spinner—20
	Dark Blue Quill—16 or 18
	Dark Brown Spinner—16 or 18
	Pale Olive Dun—20
	Dark Red Quill—16
		Brown Drake—12
		Salmon Fly—6
		Light Rusty Spinner—18 or 20
		Dark Rusty Spinner—18
		Great Red Spinner—12
		Pale Morning Dun and
		   Spinner—16 or 18

July		

Pale Morning Dun—16 or 18
Quill Gordon—12
Western Green Drake—12
Gray Drake—12
Speckle-Winged Dun and
   Spinner—14 or 18
Blue Dun—18
Dark Brown Dun—20
Dark Brown Spinner—20
Dark Blue Quill—18
Dark Brown Spinner—18
Pale Olive Dun—20 and 24
Dark Brown Spinner—24
Trico Spinner—24
Salmon Spinner—12
Pale Brown Dun—12
Dark Brown Dun—14
	Pale Morning Dun—16 or 18
	Salmon Fly—6
	Speckle-Winged Dun and
	   Spinner—14 or 16
	Western Green Drake—12
	Quill Gordon—12
	Red Quill—14, 16, and 18
	Dark Red Quill—14
	Dark Blue Quill—18
	Dark Brown Spinner—18
		Pale Morning Dun—16 or 18
		Salmon Fly—6
		Ginger Quill—12
		Light Cahill—12
		Pink Lady—12
		Salmon Spinner—12
		Red Quill—16
		Dark Red Quill—14
		Red Quill—16
		Cream Spinner—16
		Blue-Winged Olive Dun—14

MORNING	AFTERNOON	EVENING

August

MORNING	AFTERNOON	EVENING
Dark Blue Quill—18	Dark Blue Quill—18	Pale Evening Dun—14
Dark Brown Spinner—18	Dark Brown Spinner—18	Gray Fox—14
Gray Drake—12	Gray Drake—12	Pale Evening Spinner—14
Pale Olive Dun—20 and 24	Blue Dun—18 or 20	Ginger Quill—14
Trico Spinner—24	Red Quill—14 and 16	Brown Quill Spinner—12
Dark Brown Spinner—24	Pale Morning Dun—16 or 18	Cream Spinner—16
Pale Morning Dun—16 or 18	Gray Fox—14	Gray Fox—14
Ginger Quill—14		
Red Quill—14 or 16		

September

MORNING	AFTERNOON	EVENING
Dark Blue Quill—18	Gray Fox—14	Gray Fox—14
Dark Brown Spinner—18 and 24	Pale Evening Dun—14	Ginger Quill—14
Blue Dun—18 and 20	Dark Blue Quill–18	Brown Quill Spinner—12
Pale Olive Dun—24	Blue Dun—18 and 20	Dark Rusty Spinner—20
Trico Spinner—24	Dark Brown Spinner—18	Pale Evening Spinner–14
Speckle-Winged Dun and Spinner—14 or 16	Speckle-Winged Dun and Spinner—14 and 16	Cream Spinner—16
Ginger Quill—14		

October

MORNING	AFTERNOON	EVENING
Trico—20–24	October Caddis—6–10	

How Many Hatches Can You See?

Many anglers tell me that I spend too much time talking about the hatches and how important they are. Many say they've never seen a hatch. They complain that they've been fishing a short while and never seen insects on the surface. Read this note I received from a beginning fly-fisher:

Dear Mr. Meck,
I don't know if you will remember this or not but it was a turning point in my life that I will never forget. Six years ago a friend and I read your book on Pennsylvania trout streams and decided that we had to take a trip and try fly-fishing for trout. At the time I was living in Columbus, Ohio, and my friend, Robert Johnson, and I were avid smallmouth bass fishermen. Ohio has very little trout water and Robert and I had limited experience on fly-rods so we had never really done any trout fishing. We read your book cover to cover and somehow came up with Slate Run as the best trout water in the state. We set out the first week of June and camped up on the Francis Branch of Slate Run.

The Minipi River in Labrador with an angler getting ready for the green drake hatch

The first day I think we were so excited that we were on the water fishing an hour before it got light. We fished all day without a break and didn't bring in the first fish. By the end of the day we were completely disgusted and ready to go home. We thought we had made a huge mistake. That night we were sitting on the steel one-lane bridge just upstream (Pine Creek) from Slate Run contemplating what to do when a guy came up and asked us how the fishing was. We gave him our whole sob story and told him that this book had really led us on a wild goose chase. I don't know if it was just fate or an act of God but that guy was you. You showed us all the green drakes in the air and said, "Get your stuff and meet me down at the water." Robert and I couldn't move fast enough. We didn't know what a green drake was but if you thought it was good we were all for it. You showed us where to fish and what to fish with and even gave us some flies . . . I still have the Patriot you gave me. We were catching fish until well after dark.

I have since moved to Kentucky. I wouldn't say it comes close to Pennsylvania as far as trout water goes but it was a huge step up from Ohio. Robert still lives in Ohio. We have gone back to Slate Run that same week every year since. We gave up the camping a couple of years ago and started spending the week at Hotel Manor. It gets better every year we are there. We plan on going that same week every year until we can't do it anymore. I can't imagine what would have happened to us if you hadn't happened along that night . . . I probably would have given up fly-fishing all together. Robert and I have told that story in Slate Run so many times that we have actually had people that we don't know come up to us and ask to hear the "Meck" story. I have always wanted to tell you thanks. I can't think of any one event that had such an impact on my life like those few hours fishing with you did. Thanks again,

Keith Abrams

Keith and his friend had fished all day in late May and never saw a mayfly. They were ready to quit before the hatches and spinners appeared. Since that incident they have become dedicated, avid fly-fishers.

It's also important to know just how many possible hatches you'll be confronted with each time you go fly-fishing. For example, if you plan to fly-fish in mid-March you might see one mayfly hatch, the little blue-winged olive dun (BWOD), in the East and Midwest. If you fish western waters at that time—especially the coastal West—you might see two hatches. That's easy enough: Carry a couple of patterns to match the hatches and you can be fairly confident. Take special note when the peak in the number of hatches appears in the different parts of the country. If you fly-fish streams and rivers in the East and Midwest in late May and early June, you have potentially the greatest number of hatches to match. That peak of hatches on western waters, however, doesn't occur until late June or early July. These two times should be the best time for you to fish a hatch. Table I.2 shows these peaks vividly.

Here's where you're confronted with many decisions. Add to this number the spinners of these species and you see how confusing matching the hatch can be.

PATTERN SELECTION

If you've fished the hatches for any length of time, you already know that trying to match a hatch can be extremely frustrating. How many different patterns do I take with me when I fish the hatches? I carry dozens of fly boxes with thousands of patterns. After that fiasco with the brown drake I'm always afraid that I'll be confronted with a hatch for which I have no match. Furthermore, I've often encountered situations where one pattern copying a hatch catches trout and others supposedly imitating the same hatch don't. There are dozens of Quill Gordon, Hendrickson, and Blue Quill patterns. Which one will be most effective?

This leads to another question: Do you want to match the hatch exactly? Read "To Match or Not to Match the Hatch" in chapter 4.

So what can you do to make pattern selection easier? You can use the *conventional patterns* to match the hatch and copy each and every important mayfly. That's what I do. There are, however, other ways you can select a pattern to match a hatch.

Pine Creek in north central Pennsylvania holds the great brown drake hatch.

You can generalize the body, tail, leg, and wing colors and limit your number of patterns to a manageable few. In this book I'll call this limited number (31) of patterns needed to match most duns and spinners *special patterns*. With a third alternative, *restricted patterns*, you'll limit your number of patterns to a very few—in this case five well-known patterns to match the four major colors of mayfly duns—and use those patterns in several sizes to match many of the hatches. You might also select a *suggestive pattern* like the Stimulator. (And when I become frustrated,

I sometimes even try *attractor patterns*.)

You'll find the four colors you need to match the hatches in chapter 10. Also in that chapter, under "Conventional Patterns," you'll find more than 100 fly recipes you can use to match the hatches. Then there's a section devoted to "Special Patterns"—31 flies that will match most of the hatches and spinner falls you'll ever encounter. Finally, there's a section in chapter 10 that I call the "Restricted Patterns"—the Adams, March Brown, Willow Special, Light Cahill, and Blue-Winged Olive Dun. With these five patterns, in several sizes, you can match the vast majority of hatches.

Chapters 5 through 9 feature hatch charts for each season of the year, in the East, Midwest, and West. In these charts you'll see my recommended conventional, special, and restricted patterns. Let's look at two entries in chapter 6, the blue quill (*Paraleptophlebia adoptiva*) and little blue-winged olive dun (*Baetis tricaudatus*).

TABLE I.3: Sample Entries

1. Conventional Pattern Name Dun/Spinner	2. Scientific Name	3. Rating	4. Approximate Beginning Emergence Date (Spinner)	5. Time of Day	6. Size	7. Special Pattern Suggestion Dun/Spinner	8. Restricted Pattern
Little Blue-Winged Olive Dun	*Baetis tricaudatus*	1	March 15	Early afternoon	18–20	1	BWOD
Rusty Spinner		3		Afternoon		12	
Blue Quill	*Paraleptophlebia adoptiva*	1	April 1	Early afternoon	18	3	Adams
Dark Brown Spinner		3		Late afternoon		14	

Look at columns 1, 7, and 8 in table I.3. In column 1 I suggest the conventional match-the-hatch pattern. In column 7 I list a special pattern to match the hatch; as I stated earlier, in all there are 31 of these patterns to match most of the hatches. In column 8 I indicate how to copy many of the hatches with five patterns in several colors. So take your choice. If you want to carry hundreds of patterns in many sizes, like I do, then use the conventional (column 1) method. If you want to limit your number of patterns, you can choose column 7 or 8. Again, you'll see patterns for all three methods in chapter 10.

We'll look at many of the more common hatches and patterns to match them in the following chapters. And I'll try to make it simple. In chapter 4 I'll give you a general description of many of the more common hatches and emergence charts for them. Chapter 4 also has plenty of charts and figures to help make hatch identification and pattern selection easier.

Chapters 5 through 9 hold a wealth of information like hatch charts and pattern suggestions. Study these charts carefully.

In chapter 5 we'll examine the early-spring hatches—gray hatches and gray flies. I'll tell you where you can find these hatches, when they appear, and even suggest some patterns that match more than one hatch.

Chapter 6 examines the summer morning and afternoon hatches found on streams across the United States. As I mentioned already, the hatches found at this time of year are largely gray or olive. I'll list a few patterns that match most of them. Summer evenings hold plenty of mayfly hatches, and many of these are light in color. In chapter 7 we'll look at these cream-, white-, yellow-, and pink-bodied mayflies.

There are some notable exceptions to the rule that cream mayflies emerge on summer evenings. Important dark mayflies including the brown drake and slate drake also appear at this time of day. We'll take a closer look at some of these darker summer mayflies in chapter 8.

When fall arrives hatches again revert mainly to the colors of early spring—gray and olive. That's when the little blue-winged olives reappear, along with slate drakes and blue quills. Chapter 9 looks at the fall hatches.

What about stonefly and caddisfly hatches? Chapter 3 examines the role of these downwings and some easy methods to match these hatches.

Up to this point I've said little about spinners and their role as a source of food for trout. Chapter 2 looks at spinners and an easy way to be prepared for most spinner falls.

How do temperature, and weather in general, affect the hatches? Chapter 11 looks at these considerations. Chapter 12, "A Final Hatch," reviews the basic color patterns found throughout the year.

Have a great trip through the book—and best wishes for a lifetime of fishing the hatches successfully.

1. WHAT TROUT EAT ────

What food items do trout most often eat? Paul Needham completed one of the best studies on this question more than 60 years ago. He examined the diets of the different trout species in May, June, and July, reporting his findings in his definitive book *Trout Streams*. I've condensed some of his findings in tables 1.1 and 1.2.

The figures in table 1.1 include larvae (or nymphs) and adults. (I'll explain the terms *nymph, larva, mayfly,* and *caddisfly* in the upcoming pages.) Brown trout take the most mayflies of any of the three trout species—79 percent. Of the total mayflies taken, *90 percent* were nymphs and only *10 percent* were duns and spinners. (The results would of course differ greatly just after a hatch or spinner fall.) So the most important type of food these brown trout took was mayfly nymphs. As we'll see later, the nymph is the underwater or larval stage of the mayfly. That means a wet fly copying a nymph should generally be more effective than a dry fly—and in fact more often than not the wet fly *will* catch more trout than a dry fly. How am I so certain? I've fished the tandem almost exclusively for more than 10 years. On an average day I'll catch eight or nine trout on the beadhead Pheasant Tail Nymph for every one or two trout I catch on the Patriot dry fly. There are exceptions—I'll never forget that evening on the Pere Marquette River in Michigan when I finally tore off the wet-fly part of my tandem. I resorted to the dry fly only and caught dozens of trout. The dry fly often seems to work best in the evening near dusk.

Table 1.1 shows that mayflies make up 37 percent of a rainbow trout's diet (again, as tested in May, June, and July). Of that total, 77 percent were nymphs and 23 percent adults. Again, since nymphs live underwater, a wet fly should produce more trout than a dry fly.

Mayflies were not as important to brook trout as they were to the other two species. Why? Usually the areas where brook trout occur naturally hold fewer mayflies. Thus mayflies, both adults and nymphs, made up only 17 percent of a brook trout's diet. It should also be noted that the stomachs of the brook trout were checked from April through the following March.

What can you deduce from these findings, and how can this help you decide what pattern to use? As I suggested earlier, a pattern copying a nymph should be more effective more times of the year than a dry fly imitating the mayfly adult.

Downwing patterns (patterns whose wings lie flat over the body, as opposed to the upright wings of mayflies) are used to copy adult stoneflies and caddisflies (see chapter 3). Copying caddisflies especially should be an important part of your repertoire. Take a look at table 1.2: You'll see that, again, trout eat few caddisfly adults. Why? Trout often expend more energy attempting to catch these quick-winged caddis than they can gain by catching the odd one. Trout, like most other creatures, attempt to catch the insects that are easiest and most vulnerable. The adult caddis is difficult to catch, while the emerging pupae and larvae are much easier.

TABLE 1.1: What Different Trout Feed On—Types of Food[+]

Type of Food by Percent*	Brown Trout	Rainbow Trout	Brook Trout
Mayflies	79	37	17.6
Caddisflies	10	19	30
Stoneflies	1	3.3	1.5
Midges	2.5	18	18.5
Terrestrials**	3.3	16.5	23
Alderflies		1	
Other fish	0.3	0.5	0.5
Slugs	1.3	1.1	
Crayfish, scuds, and shrimp	1	1	2.5

+Adapted from Trout Streams *by Needham.*
*Includes both adults and nymphs of midges, stoneflies, caddisflies, and mayflies (see table 1.2 for adults only).
**Includes grasshoppers, beetles, ants, bees, and others landborne insects.*

Let's take a closer look at some of the food items that trout eat.

MAYFLIES

Mayflies make up the largest part of most trout's food. In the entire *life cycle* (the development from an egg to an egg-laying adult) of a mayfly, trout most often eat the *nymph* or *larva*—an insect still in the stage where it lives underwater. Mayflies belong to the family Ephemeroptera. *Ephemeroptera* (it's related to the word *ephemeral*) means "short lived." You'll see in the following description that mayflies live out of water for only one to three days and then they die. The nymphs or larvae and egg of many mayflies live approximately 362 days, however—all underwater.

Many hatch terms may be foreign to the beginning fly-fisher: *hatch, spinner, dun, spinner fall, nymph, natural, life cycle,* and so on. To understand why trout take wet flies, dry flies, and nymphs, though, it's essential to have a basic understanding of the biology of the aquatic insects on which they feed and so come to understand

TABLE 1.2: Percentage of Adults Eaten by Different Trout*

Type of Trout	Caddisfly Adults	Midge Adults	Mayfly Adults
Brown	1.1	2.8	53.9
Rainbow	1.4	15.8	27.7
Brook	4.1	22.1	13.1

*Adapted from Trout Streams by Needham.

these terms. Let's examine a typical life cycle of a mayfly, which for most species is a one-year period. In this time the insect changes from egg, to nymph, to adult, to egg-laying adult before it finally dies.

Female *spinners* mate with male spinners (anglers call the mating stage a spinner; scientists often call it an *imago*) and lay their eggs in one of several different ways. Some sit on the water to deposit the fertilized eggs, others drop the eggs while flying above the water, and still others sit on the water for a short period, deposit their eggs, and then take flight again. Hendricksons, pale morning duns, and sulphurs (all *Ephemerella* species and all in the chart on pages 27–36) carry their eggs in a ball or sac under the female's abdomen and drop them into the water. After depositing their eggs, female spinners die.

The fertilized eggs take several weeks to hatch into nymphs. In some species (like the trico and white fly), eggs that are laid in fall don't hatch into nymphs until the following May—a way of protecting the nymph against harsh winters (see table 1.3).

Nymphs usually live in specific locations in a stream, river, or lake. Some closely related mayflies like the yellow drake, brown drake, and green drake (all *Ephemera* species) burrow in loose gravel. Others, like the big slate drake and all other *Hexagenia* species, burrow in mud or silt. Anglers refer to all of these mayfly nymphs as *burrowers*. They live out their entire life in a burrow, feeding as they grow. Many of the burrowers are large, and when they appear on the surface they create great hatches. *Most burrowers emerge at dusk or dark.*

Light Cahills, quill Gordons, and many others (*Stenonema* and *Epeorus* species in the chart on pages 29– 30) cling to rocks. Because of this we often call these mayflies *clingers*. Most live in moderate to faster water. If you pick up a rock in a riffle on your favorite stream, you should find some of these mayfly larvae. To help them cope with fast-water conditions, clinger nymphs have flattened bodies.

Still others, like the blue-winged olives (some *Drunella* and *Ephemerella* species), live on or in aquatic weeds. These and other nymphs are called *swimmers* and move about freely on the bottom of the stream. Most of these are fast-moving nymphs (like *Isonychia*).

Not only are nymphs specific in their habitat, but many are also particular about the velocity of the water where they live. Slate drakes (*Isonychia*) usually inhabit fast-water sections of a stream. Hendricksons (*Ephemerella subvaria*) are found in all types of water, but yellow drakes (*Ephemera varia*) customarily occupy slower areas, usually pools of a stream. Other nymphs, like the speckle-winged dun (*Callibaetis*), regularly inhabit ponds and lakes.

Mayflies that are alike in physical characteristics and can procreate (breed) are called members of the same *species*. Members of a species (like the Hendrickson) can vary considerably in color and size from stream to stream—and even on the same stream. Sometimes some members of a species are different enough to create an even finer distinction, a *subspecies*.

Although there are numerous exceptions, most mayfly species live underwater for about 362 days as eggs and nymphs. The green drake has a two-year life cycle and lives in a burrow for almost that whole time. As the nymph feeds and grows, it regularly sheds its outer skin, or *exoskeleton*, and develops a new one. Some species—depending on their size and the length of time they live as nymphs—go through five or more of these transformations, called *instars*, as they continue to grow.

Approximately a year after the eggs were fertilized, the nymph is ready to emerge on the surface as an air-breathing mayfly (see table 1.4). When this time arrives, the nymph begins to move toward the surface. A given species can emerge in good numbers as a *concentrated* hatch or appear in fewer numbers over a longer time as a *sporadic* hatch. At or near the surface, the nymph splits its skin dorsally and appears as a mayfly *dun:* an immature, nonmating adult (or *subimago*). There are exceptions, however. Some mayflies, like the white fly female (*Ephoron* species), breed as duns. The process of changing from an underwater insect to an air breathing one often takes time. Anglers often call this stage, the transformation from a nymph to a dun, the *emerger*. It is the most vulnerable part of the mayfly's entire life cycle (except for the dead spinners, of course). Trout sense their prey's defenselessness at this stage and readily feed on nymphs that are changing into duns. The air-breathing mayfly dun rests on the water for anywhere from a split second to several minutes, depending on the species and the weather, before flying away. Abnormally cold weather, especially in spring and fall, delays or prevents the dun from taking flight.

Once the dun has emerged, it has to escape from the surface or die. If it appears on an abnormally cool day, it might not escape, and it will die. Overcast, drizzly conditions often prevent duns from taking off even in midsummer. These conditions are of special importance to the dry-fly fisherman, since they create a hatch. Some species take much longer to transform from nymph to dun. Those species that emerge out of the water (gray drakes and slate drakes) are generally slower changing from a nymph to a dun than are those that emerge on the water's surface. Duns are readily eaten not only by trout, but also by birds like swallows and fly-catchers. In fact, I often look for feeding birds near the surface to determine if a hatch is in progress.

If and when the dun escapes, it flies toward a nearby branch to rest. On extremely cold, miserable days, many duns struggle to reach rocks or debris on the shoreline and rest there. After resting for anywhere from a couple of hours to a day or more, the dun again goes through a change, losing its outer skin to become a *spinner* (also called an adult or *imago*) with glassy, clear wings. This spinner is a mating adult. Most duns that change to a spinner in a couple of hours (like the white fly or *Ephoron,* and the trico) emerge in August. Often, in the evening, male spinners form a swarm over or near the water, waiting for females to join them. The spinner has more choices

Mayfly

than the dun. If the dun appears in cool weather, it might die. The spinner, however, can delay its mating flight for a day or two until better weather appears. When the females enter the swarm, the males impregnate them; the females then move toward the water's surface and deposit their fertilized eggs. Mayflies live out of the water as air-breathing duns and spinners usually less than five days. This is a very generalized description, and there are many exceptions.

When the term *hatch* is used in this book, it usually refers to mayfly duns (although it can refer to stoneflies, caddisflies, midges, and others) emerging on the surface. *Spinner fall* is the time when females (and in some instances males) return to the water to deposit eggs and fall onto the surface *spent,* or with wings outstretched. *Natural* refers to the nymph, dun, or spinner of a species. The *artificial* is the pattern you use to copy the insect.

Some of the Major Mayfly Species
What's the mayfly's place in the animal kingdom? Here's a brief look at where it fits.

Kingdom: Animal (all animals from one celled to human)
Class: Insecta (all insects with three pairs of legs and one set of antennae)
Order: Ephemeroptera (meaning "short lived," this order includes all mayflies)

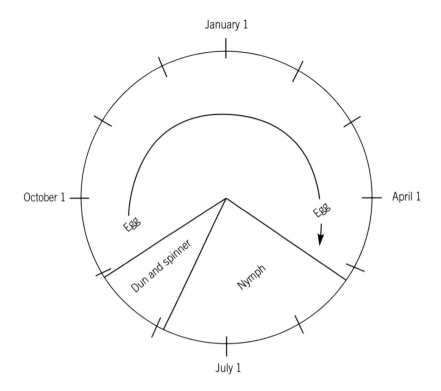

TABLE 1.3. Life cycle of the white mayfly (*Ephron* species). Egg waits until spring to develop into nymph.

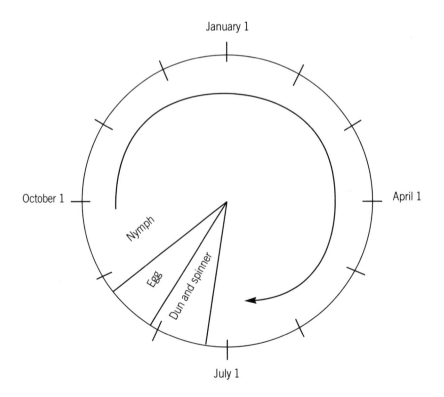

TABLE 1.4: Life cycle of a blue quill *(Paraleptophlebia debilis)*

Family: Ephemeridae (most are burrowing or digging mayflies and are further differentiated by the veins in their wings)
Genus: *Ephemera* (burrowers that have dark shading on their front wing)
Species: *simulans* (called the brown drake by anglers, it is distinguished by its various body parts)

Think of the above chart as a sort of address. Compare it to an address for an individual:

> Planet: Earth
> Country: United States
> State: Pennsylvania
> County: Centre
> Town: Cahill
> Street: Mayfly Drive
> Number: 10

Both the classification and the street address get more specific as they descend. In the case of the classification, the farther you descend the chain, the more alike the animals become.

Let's examine several groups of the more important mayflies. You'll see how they all fit into the scheme of things—and where you can find these hatches. (Please note that "E" represents "East," "M" represents "Midwest," and "W" represents "West.")

I. Burrowers
These mayfly nymphs actually burrow into the substrate and live there for one or more years.

A. Family Ephemeridae

1. Genus Ephemera
These are moderate to large (hook size 6 to 14) burrowing mayflies. The nymph burrows in coarse gravel. Most of these mayfly duns emerge and the spinners fall near or after dusk in late May, June, and July. All have three tails; the wings of the duns and spinners are heavily spotted. These are the famous drake hatches and are common on Penns Creek (Pennsylvania), the Delaware River (New York), the Housatonic River (Connecticut), the Minipi River (Labrador), Silver Creek (Idaho), and Henry's Fork (Idaho). Body colors are cream, yellow, or tan, and duns emerge in the evening.

Some common species:

Ephemera guttulata (E)
This is the famous green drake. It's a large mayfly that emerges near the end of May

and farther north well into June. The dun emerges around 9 PM; the spinner (the coffin fly) usually appears over the stream a day or two later. The tannish gray nymph is a burrowing one and lives underwater for two years before it emerges. See chapter 4 for more information.

Ephemera simulans (E, M, and W)

This, the brown drake, is one of only a handful of mayfly species found in all three regions of the United States. It appears around the same time as the green drake, but usually on any given stream for less than a week. Michigan, Wisconsin, and northern Pennsylvania streams and rivers hold great hatches. Silver Creek and Henry's Fork in Idaho boast heavy brown drake hatches. (See chapter 8 for more information.)

Ephemera varia (E and M)
Ephemera compar (W)

2. Genus *Hexagenia*

These are large mayflies (hook size 4 to 12). The nymph burrows in silt and the duns emerge at or well past dark. These often emerge in enormous numbers in June, July, and August on lakes of the Northeast and the West, and rivers and streams in the Midwest. *Hexagenia rigida* is common in Labrador in late July and early August. *H. munda* (called the brown drake by the locals) is a common hatch in streams like the Yellow Breeches in south-central Pennsylvania and Mossy Creek in Virginia. *Hexagenia* mayflies often have a pale yellow, cream-yellow, or tannish abdomen (belly) and emerge at dusk or after. The wings of the duns are heavily barred; all have two tails (a middle tail is vestigial or barely visible).

Some common species:
Hexagenia limbata (E, M, and W) (see chapter 8)
Hexagenia atrocaudata (E and M)
Hexagenia rigida (E and M) (see chapter 7)

3. Genus *Litobrancha*

These nymphs are often found on small streams—one of the few large hatches to occur on them. Duns often emerge under a heavy canopy in the early afternoon. Native trout in small streams often go on a feeding binge when this hatch appears in late May and early June. The dun has two tails, with just a hint of a middle one. The body is dark gray; duns emerge in the afternoon.

One common species:
Litobrancha recurvata (E and M)

B. Family Potamanthidae

1. Genus *Anthopotamus*

These mayfly nymphs are also burrowers. The adults are fairly large (hook size 10 to 14); they're usually yellow to yellow-orange and often appear on large waters during June and July evenings. The adults all have three tails, and the middle tail in males is somewhat shorter than the outer two. The bodies are cream or orange-cream; duns emerge at night. These are rare on western rivers.

Some common species:
Anthopotamus distinctus (E and M)
Anthopotamus rufus (E and M)

C. Family Polymitarcydae

A family of burrowing nymphs.

1. Genus *Ephoron*

The nymphs are usually gray to grayish tan in color, whereas the adults are almost white. These burrowers often appear near dusk in July, August, and early September. The females (which have three tails) never change from a dun to spinner, but the males (two tails) do. The legs of all of these mayflies are atrophied (stubby). You can identify males in flight because they often carry part of their pellicle (the shuck of the dun) behind them; they resemble little drag-racing cars with parachutes. The mating flight rarely takes place more than 5 feet above the surface. The bodies of the duns are cream to white, and they appear at night.

The eggs of these mayflies usually go into *diapause* (resting stage) once they're laid; they don't develop until the following May.

Some common species:
Ephoron leukon (E and M)
Ephoron album (M and W)

II. Clingers

A. Family Heptageniidae

These are the rock clingers. Look for the dark brown to brownish black nymphs on the underside of rocks in faster water. All adults have two tails, and most are fairly large. Many duns have cream to yellow to light brown bodies.

1. Genus *Stenonema*

These are fairly large mayflies—from size 10 to 16. Most appear in summer at dusk, and are often yellow. Many of the species in this family can be copied with a Light Cahill pattern. All adults have two tails. This genus contains many of the more famous hatches, like the March brown and light Cahill. Bodies are cream to yellow and appear in the afternoon to evening. These are rare on western rivers.

Some common species:

Stenonema vicarium (E and M)

Stenonema modestum (E and M)

Stenonema ithaca (E)

2. Genus *Stenacron*

These are large mayflies (size 12 to 14) that most often appear in early evening in late May and June. The female often has an orange body; the male, a yellow one. All adults have two tails. Duns appear in the evening. They're rare on western rivers.

One common species:

Stenacron interpunctatum canadense (E, M, and W)

3. Genus *Heptagenia*

These are medium-sized mayflies (hook size 14 to 18), most often with a pale yellow or tan body; many have olive reflections on their bodies. The wings of the duns and spinners are heavily marked. Hatches most often occur in the evening, and most of the duns escape rapidly from the surface. Hatches occur in late May, June, July, and August. All adults have two tails. Duns emerge in the evening.

Some common species

Heptagenia elegantula (W)

Heptagenia solitaria (W)

Heptagenia pulla (E and M)

Heptagenia marginalis (E and M)

4. Genus *Leucrocuta*

Recently broken off from the *Heptagenia* genus, these medium-sized mayflies are most often pale yellow in color. Duns usually escape rapidly. Some species appear late in the fishing season and can be important. Duns emerge in the evening.

Some common species:

Leucrocuta aphrodite (E and M)

Leucrocuta hebe (E and M)

Leucrocuta walshi (E and M)

5. Genus *Epeorus*

These medium- to fairly large-sized mayflies are most often dark brown to gray to creamish yellow in color. All adults have two tails. Unlike most other mayflies, some members of this genus split their nymphal skin near the bottom and swim to the surface as duns. Old-fashioned wet flies work well for these hatches. Cream-colored species appear in the evening, and darker species in the afternoon.

Some common species:

Epeorus albertae (W)
Epeorus vitreus (E and M)
Epeorus longimanus (W)
Epeorus pleuralis (E)

6. Genus *Rhithrogena*

Most important *Rhithrogena* species are found in the West. Nymphs are found in fast water. Many of these hatches appear during the day in June, July, and August. One of the most important hatches, however—*R. morrisoni*—appears from February to May, especially on western coastal and near-coastal trout rivers. Most duns are light to dark brown and appear in the morning and afternoon. All adults have two tails (see chapter 4).

Some common species:

Rhithrogena hagani (W)
Rhithrogena futilis (W)
Rhithrogena undulata (M and W)
Rhithrogena morrisoni (W)

7. Genus *Cinygmula*

Most species are found in the West and range in body color from pale brown to dark brown. All adults have two tails; most emerge in the morning.

Some common species:

Cinygmula reticulata (W)
Cinygmula ramaleyi (W)

8. Genus *Cinygma*

Many are light colored and appear on western waters in the evening. They can often be copied with Light Cahill patterns. The duns emerge in the evening.

One common species:

Cinygma dimicki (W)

III. Swimmers and Crawlers

A. Family Ephemerellidae

Until a few years ago all of these genera were placed in the *Ephemerella* genus. Now they have been distributed into several genera. All have three tails and swim freely or live in aquatic weeds. Most are fairly large (size 12 to 18), and many have olive or olive-tinged bodies.

1. Genus *Drunella*

Often these mayfly duns have olive bodies; anglers call them blue-winged olives. Most appear during the day (often around midday), and some can create great hatches in May, June, and July. Spinners often return to lay eggs in the evening and are usually dark olive. Most range in size from 14 to 18 (see chapter 4).

Some common species:
Drunella flavilinea (W)
Drunella cornuta (E and M)
Drunella cornutella (E and M)
Drunella grandis (W)
Drunella doddsi (W)
Drunella walkeri (E and M)
Drunella lata (E and M)

2. Genus *Ephemerella*

This genus contains some of the most famous hatches in the United States, including the sulphur, pale morning dun, and Hendrickson. These mayflies often appear early in the season. All are pale yellow to olive-yellow in color except *Ephemerella subvaria*. The cream- and olive-colored mayflies emerge in the evening, and the darker ones in the afternoon (*E. inermis* and *E. infrequens* are exceptions; see chapter 5).

Some common species:
Ephemerella subvaria (E and W)
Ephemerella invaria (E and M)
Ephemerella dorothea (E and M)
Ephemerella rotunda (E and M)
Ephemerella infrequens (W)
Ephemerella inermis (W)
Ephemerella needhami (E and M)
Ephemerella septentrionalis (E and M)

3. Genus *Timpanoga*

Many of these are also olive in color. They emerge during the day, but are rather small.

One common species:
Timpanoga simplex (E and M)

4. Genus *Attenuella*

Also olive in color, this hatch can be important in the East. The insects emerge in the late morning.

One common species:

Attenuella attenuata (E)

5. Genus *Eurylophella*

These medium-sized mayflies are the typical chocolate duns that appear in late May and early June around midday. Hatches can bring trout to the surface. The species emerges in the late morning.

Some common species:

Eurylophella bicolor (E and M)
Eurylophella funerialis (E and M)

6. Genus *Serratella*

These are small mayflies, some very dark in color.

One common species:

Serratella deficiens (E, M, and W)

B. Family Siphlonuridae

A relatively primitive family. These are large mayflies that often have dark gray bodies.

1. Genus *Isonychia*

These highly mobile nymphs often emerge on exposed rocks in the stream. *Isonychia bicolor* has two generations per year—one emerging in late May and June, the other in September and October. The adults are large and dark brownish gray. The spinners, usually dark maroon in color, are often important in the evening. All have three tails and often appear in the early evening (see chapter 7).

One common species:

Isonychia bicolor (E and M)

2. Genus *Siphlonurus*

These are the gray drakes mainly found in the Midwest and West, and to a more limited extent in the East. They're large mayflies that crawl out of the surface by way of a weed or plant along the stream bank. Duns—often unimportant—generally emerge in the morning. Spinner falls are important in the evening in late May and June in the Midwest and in July and August in the West. All have three tails.

Some common species:

Siphlonurus quebecensis (W)
Siphlonurus occidentalis (E and M)
Siphlonurus mirus (E)

C. Family Amelitidae

1. Genus *Ameletus*

Ameletus species are more common in the West and most are fairly large and dark brown. *A. ludens* appears on eastern waters in April and is *parthenogenic*—the female does not need a male to mate but lays fertilized eggs without his help. You will find few males; most are females. Adults have two tails. They emerge during the day.

Some common species:
Ameletus ludens (E and M)
Ameletus cooki (W)

D. Family Leptohypidae

1. Genus *Tricorythodes*

Members of these small-bodied but extremely important species most often appear in July, August, and September. Some hatches appear almost year-round in the Southwest. Hatches appear and spinners fall most often in the morning; length and time depend on the temperature. All have three tails. The sexes are very different in coloration. Female spinners are white with a dark brown thorax, whereas the male spinner is dark brown. Male duns emerge usually at night, and the female duns at dawn. This is one of the very few male spinners that can be important to copy (see chapter 4).

Some common species:
Tricorythodes allectus (E and M)
Tricorythodes minutus (E, M, and W)
Tricorythodes fictus (W)

E. Family Caenidae

1. Genus *Caenis*

These are extremely small white mayflies (hook size 24 or 26) that often appear in huge numbers in July and August near dark. Spinner falls generally occur in the morning. All have three tails. An unusual number of the members of this genus are found in all three areas of the United States. They emerge in the evening.

Some common species:

Caenis hilaris (E, M, and W)

Caenis anceps (E and M)

Caenis simulans (E, M, and W)

F. Family Metretopodidae

1. Genus *Siphloplecton*

A dark gray mayfly that appears as far north as Labrador. Duns appear in April in the United States and as late as June in Labrador. Duns emerge in the day.

One common species:

Siphloplecton basale (E and M)

G. Family Baetidae

1. Genus *Baetis*

Possibly the most common hatches across the United States, these mayflies are small with two tails and often have more than one brood or generation each year. What they lack in size, they often make up for in quantity. Hatches often occur on miserable-weather days. Many of these species are called little blue-winged olives by anglers. Some are believed to be *parthenogenic* (females can fertilize eggs without a male) at times. Eggs of some species wait until spring to develop into nymphs. Expect to see many of these in spring and fall. The bodies are usually grayish olive; duns often emerge in the afternoon (see chapter 7).

Some common species:

Baetis tricaudatus (E, M, and W)

Baetis levitans (E and M)

Baetis intercalaris (E, M, and SW)

Baetis bicaudatus (W)

2. Genus *Callibaetis*

These fairly large dark gray to dark brown mayflies bear many generations each year. They often begin appearing as early as April, usually in the morning. Look for these three-tailed mayflies to appear in very slow sections of streams and rivers and most lakes and ponds of the West. Hatches most often appear in highly alkaline waters. Adults have two tails (nymphs have three).

Some common species:

Callibaetis skokianus (E and M)

Callibaetis americanus (W)

3. Genus *Plauditus*

Many of these species were once placed in the genus *Pseudocloeon*. I have seen good hatches of *Plauditus veteris* in early October. This and other species can be copied by a Little Blue-Winged Olive Dun. These mayflies have no hind wing. They have olive-gray bodies and appear in the afternoon.

Some common species:

Plauditus veteris (E and M)
Plauditus punctiventris (E, M, and W)
Plauditus virilis (E, M, and W)

4. Genus *Diphetor*

Until recently members of this genus were part of *Baetis*. These are very small, dark mayflies and appear in the afternoon.

One common species:

Diphetor hageni (E, M, and W)

5. Genus *Acentrella*

As with most Baetidae, these are small gray-olive mayflies with several broods each year. Until recently they were placed in the genus *Pseudocloeon*. These mayflies can produce important hatches because they can appear in great numbers. Duns appear in the afternoon.

One common species:

Acentrella turbida (E, M, and W)

6. Genus *Pseudocloeon*

These also are small gray mayflies with more than one generation per year. They're usually copied with Little Blue-Winged Olives or Blue Duns in a size 20 or smaller.

Some common species:

Pseudocloeon dardanum (E, M, and W)
Pseudocloeon propinquum (E, M, and W)

H. Family Lepthophlebiidae

1. Genus *Paraleptophlebia*

One of the most common mayflies of the United States, these are fairly small (size 18) but extremely important as a source of food for trout. Most can be copied with a size 18 Blue Quill imitation. There are 31 species found in the United States. This three-tailed genus is found on small to large trout streams and rivers. Duns are dark gray and appear in the morning and afternoon.

Some common species:
Paraleptophlebia adoptiva (E and M)
Paraleptophlebia memorialis (W)
Paraleptophlebia guttata (E and M)
Paraleptophlebia mollis (E and M)
Paraleptophlebia heteronea (W)
Paraleptophlebia vaciva (W)

2. Genus *Leptophlebia*

Until a few years ago I thought that these insects were found on only marginal trout waters. More recently I've learned that these large dark brown mayflies exist on many small mountain streams in late April. The middle tail is half the size of the outer two. These are fairly large, dark brown mayflies and appear in the afternoon. The nymphs often migrate before they emerge.

Some common species:
Leptophlebia cupida (E and M)
Leptophlebia nebulosa (E, M, and W)

CADDISFLIES

As you can see from table 1.1, caddisflies are second in importance as food for trout. You'll find these mothlike insects on most rivers and streams across the United States. If you glance at table 1.2 you'll note another interesting feature: Few trout take the adult caddisfly. Why? A look at the life cycle will tell us.

Caddisflies (order Trichoptera) and stoneflies (order Plecoptera) are similar to the mayfly in their development. Anglers often call these insects *downwings*

Caddisfly

because of the configuration of their wings (folded down over their back) when at rest. Stoneflies and mayflies, however, lack one stage of the complete insect life cycle and are, therefore, considered to have an *incomplete metamorphosis* (change in form). Caddisflies do pass through this phase, called the *pupa* or resting phase (diapause). This resting period usually lasts several weeks.

Caddisfly larvae, like mayfly nymphs, are specific in the location where they live. Unlike stonefly and mayfly nymphs, however, caddis larvae (remember, larvae are the underwater phase of caddisflies) lack the tough outer protective shell called the *exoskeleton.* Therefore, some caddis (but not all) construct a protective shelter or case made of sticks or stones. Caddisflies can be grouped according to the type of case they build. Some, like the green caddis (*Rhyacophila*), are free swimmers on the bottom and construct no shelter. Other important caddis, like grannoms (*Brachycentrus),* build a case of twigs. Still others build a cover in the form of a net (the little black caddis); the dark blue sedge (*Psilotreta)* makes a case of coarse stone fragments. Inside its case, the larva turns into a pupa. You can often predict what species you'll encounter in a stream by what's available for the larvae to use for cases.

Some caddisflies, like the grannom, can be found in many waters across the United States. The genus *Brachycentrus* creates many of the so-called grannom hatches. (See chapter 3 for more information.)

Some of the More Important Caddisfly Species

A. Family Hydropsychidae

The larvae of this family use silken catch nets as a sort of protection or retreat. Some species create great hatches—often in late May—across the United States.

1. Genus *Symphitopsychae*

These often tan-bodied adults are often called the spotted sedges and appear in numbers in the East and Midwest in late May. They make a silklike net.

One common species:

Symphitopsychae slossanae (E and M)

B. Family Brachycentridae

These larvae live mostly in wood structures, although some members build protection of stones. It's an extremely important family, found across the United States.

1. Genus *Brachycentrus*

This genus creates the famous grannom hatch in the East and Midwest and the "Mother's Day" hatches in the West. Hatches most often appear from mid-April (in the East and Midwest) to mid-May (in the West). Bodies of many of these species are dark brown to black and can be copied with a size 12 to 16, black-bodied downwing.

Some common species:

Brachycentrus americanus (W)

Brachycentrus fuliginosis (E and M)

Brachycentrus numerosis (E, M, and W)

C. Family Rhyacophilidae

1. Genus *Rhyacophila*

Found across the United States, these cad-disflies are often called green caddis by anglers. Since they have no case, in their larval stage they are taken readily by trout.

Some common species:
Rhyacophila lobifera (E and M)
Rhyacophila grandis (W)
Rhyacophila basalis (W)

Stonefly

STONEFLIES

Stonefly nymphs live on underwater rocks. When they're ready to emerge, most of the nymphs swim to an exposed rock or to shore and crawl out of the water to emerge. Therefore, emerging adults are of less importance to trout than are other aquatic families. Still, the nymphs can be a significant source of food, especially when they're migrating toward shore to emerge. You'll note in Table 1.2 that adult stoneflies are omitted completely as trout food. Some of the little black stoneflies, common across the United States in January, February, and March, do become an important food source both as nymphs and as adults.

Some of the More Important Stoneflies

A. Family Capniidae

1. Genus *Capnia*

These small, often black stoneflies often appear nationwide in January, February, and March. Hatches can be heavy on streams and bring trout to the surface even in midwinter.

One common species:
Capnia vernalis (E and M)

2. Genus *Eucapnopsis*

This the great black stonefly hatch of the Southwest. You'll find the insects appearing in January and February.

One common species:
Eucapnopsis brevicauda (W)

B. Family Pteronarcyidae

1. Genus *Pteronarcys*

These are the giant stoneflies and most often appear from late May through much of June and early July. Hatches are much heavier in the West, but on rivers like the Delaware in New York and Wills Creek and Stonycreek River in southwestern Pennsylvania, hatches can be extremely heavy.

Some common species:

Pteronarcys dorsata (E and M)

Pteronarcys californica (W)

C. Family Perlodidae

1. Genus *Isoperla*

This important genus contains the light stonefly found in the East in early May and the yellow stonefly that appears much of June.

Some common species:

Isoperla signata (E)

Isoperla bilineata (E)

D. Family Chloroperlidae

1. Genus *Alloperla*

Many of these stoneflies are small (size 16 to 18) and green in color. You'll find them most often on eastern waters in June.

One common species:

Alloperla imbecilla (E)

2. Genus *Sweltsa*

A very important species on many western waters. You'll find great hatches on Montana's Kootenai and Bitterroot Rivers. Many species are called olive stoneflies.

One common species:

Sweltsa coloradensis (W)

MIDGES

Midges are small insects that spend their larval lives in the water. When they emerge, midge adults or chironomids look like mosquitoes. Midges, mosquitoes, and craneflies are members of the two-winged family of insects, Diptera.

Midges are found on just about every stream and river across the continent. You can see from the tables that midges are extremely important as both wet- and dry-fly patterns. Many of our western rivers—including the Fryingpan and Cache la Poudre in Colorado, the Colorado River in Arizona, and the San Juan in New Mexico—harbor chironomid hatches almost daily throughout the year. Add to these great midge hatches in the East and Midwest

Midge

and you'll see why these small true flies are important to copy. Don't overlook wet-fly patterns like the Zebra Midge, which works on all streams and rivers across the country.

TERRESTRIALS

Those landborne insects that occasionally find their way onto the water's surface are called *terrestrials*. They include beetles, grasshoppers, crickets, ants, jassids, and others. In addition to landborne beetles, there are many aquatic forms of beetles that spend their larval life in water. Terrestrials are of especial importance in June, July, and August. You can often detect a rise to terrestrials; at other times, trout feed on them almost imperceptibly near stream banks in heavily shaded stretches. Note the numbers taken by trout in table 1.1.

CRAYFISH, SCUDS, AND SHRIMP

Members of the orders Decapoda and Amphipoda, crayfish, shrimp, and scuds are important sources of trout food. Trout can feed on these decapods and amphipods any time of the year. Members of these species spend 100 percent of their time underwater. Scuds and shrimp are especially important to trout in limestone or alkaline streams, rivers, and lakes.

Anglers have come up with excellent imitations of crayfish, scuds, and shrimp. Carry a good supply to copy these.

2. SPINNERS ————————————

Spinners can be an important part of a trout's diet. You've learned what a spinner is in chapter 1: an adult mayfly capable of breeding and laying eggs. After mating, spinners often fall dead or dying onto the surface in unbelievable numbers.

On the Beaverkill in New York I've been confronted during many summer evenings by three and four different spinners falling at the same time. Predicting which spinner each rising trout is taking can be frustrating at best. There are four predominant colors in spinner patterns—brown, cream (including white and yellow), dark gray (including black), and dark olive. With various shades of these basic colors you can match most spinner falls. You'll see suggested patterns for the spinners in each chart in chapters 5 through 9. Suggested patterns are listed in chapter 10.

Just when can you expect to see a spinner fall? Are they as predictable as mayfly hatches? Yes, they are. I noted earlier that mayfly duns tend to emerge at the most comfortable time of day. In spring and fall that time is afternoon to early evening. Spinners appear at the same time. In early spring that "most comfortable time" is from noon to 5 PM. Moreover, just about every spinner fall you'll hit at this time of the year will be brown to dark brown in color. Brown spinners reign supreme in early spring.

In summer the most comfortable time of day is early morning and evening, and that's when the majority of spinners fall. On summer evenings you'll encounter two major colors—cream and brown (with a few dark olives and dark grays). In the morning you'll again find mainly brown spinners falling—the pale morning spinner, trico (the male has a dark brown body, whereas the female's is mainly cream), and blue quill (there are 30 species; the female has a dark brown body while the male often has a dark brown tip, with the remainder of his body hyaline or white). In addition, in the West you'll find several species (duns and some spinners) that appear in both the morning and the evening during the summer months. This is possibly a protective device against bad weather.

In fall spinners again appear over the surface in the late afternoon, and once more you'll see spinners with mostly brown bodies. That's it—it's that simple. Table 2.3 shows when to expect spinner falls and what color most of these are.

But weather affects spinner falls possibly more than it does the hatches. I've seen coffin flies, brown drakes, yellow drakes, and other spinners lay eggs and fall onto the surface in the morning; normally these spinners appear on the surface spent in the evening. I've also seen heavy rusty spinner (spinner of the blue-winged olive dun) falls around 5:30 PM in January on the Salt River near Phoenix, Arizona. Cold or rainy weather can shut off a spinner fall. I've seen brown drake (*Ephemera simulans*) and hex (*Hexagenia limbata*) spinners in the air, but they return to trees as the evening cools. On other occasions they're in the trees, and they remain there because of the weather. You'll learn more about weather and other factors in chapter 11.

To tie patterns to match spinner falls, I've included four colors with many shades in chapter 10. A couple of words of caution: What's brown to me might be reddish brown to you. Also, the color of a mayfly can vary from one river to another. We'll look at this further in chapter 11.

BIG SPINNERS VERSUS SMALL SPINNERS

At what time of day do the vast majority of large mayfly spinners mate? If you see a spinner fall in the morning, what size and color will it probably be? These are questions to which you might think there is no answer—but there is. *Most big mayfly spinners (and big mayfly duns) appear in the evening—under the cover of partial light.* There are some exceptions, like the western green drake and some of the blue-winged olives. If mayflies (spinners) appear during the day in summer, they're probably small. If they're large, then they're probably dark. Have a look at the most

TABLE 2.1: Spinner Falls Common on Summer Mornings

Spinner	Hatch	Morning	Afternoon	Evening	Size
Dark brown spinner	*Paraleptophlebia* (30 species)	Yes	Occasionally	Occasionally	18–20
Trico spinner	*Tricorythodes* (several species)	Yes	Occasionally (in September and October)	Rare	24
Pale morning spinner	*Ephemerella inermis, E. infrequens*	Yes	Yes	Rare	16–18
Dark rusty spinner	*Cinygmula reticulata*	Yes	Occasionally	Rare	14

common morning mayfly spinner falls during the summer months in table 2.1.

FISHING THE SPINNER

Warning—what I'm about to say will be sacrilegious to many anglers: If you have no success with your spinner imitation, sink the pattern.

Sink the darn pattern? How does that help? What does that do? Think about it for a second. You're in the middle of a heavy spinner fall and you see only a few trout rising. Why aren't they feeding? Well, if water temperature and other conditions are proper, then the trout just might be feeding under the surface on spinners. If your pattern doesn't seem to be catching trout—whether it's copying a dun or a spinner—try tugging it under the surface.

Have you ever tried fishing directly downstream? I use this technique quite frequently when I'm working spinner falls on heavily fished waters. I make a slack-leader cast with plenty of S-curves in the leader directly upriver from a rising trout. This technique (see the story below about it) seems to work quite effectively, but I tend to miss more trout because I'm pulling the hook out of their mouths.

To prepare for the unexpected, I carry a series of patterns in different sizes and colors. If you follow the suggestions for patterns in chapter 10, you should be prepared for the vast majority of spinner falls.

BUILDING YOUR INVENTORY OF SPINNER PATTERNS

You can match most spinner falls by carrying one box with a series of spinner patterns with you. I first discussed this in *How to Catch More Trout*. If that box holds 64 compartments, here are the recommended patterns to take with you. This selection will match more than 95 percent of the hatches you'll see. For those special spinner falls like the Michigan caddis, carry some special patterns.

You'll find a restricted list of patterns for spinners in chapter 10. To review, restricted patterns are six fairly common patterns that I've designated to copy the spinner of many of the major hatches. In chapter 10 you'll also find recipes for the conventional

TABLE 2.2: Recommended Spinner Patterns*

	Cream (White)	Yellow	Tan	Brown	Dark Brown	Reddish Brown (including maroon)	Dark Olive	Black	Gray
10	X	X	X	X	X	X	X	X	X
12	X	X	X	X	X	X	X	X	X
14	X	X	X	X	X	X	X	X	X
16	X	X	X	X	X	X	X	X	X
18	X	X	X	X	X	X	X	X	X
20	X	X	X	X	X	X	X	X	X
22	X	X	X	X	X	X	X	X	X
24	X	X	X	X	X	X	X	X	X

Adapted from How to Catch More Trout

spinner patterns. Conventional patterns are the normal imitation of each species you fish. Check out table 10.9; the colors listed there will copy the vast majority of spinners. If you'd like to add another color or two, add some spinners with dark gray and maroon bodies. There are plenty of wing materials available. I use organza (from craft shops) or white or gray poly yarn. On some of the larger patterns, I tie in a hackle or two, then clip it off on the top and bottom to form a large wing.

SPOTLIGHT ON SPINNERS

Andre Lijoi of Hanover, Pennsylvania, just completed a memorable day—eight straight hours of fly-fishing over a series of tremendous hatches. On that cold, cloudy late-May day Andre and his friend Jim Herde of Tucson, Arizona, had fished while heavy sulphur and green drake hatches vied for the angler's and the trout's attention. Huge green drakes emerged in respectable numbers for more than five hours. Not once during that entire afternoon and early evening did the two anglers see a lull in the hatches. Just before sunset the three of us met at a heavy riffle and reminisced about the great hatches we had experienced while we made a few final casts into a riffle in front of us. Then it happened—subtle, almost continuous rises just before dark in that riffle suggested that the trout had now keyed in on my old nemesis—spinners. Many of these rises occurred in areas

A male sulphur spinner (*Ephemerella rotunda*)

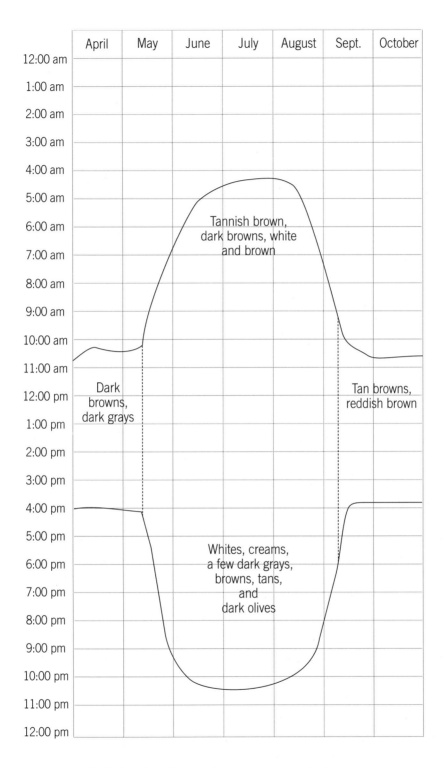

TABLE 2.3: When spinners appear and what color they are

A jenny spinner *(Leptophlebia johnsoni)*

behind submerged rocks where an angler struggles to accomplish the impossible: a drag-free float.

"Spinners," I said, "they're taking spinners." I hurriedly glanced a few feet above the riffle and saw thousands of females laden with bright orange egg sacs. Twenty feet above the same riffle we noticed another layer of larger mayfly spinners carrying out their nuptial flight. Yesterday's sulphur duns transformed into that night's sulphur spinners. Above the layer of sulphurs, ginger quills were ready to take their turn at laying eggs on the surface, then dying spent-winged. The three of us spread out over the riffle and flat water below to fish this added bonus. For the next 45 minutes we had a fitting end to an unbelievable day of matching the hatches.

For the first half of that spinner fall, trout occasionally took our Sulphur Spinner patterns—but only when we floated the imitation perfectly drag-free, and most often when we fished upriver from the risers and let the imitation drift down over them. For many years I have strongly felt that a drag-free float takes on more significance when fishing spinner falls than it does during a hatch of duns. To produce a drag-free float I use a slack-leader cast first developed by the Dean of Fly-Fishers, George Harvey. On the last false cast I stop the fly abruptly, making many S-curves in the leader on the surface. I make the tippet as long as 3 feet to help produce those drag-free floats.

I finally drifted the Sulphur Spinner downriver and began catching a few trout— but as soon as my friends joined me, the trout began refusing the Sulphur Spinner pattern completely. I now noticed a larger spent mayfly on the water and suggested that we switch to a Ginger Quill Spinner pattern. Within minutes after switching to a size 14 Ginger Quill Spinner, Andre caught four trout. Jim fished over several trout rising in the flat water below. Jim felt he could achieve a longer drag-free float on this flatter water than on the pocket water above.

Eventually we had no choice but to leave the river—darkness had completely set in. We had extended our fishing trip by almost an hour fishing two serendipitous spinner falls. For the next two weeks I fished the same riffle several additional times when sulphur and ginger quill spinners fell—each time with good success, as long as I fished the spinner patterns totally drag-free.

Anglers eagerly fly-fish over April hatches like the Hendrickson, blue quill, and black quill, but often overlook the potentially great spinner falls these same insects present. I've witnessed spectacular falls as early as mid-April with the red quill spinner (the spinner of the Hendrickson) and dark brown spinner (the early blue quill). In the Southwest I've fished over great rusty spinner falls on Arizona's Salt River (if the river isn't lowered for water conservation) in January just at dusk.

During the summer you expect to see most falls just at dusk. Not so on these early-season mating flights. Most of these occur in the afternoon or very early evening. Once the Hendrickson or blue quill hatch has first emerged in numbers, you can estimate spinner falls to occur a day or two later, depending on the weather. Other dark brown spinners (all members of the genus *Paraleptophlebia*) that appear

A dark olive spinner with eggs *(Drunella walkeri)*

later in the season seldom produce the concentrated spinner fall that this early species (*P. adoptiva*) does. I've witnessed clouds of dark brown spinners on April afternoons on streams as small as White Deer Creek in central Pennsylvania, and sensational red quill spinner falls in late afternoon on the Delaware River and dozens of other streams and rivers in the Northeast and Midwest.

As I said earlier, it's not uncommon to see more than one spinner fall in progress on a stream. On highly productive streams like the Beaverkill in New York in May or June, you can expect to see several spinner falls at dusk. I've often switched three or four patterns trying to keep up with what spentwings the trout were feeding on. Spinners were once my nemesis—but they're nemesis no more. I've learned a lot about these frustrating mating adults in the past 40 years. In addition to drag-fee floats, taking advantage of the early-season spentwings, and recognizing that more than one spinner fall can occur at the same time, there are several other important principles that you should follow for successful spinner fishing. The first—and this is crucial—is to match the color of the spinner as closely as possible.

Let me explain. I talked earlier about the haunting brown drake spinner fall Jim Heltzel and I witnessed almost 30 years ago on Pine Creek in north-central Pennsylvania. Within minutes of our arrival, I was watching the heaviest spinner fall of my adult fishing life. Hundreds of thousands of brown drake spinners appeared over the stream at the mouth of Cedar Run. In the next half hour I had probably 100 trout rising within casting distance. Trout fed freely on spent female spinners that had just exuded fertilized eggs back into the water, producing next year's generation. I stood awestruck at the spinner fall, but I was unable to match it with any appropriate imitation. Baffled by this unknown mayfly, I tried a March Brown and then a Black Quill, but came up with only one trout. Talk about frustrating fishing trips. When I headed back to the car that evening, I vowed never to be ill prepared for another spinner fall.

Since that trip I've become convinced that the key is matching the color and size of the spent spinner. If you can do this, you'll increase tremendously your chances of success. Even in the half light of dusk, color and size remain important.

Years later I hit spectacular brown drake spinner falls on Silver Creek and Henry's Fork in Idaho. The same species that caused the feeding frenzy in the East appears on these Idaho rivers in great numbers—usually the last half of June. (See a discussion of the brown drake in chapter 8.) I fished those long flat sections so common on the Railroad Ranch area of Henry's Fork. Here spentwings dotted the surface for a couple of hours, and the long flats made it much easier for me to detect and cast to rising trout than had been the case on some of the faster riffles. Here also the spinner fall continued for a much longer time than it did in the East. After my frustrating experience with the drake fall on Pine Creek, I'd come fully prepared

A red quill spinner

for the western counterpart. The very same spinner pattern I finally devised for the eastern spinner fall performed well in the half light of those early-summer nights in Idaho. Several years later that same Brown Drake Spinner pattern would serve me well on Michigan rivers like the AuSable.

When you look at most naturals, the body of the spinner is one color—not so with the brown drake. Matching that gray, yellowish tan body color took several years, but the resulting fly works. You find a unique method for tying this (the Twisted Spinner) and other spinner patterns—including getting those marking on the side of the body—in chapter 10.

Just ask Bob Budd of Altoona, Pennsylvania, if color isn't dramatically important when matching a spinner fall. Many streams and rivers across the United States hold great blue-winged olive dun hatches. Duns often escape rapidly, except on those occasional cold, damp dreary days of early summer when they can't get off the surface. Spinners of several species (*Drunella lata* and *D. cornutella*), however, appear nightly on the surface for several weeks, and trout feed on them freely. For more than a season this hatch frustrated me. I thought I matched the fall with a lifelike size 16 Dark Olive Spinner, but most of the trout refused the pattern. Not until I examined the spinner closely and matched it with an olive-black pattern did I see any success. I mixed 1 part of dark olive to about 10 parts of black to make the correct body color. I handed Bob Budd one of these patterns during a spinner fall, and he too noticed the higher success ratio immediately.

A Montana Bighorn trout caught during a pale morning spinner fall

Another point to remember is that too often, we key on duns on the surface and forget to look skyward to see the tremendous flights of spinners. On many productive streams, look up to 100 feet above the surface for mating flights. With most of the drakes (green, yellow, and brown), males stay near trees along the shore. You can distinguish males from females by the undulating or up-and-down flight of many of the former. With the exception of tricos and some jenny spinners (males of the genus *Paraleptophlebia*), male spinners tend to die away from the stream's surface and are less important than females.

How do you know when a spinner fall will occur? The more you know about the habits of the mayfly hatch you're fishing, the better prepared you'll be. Many duns like the gray drakes of the Midwest emerge sporadically during the day but reappear on the surface as spinners in unbelievable numbers. It's easy to forget that many mayflies emerge sporadically throughout the day without the burst of activity we often associate with hatches. Not only do spinners concentrate their activity at dusk, but they're generally very predictable as well—often you can meet the same spinner fall for several weeks with planned regularity.

One of the Midwest's most important spinner falls evolves from a sporadic hatch. Just ask Dick Pobst, Glenn Blackwood, or Wade Seley about the gray drake spinner fall on Michigan rivers. At one time all three worked at the Thornapple

Orvis Shop just outside Grand Rapids, Michigan. Several years ago all three regularly fly-fished the spinner fall of the gray drake on the Rogue and Pere Marquette Rivers. Dick wrote an excellent book on the hatches—it's a classic. Glenn now operates the Great Lakes Fly Shop in Grand Rapids. The spinner is much more predictable and productive than is the dun. Nymphs usually crawl out of the water on vegetation to emerge. These three anglers, and thousands of others, travel nightly to fish over spinner falls created by this sporadic emerger.

"It's a very predictable spinner—without a doubt it's the most important spinner fall on the Pere Marquette," says Glenn Blackwood about the gray drake. "From mid-May through much of June we arrive at the Rogue or Pere Marquette Rivers just before dusk and we're confident we'll see this tremendous spinner fall."

Has fishing spinner falls frustrated you? Have you had meager success when fishing spentwings? Then remember these simple rules. Make the cast as drag-free as possible; try fishing the spinner imitation from an upstream position; don't overlook those early-season spinner falls; match the color and size of the adult as closely as possible; and remember that sporadic duns can create concentrated spinner falls. Following these few simple rules can lessen some of the frustrations with spentwings.

3. DOWNWINGS

If you've read chapter 1, then you already know how important caddisflies and stoneflies are. Anglers often call these two orders of aquatic insects downwings because of the way the wings lie at rest. You'll find some of the more important stoneflies and caddisflies listed in the charts below. However—and this goes especially for caddisflies—there are hundreds of species with almost identical body, wing, and leg colors. Identification, especially on the stream, can be impossible. Except for a few well-known caddis hatches like the grannom and some of the more important stoneflies like the salmon fly, many downwings remain unidentified. But matching the downwings can be simple—just carry imitations in several colors and sizes, and you can easily match the majority of hatches. You'll see those colors shortly.

Stoneflies have very short tails—caddisflies have none. So don't forget to add a few short tail fibers for patterns if you want to copy stoneflies. Or you can use one of the downwing patterns at the end of the chapter that have wings extending well back over the bend of the hook. These wings can act as a tail and balance the body.

Colors for the downwings? As with mayflies, there are four basic colors with

TABLE 3.1: Downwing Patterns

	6	8	10	12	14	16	18	20
1. Cream				X	X	X	X	X
2. Yellow		X	X	X	X	X	X	X
3. Tan				X	X	X	X	X
4. Brown			X	X	X	X	X	
5. Dark brown				X	X	X	X	
6. Black			X	X	X	X	X	X
7. Olive			X	X	X	X	X	X
8. Olive green				X	X	X	X	
9. Bright green					X	X	X	
10. Dark gray	X	X	X					
11. Light orange					X	X		
12. Dark orange	X	X						

plenty of shades in between. You'll find olive (including green), gray (including black), brown, and cream (including yellow and orange).

I talked about downwings and their life cycles in chapter 1, but let's review it here. Caddisflies (order Trichoptera) and stoneflies (order Plecoptera) are similar to the mayfly in their development. Stoneflies and mayflies, however, lack one stage of the complete insect life cycle and are, therefore, considered to have incomplete metamorphoses. Caddisflies do pass through this phase, however: the pupa or resting phase (diapause). This period usually lasts several weeks.

Stonefly nymphs take one to three years to develop, depending on the species. You'll see different sizes of salmon fly (*Pteronarcys californica*) nymphs on western

TABLE 3.2: Downwing Hatches on Western Streams and Rivers

Common Name	Species	Date	Hook	Time of Day
Little black stonefly	*Eucapnopsis brevicauda*	February–April	16	Afternoon
Little golden stonefly	*Skawala parallela*	April 1	18	Afternoon
Little brown stonefly	*Amphinemura* spp.	April 1	16	Afternoon
Early brown stonefly	*Strophopteryx occidentalis*	May 1	14	Afternoon
Grannom (c)	*Brachycentrus occidentalis*	May 1	16	Evening
Salmon fly	*Pteronarcys californica*	May 20	6	Morning
Little yellow stonefly	*Sweltsa coloradensis*	May 20	16	Evening
Green sedge (c)	*Rhyacophila bifila*	May 20	14	Afternoon and evening
Golden stonefly	*Calineuria californica*	June 1	6	Afternoon
Willow fly (s)	*Hesperoperla pacifica*	June 1	6	Variable
Little yellow stonefly	*Isoperla* spp.	June 5	16	Afternoon
Dark brown caddis	*Arctopsyche grandis*	June 5	14	Morning
Spotted sedge (c)	*Hydropsyche cockerellia*	June 12	12–14	Evening
Green caddis	*Rhyacophila vagrita*	June 15	12–14	Evening
Yellow caddis	*Oecetis* spp.	June 15	14–16	Evening
Brown caddis	*Oecetis* spp.	June 15	14–16	Evening
Golden stonefly	*Hesperoperla pacifica*	June 15	4	Evening
Little sister sedge (c)	*Cheumatopsyche campyla*	July 1	14–16	Evening
October caddis	*Discosmoecus jucundus*	September 10	12	Late morning and afternoon

TABLE 3.3: Hatches on Eastern and Midwestern Streams and Rivers

Common Name	Species	Date	Hook	Time of Day
Little black stonefly	*Capnia vernalis*	February 1	14–18	Afternoon
Early brown stonefly	*Strophopteryx faciata*	April 10	14	Afternoon
Little black stonefly	*Chimarra atterima*	April 20	16	Afternoon
Grannom (c)	*Brachycentrus fulliginosis*	April 22	12–16	Afternoon
Grannom (c)	*Brachycentrus numerosis*	April 22	10–14	Afternoon
Cream caddis	*Psilotreta* spp.	April 25	14	Afternoon
Light stonefly	*Isoperla signata*	May 8	14	Afternoon
Green caddis	*Rhyacophilia lobifera*	May 8	14–16	Afternoon
Dark brown caddis	*Diplectrona modesta*	May 15	12	Afternoon
Spotted sedge (c)	*Symphitopsyche slossanae*	May 23	14	Afternoon
Giant stonefly	*Pteronarcys dorsata*	May 25	8	Evening
Yellow sally (c)	*Isoperla bilineata*	June 1	14–16	Afternoon and evening
Little green stonefly	*Alloperla imbecilla*	June 1	16	Afternoon and evening
Great stonefly	*Phasganophora capitata*	June 1	10	Afternoon and evening
Dark blue sedge (c)	*Psilotreta frontalis*	June 1	14	Evening
Green caddis	*Rhyacophila* spp.	July 1	14	Morning
Autumn sedge	*Neophylax* spp.	September 15	10–14	Afternoon

s = stonefly   c = caddisfly

waters because they take three years to complete their life cycle. When they do emerge, mating usually takes place while they're resting on some surface rather than while they're in flight.

You can see by the brief description of the life cycles of mayflies, stoneflies, and caddisflies that the nymph or larva of a species is available to trout almost every day of the year, whereas the adult is available for only about a few days in an entire year. Nymph fishing by a skilled angler will usually outperform fly-fishing using dry flies—*when there is no hatch*.

Until this chapter I have mentioned little about caddisflies in this book. This order, Trichoptera, might be able to withstand a greater degree of pollution than some other orders of aquatic insects, especially mayflies. You'll find caddisflies

Michigan's Muskegon River holds great September caddis hatches.

emerging from mid-April through October on many waters. On many streams you'll find the heaviest caddis activity from late April until mid-May. I often call this time of the fishing season "caddis time." Usually the early mayfly hatches like the blue quill, quill Gordon, and Hendrickson have ended by early May. For the next two weeks you'll find plenty of downwings appearing.

TANDEM CONNECTION

"The tandem is the best way to fish the emerger," says Tom Finkbiner. Tom should know: He's been helping anglers catch trout on Pine Creek in north-central Pennsylvania during the cream caddis hatch for years. What is the tandem? Western anglers have used this method for years. With the tandem you use a dry fly, then attach a tippet to the bend of the hook of that pattern. I usually prefer a 2- to 3-foot piece of tippet material, depending on the velocity and depth of the water. Tie the wet-fly pattern on the end of the tippet that's attached to the dry fly. I add a bit of weight to the emerger pattern when I tie it to keep it under the surface. Add the weight to the body of the wet fly; don't attempt to add a lead shot to the tippet. When you're fishing a cream caddis hatch, you can then use a high-floating dry-fly caddis and attach a Cream Caddis Emerger (try some with a beadhead) to the tippet. With this method you cover trout coming to the surface *and* those feeding just under the surface. With just a few minutes of practice, you'll find it extremely easy casting the two flies at one time.

Craig Josephson fished the Yellow Breeches in south-central Pennsylvania in late June with an unusual tandem connection. He used a fluttering Green Caddis dry with a beadhead Green Caddis on the point fly. This is an excellent way to fish streams and rivers that hold good caddis hatches. If trout chase the emerger during a hatch, then they'll strike the wet fly; if they're feeding on top, they'll take the dry fly. You can use the tandem in other ways during caddis hatches. If you want to see the floating pattern better, use an attractor pattern like the Patriot or other larger upright winged-type pattern with a caddis emerger or larva tied behind it.

GENERAL TYING INSTRUCTIONS

If you've tied flies for a while, you already know there are many ways to copy caddisflies. With the advent of new synthetics, you can add a Z-lon tail to some of your patterns to suggest the pupal shuck. If you look at the body of a caddisfly, you'll see that it's short and definitely ribbed. Try to do the same with your imitation. Keep each wrap separate to suggest the ribbing, and don't make the body too long.

Shucks have grown in importance recently in fly-fishing. They copy nymphal or pupal cases still attached to the mayfly or caddisfly. Fly-fishers add these to many mayfly patterns. More recently some fly-tyers have begun to add them to their caddisfly patterns. If you include a shuck on some of your caddisfly patterns, you have an added bonus: The shuck, extending back over the bend of the hook, acts as a tail and gives the fly more ballast. I tie most of these shucks with pale tan Z-lon.

I prefer elk hair over deer hair for the wings of most caddis patterns, but the former is not as easy to tie in. When cutting off the hair after tying it in, clip it at an angle so you can add the hackle and complete the head. Elk hair floats well and produces an excellent downwing pattern.

Montana's Madison River in early July holds a great salmon fly hatch.

A fluttering Green Caddis with a shuck

If you add a hackle in front of the wing to produce a fluttering caddis, make certain you add a short one. If you're tying a size 12 Green Caddis, for instance, then use a size 16 hackle. If you use a larger hackle, you might want to clip it off on the bottom.

Many anglers prefer another type of floating caddis pattern. They dub a poly body, then palmer a hackle over it. The famous Henryville pattern features this type of body. Some anglers prefer lower-riding patterns and omit the hackle altogether. Using this last type of downwing, without any hackle, allows you to sink the pattern, if necessary, just under the surface, but it's much less detectable on the surface.

Next time you see a caddis hatch, grab one and examine it. If you look closely at the body, you'll see that it's small and often noticeably segmented. Try to copy the natural as much as possible.

I recently came up with an unusual way of tying downwing patterns. If I want to tie a normal size 14 caddisfly, I use a size 16 hook. Tie in your desired color of poly yarn just a little bit forward of the bend of the hook. Take the other end of the poly and attach it to a hackle pliers. Spin the poly with the hackle pliers about 20 times. Now bring the poly—attached to the hackle pliers—toward the end attached at the shank of the hook. Use a bodkin to make the poly curl where you want it to. The poly will now curl and form a perfect body. Place this as an extended body and tie it in just in front of the bend of the hook. Don't make the extended body too long; if you do, it will constantly twist around the bend of the hook. Next, tie in a bunch of elk hair as a wing. Make certain that this wing is just a tad longer than the body. Since most of the body and the wing are extended, the wing acts as a tail—holding the pattern fairly high and making it much more buoyant.

Try this new method to copy all downwings—it's really an effective way to float the downwing and match the hatches.

TACTICS FOR CADDIS HATCHES

When fishing caddisfly hatches, remember these two principles—movement and depth. *Movement* refers to twitching or skittering the dry fly and twitching the emerging pupa. *Depth* refers to where you're fishing the pattern. If trout refuse your dry-fly pattern, sink it just under the surface. If that doesn't work, try an emerging pattern. Let's examine both tactics in more detail.

Whether it's called the Mother's Day hatch (in the West) or the grannom hatch (in the East and Midwest; there's a story about this hatch later), this member of the genus *Brachycentrus* produces fantastic matching-the-hatch opportunities in April and May. Several years ago I fished a grannom hatch on Spruce Creek in central Pennsylvania in late April. I cast over half a dozen rising trout and had nothing to show for it—all refused my dry fly. In a fit of frustration I lifted my rod tip and moved the downwing across and in front of a rising trout in a skittering motion. At the first movement a brown trout took the pattern. Within half an hour six more trout took that moving pattern. Don't overlook this method, especially if trout have refused a drag-free float.

A Deer Head Black Caddis

While fishing the green caddis on the Little Juniata River one day, I varied the movement of my submerged emerging pupa pattern. I tied on a soft-hackle wet fly and alternated retrieves, fishing one with a dead drift and the next with a twitch or jerking motion. *In more than 500 casts during that particular experiment I caught twice as many trout on the pattern I twitched than I did on the one using a dead drift.* Vary the movement of wet and dry flies when you fish caddis hatches. It works!

In addition to movement, depth plays an important part in fishing a caddis hatch. Unlike mayflies, adult caddisflies usually escape from the surface rapidly. Because of this quick getaway, trout often shun the freshly emerged adults in order to chase the underwater emerging caddis. Trout will on occasion take a dry fly, especially when the adult female comes back to the surface to lay eggs. Adults dive under the water sometimes to lay eggs, and trout feed on them then. Trout often seem to prefer an underwater pattern.

GRANNOMS—EAST AND WEST

Wherever you fish in early to midspring, make certain you carry plenty of Green and Black Caddis patterns—this is the time when the grannom appears in all areas of the United States. Members of this genus vary in size from a 10 or 12 on Penns Creek in central Pennsylvania to a size 14 or 16 to copy the hatch on the Yakima River in Washington. Closely related hatches occur in the East and Midwest from the middle of April to early May. In the West they appear around mid-May. Because of its timing, western anglers call this the Mother's Day hatch. Whatever you call it, this hatch can be one of the most important of the year on many streams and rivers. The genus *Brachycentrus* builds a derricklike wooden structure as a protective case for the larva.

I'll never forget my own first encounter with the western hatch on the Yakima River in central Washington. We fished this great river for a week to produce a video for Kodak. Dave Engerbrettson, a writer from eastern Washington, fished out of one boat, and I fished out of another. Al Novotny of Casper, Wyoming, produced the film; Craig Shuman and Jack Mitchell were our expert guides for the week. (Yes, it took that long to produce a 45-minute video!)

We were in luck: The Mother's Day hatch had already begun and trout were feeding on the surface. No need to dredge them up with a wet fly. As I glanced toward the far shore of this 150-foot-wide river, I saw thousands of adult caddis flying near the bushes. An occasional rainbow took one of the many naturals that inadvertently fell onto the surface.

Dave and I began fishing as soon as we got in the boat. Al Novotny placed his video equipment in a third boat. The minute we began casting Al shouted in a serious tone, "Okay—catch a trout." Evidently the trout were not aware that they were to strike on command.

It didn't, however, take long for Dave to hook up with a Yakima rainbow—and I hooked one shortly thereafter. For the first three days we worked on the video, caddisflies emerged and laid eggs, and we caught plenty of trout on a black down-wing pattern.

Look for this hatch on some of the best western rivers like the Yellowstone and the Bitterroot in Montana. It arrives in April on the Delaware River in New York and on Penns, Big Fishing, Sugar, and Spruce Creeks in Pennsylvania. Sugar Creek in the northwestern part of the state hosts one of the heaviest hatches I've ever seen on a small stream. These eastern hatches usually occur around the middle of April.

Wherever you see this hatch, be prepared with plenty of black-bodied patterns—as well as some olive-green-bodied ones—in sizes 10 through 16.

TAN CADDIS

A size 16 Tan Caddis has taken more trout for me from June through August than any other downwing pattern I've ever used. It has consistently caught trout on such disparate waters as the Firehole River in Yellowstone National Park, Clark Fork near Anaconda, Montana, the Ruby River near Alder, Montana, and the Lackawanna River near Scranton, Pennsylvania.

Nick Nicklas, Jerry Meck, and I fly-fished the Firehole in late June almost a decade ago. As I entered the warm water, I immediately checked the temperature. Even in the nearly 80-degree water, heavy rainbows rose to a number of tan caddis in a riffle entering a sizable pool. Nick, Jerry, and I tied on size 16 Tan Caddis and fished the riffles of this productive trout river. Ten Firehole trout took our downwings on that late-June afternoon.

The Tan Caddis also works exceptionally well on northeastern streams and rivers during the summer. For years many anglers thought of Pennsylvania's Lackawanna River as a cruel joke. Mine acid prevented any trout from living in its lower 10 miles. Abandoned mining, sewage treatment, and other cleanup projects affected this river tremendously in the past three decades. About 20 years ago some local anglers like Jim Misiura discovered some stream-bred brown trout in the river. In the following two decades of fishing the stream, Jim has caught brown trout as large as 24 inches long.

Jim invited me to the river in early June a couple of years ago. We entered the river near the town of Archbald. Just across the river an abandoned mine poured its acid-tainted water into the Lackawanna. How could this section of the river hold any fish? Believe it or not, in front of me two heavy trout rose. Only a few gray fox mayflies appeared that evening, along with a variety of caddis. I relied on my old summer standby—a size 16 Tan Caddis. That caddis pattern landed four heavy Lackawanna River brown trout on a pool-and-riffle section that evening.

The beadhead Olive Caddis works well in the East.

No other pattern I used, including one to match the emerging gray foxes, produced any strikes.

One of the best matching-the-hatch opportunities around comes on Montana's Ruby River in early August with a size 14 or 16 Tan Caddis. If you haven't fished the Ruby lately, you'll probably remember it as a river with little public access. The state has recently bought several additional access sites, however; you can fish a lot of water now that you couldn't just a decade ago.

One morning my son Bryan, Ken Rictor, Lynne Rotz, and I fished a section of the river just upriver from Jake and Donna McDonald's Upper Canyon Lodge. I tied on a Pheasant Tail Nymph, and Bryan used a Beadhead Tan Caddis. In an hour I landed only one small rainbow, while Bryan had caught and released more than 10 trout. Finally I asked him what he was using—and if I could borrow one of his deadly patterns. After I said "please," he finally gave me one. In the next hour I caught 10 trout.

We went back to the river later that day for the evening hatch. By 8 PM thousands of tan caddisflies emerged, and trout went crazy. I used a Tan Caddis dry fly with a Beadhead Tan Caddis behind it. That evening on two occasions I landed two trout on the two flies. What a mess!

For the next week the Tan Caddis downwing worked well on the Ruby River.

SPECIAL DOWNWING PATTERNS

You don't have to match individual caddis- or stonefly species. Just have several body colors in sizes 10 to 20, and you'll copy more 90 percent of the hatches. My favorite way to tie these is to add hackle to the body, Henryville style, and add hackle at the thorax, fluttering caddis style. By adding hackle at both locations, you create a downwing pattern that's much easier to follow. Use the same color hackle for the body and thorax areas.

1. CREAM
Thread: Cream
Body: Cream poly
Wings: Light elk
Hackle: Tan
Hook: Sizes 12–20

2. YELLOW
Thread: Yellow
Body: Yellow poly
Wings: Light elk
Hackle: Cream
Hook: Sizes 8–20

3. TAN
Thread: Tan
Body: Tan
Wings: Light elk
Hackle: Tan
Hook: Sizes 12–20

4. BROWN
Thread: Brown
Body: Brown
Wings: Dark elk
Hackle: Brown
Hook: Sizes 10–18

5. DARK BROWN
Thread: Dark brown
Body: Dark brown poly
Wings: Dark elk
Hackle: Dark brown
Hook: Sizes 12–18

6. BLACK
Thread: Black
Body: Black poly
Wings: Dark elk
Hackle: Dark elk
Hook: Sizes 10–20

7. OLIVE
Thread: Olive
Body: Olive poly
Wings: Medium elk
Hackle: Grayish tan
Hook: Sizes 10–20

8. OLIVE GREEN
Thread: Olive-green
Body: Olive-green
Wings: Medium elk
Hackle: Dark grayish tan
Hook: Sizes 12–18

9. BRIGHT GREEN
Thread: Green
Body: Green poly
Wings: Light elk
Hackle: Tan
Hook: Sizes 14–18

10. DARK GRAY
Thread: Dark gray
Body: Dark gray
Wings: Dark elk
Hackle: Dark gray
Hook: Sizes 6–10

11. LIGHT ORANGE
Thread: Orange
Body: Pale tan with
 orange reflections
Wings: Medium elk
Hackle: Tan
Hook: Sizes 14–16

12. DARK ORANGE
Thread: Orange
Body: Burnt orange poly
Wings: Dark elk
Hackle: Brown
Hook: Sizes 6–8

Conventional Downwing Patterns—East and Midwest

Caddisfly Imitations

Tan Caddis
Thread: Tan
Tail (optional): A light tan Z-lon shuck as long as the shank of the hook
Wings: Brown deer hair or elk hair
Hackle (optional): Tan, cut off underneath
Hook: Mustad 94841, sizes 14–18
Tying Notes: On many of my caddis, I cut some of the hackle off underneath to make the downwing float lower on the surface.

Deer Head Green Caddis
Copies many members of the genus *Rhyacophila*
Thread: Brown
Body: Medium olive-green poly with a gray cast, dubbed
Wings: Medium brown deer hair tied in with the butts pointing toward the bend of the hook and the tips extending out over the eye of the hook. Tie in the hair securely near the eye of the hook, then wind thread one-fourth of the way back toward the bend. Bend the deer hair back and tie it in.
Hackle: If you prefer the regular fluttering caddis, you can tie as above and add a ginger hackle where you tie in the hair. Place a drop of lacquer on the thread and finished head.
Hook: Sizes 14–16

Spotted Sedge
Copies *Symphitopsyche slossanae*
Thread: Tan
Body: Grayish tan poly, dubbed
Wings: Medium brown deer hair
Hackle: Ginger
Hook: Sizes 14–16

Dark Blue Sedge
Copies *Psilotreta frontalis*
Thread: Dark gray
Body: Dark gray poly, dubbed

Wings: Dark grayish brown deer hair
Hackle: Dark brownish black
Hook: Size 12

GRANNOM
Copies many species of the genus *Brachycentrus*
Thread: Black
Body: Dark brownish black poly (with olive reflections; some grannoms are olive-green), dubbed
Wings: Dark brown deer hair
Hackle: Dark brown
Hook: Sizes 12–16

LITTLE BLACK CADDIS
Copies *Chimarra atterima*
Thread: Black
Body: Black poly, dubbed
Wings: Dark-gray-dyed deer hair
Hackle: Dark brown
Hook: Size 16

CREAM CADDIS
Copies some *Hydropsyche* species
Thread: Tan
Body: Creamish tan poly, dubbed
Wings: Medium brown deer hair
Hackle: Ginger
Hook: Sizes 14–16

AMBER CADDIS
Copies some *Neophylax* species
Thread: Tan
Body: Tannish poly with an amber hue, dubbed
Wings: Dark brown elk hair
Hackle: Dark brown
Hook: Sizes 14–18

DARK BROWN CADDIS
Copies *Deplectrona modesta* and many other caddis species
Thread: Dark brown
Body: Dark brown poly
Wings: Dark brown deer hair
Hackle: Dark reddish brown
Hook: Size 12

CADDIS LARVA
Thread: Appropriate color (most often dark brown or black)
Tail: Olive, green, brown, yellow, black, or tan fur, dubbed and ribbed with fine wire; or use a rubber band of the appropriate color, tying it in at the bend of the hook and spiraling it to the eye
Thorax: Dark brown fur, dubbed; or a dark-brown-dyed ostrich herl, wound around the hook several times
Hook: Sizes 12–18

EMERGING CADDIS PUPA
Thread: Same color as the body color you select
Body: Olive, green, brown, yellow, black, or tan fur or poly nymph-dubbing material
Wings: Dark mallard quill sections, shorter than normal and tied in on both sides of the fly, not on top
Legs: Dark brown grouse or woodcock neck feather wound around the hook two or three times
Hook: Mustad 37160, sizes 12–18

Stonefly Imitations
EARLY BROWN STONEFLY ADULT
Copies species like *Strophopteryx fasciata*
Thread: Yellow
Tail: Short dark brown hackle fibers
Body: Dark grayish brown poly, dubbed; or peacock herl, stripped
Wings: Dark brown deer hair
Hackle: Dark brown
Hook: Sizes 12–14

EARLY BROWN STONEFLY NYMPH
Thread: Brown
Tail: Fibers from a brown pheasant tail
Body: Reddish brown opossum dubbing
Wings: Brown turkey
Hackle: Brown
Hook: Size 12

LIGHT STONEFLY ADULT
Copies species like *Isoperla signata*
Thread: Pale yellow
Tail: Short ginger hackle fibers
Body: Pale yellow poly, dubbed and ribbed with tan thread
Wings: Light tan to cream deer hair
Hackle: Ginger
Hook: Sizes 12–14

LIGHT STONEFLY NYMPH
Thread: Tan
Tail: Fibers from a brown-dyed mallard flank feather
Body: Tan fox fur or nymph dubbing
Wings: Light brown turkey
Hackle: Cree
Hook: Size 12

LITTLE GREEN STONEFLY
Copies species like *Alloperla imbecilla*
Thread: Green
Tail: Short pale cream hackle fibers
Body: Medium green poly, dubbed
Wings: Pale gray hackle tips, tied downwing
Hackle: Pale creamish green hackle
Hook: Size 16

YELLOW SALLY
Copies species like *Isoperla bilineata*
Thread: Yellow
Tail: Short cream hackle fibers
Body: Pale yellow poly, dubbed

Wings: Cream hackle tips, tied downwing
Hackle: Cree hackle
Hook: Sizes 14–16

GREAT BROWN STONEFLY ADULT
Copies species similar to *Acroneuria lycorias*
Thread: Dark brown
Tail: Short dark brown hackle fibers
Body: Dark brownish gray poly, dubbed and ribbed with yellow thread
Wings: Dark gray deer hair
Hackle: Dark brown
Hook: Sizes 10–12

GREAT BROWN STONEFLY NYMPH
Thread: Brown
Tail: Light brown hackle fibers
Body: Light brown fur or nymph dubbing
Wings: Brown turkey
Hackle: Light brown
Hook: Size 10

ACRONEURIA NYMPH
Copies many species like *Acroneuria arida*, *A. abnormis*, and *A. carolinensis*
Thread: Dark brown
Tail: Light brown hackle fibers
Body: Dark olive-brown yarn, laid over the top of pale yellow dubbing fur
Wings: Dark brown turkey
Hackle: Cree
Hook: Sizes 10–12

GREAT STONEFLY NYMPH
Copies many species like the common *Phasganophora capitata*
Thread: Tan
Tail: Soft ginger hackle fibers
Body: Dark cream below with darker brown on top
Wings: Mottled turkey quill
Hackle: Cree
Hook: Sizes 8–10

Conventional Downwing Patterns—West

Caddisfly Imitations

Green Caddis
Copies some species in genera *Rhyacophila* and *Cheumatopsyche*
Thread: Green
Body: Green poly
Wings: Brown deer body hair
Hackle (optional): Tan deer hair
Hook: Sizes 14–16

Little Black Caddis
Copies some species in genus *Chimarra*
Thread: Black
Tail (optional): Tan Z-lon shuck
Body: Black poly, dubbed. As an option, you can wind in a dark brown hackle at the bend of the hook and palmer it to the eye. Clip off the barbules on top.
Wings: Dark brown deer or elk hair
Hackle (optional): Dark brown
Shuck (optional): Tan Z-lon
Hook: Size 16

Tan Caddis
Copies many species in the genus *Hydropsyche*
Thread: Tan
Body: Tan poly, dubbed
Wings: Light brown deer hair
Hackle: Tan
Shuck (optional): Tan Z-lon
Hook: Size 14–16

Grannom
Copies many species in the genus *Brachycentrus*
Thread: Black or very dark olive-green
Body: Black or very dark green poly, dubbed
Wings: Dark deer body hair, tied downwing
Hackle (optional): Dark brown
Hook: Sizes 12–16

October Caddis

Copies several *Dicosmoecus* species

Thread: Orange

Body: Orange poly

Wings: Dark elk hair

Hackle: Dark brown

Hook: Sizes 6–8

Stonefly Imitations

Little Yellow Stonefly Adult

Copies species like *Skwala parallela*

Thread: Yellow

Tail: Short cream hackle fibers

Body: Pale yellow to yellowish olive poly, dubbed

Wings: Cream hackle tips, tied downwing

Hackle: Cree hackle

Hook: Size 16

Little Yellow Stonefly Nymph

Thread: Pale yellow

Tail: Pale yellow hackle fibers

Body: Pale yellow angora

Wings: Pale yellow mallard flank

Hackle: Pale yellow hackle

Hook: Size 16

Little Black Stonefly

Copies species like *Encopnopsis brevicanda*

Thread: Black

Tail: Short black hackle fibers

Body: Black poly, dubbed

Wings: Pale gray deer hair

Hook: Size 16

LITTLE BROWN STONEFLY

Copies some species in the genus *Amphinemura*

Thread: Dark brown

Tail: Dark brown moose mane, very short

Body: Dark brown poly

Wings: Gray deer hair

Hook: Sizes 16–18

SIMPLE SALMON

Copies species like *Pteronarcys californica*

Thread: Orange

Body: Burnt orange poly, dubbed

Wings: Dark elk hair

Hook: Mustad 94831, size 8

Tying Notes: Tie the pattern just as you would a size 14 caddis pattern. Dub in poly for a size 14 pattern, then tie in a wing. In front of the first wing dub in some more poly, then another wing, until you've finished at the eye. The final product gives the impression of a continuous wing—not five or six separate patterns.

4. AN INTRODUCTION TO THE HATCHES ———————

W e looked cursorily at what a hatch is in chapter 1. A hatch occurs when a sufficient number of mayflies, caddisflies, stoneflies, or other insects appears on the surface and trout feed on them.

Look at table 4.1, which shows the green drake hatch (*Hexagenia rigida*) appearing on the Minipi River system in Labrador. This particular green drake (some anglers in Wisconsin call *Hexagenia limbata* the green drake; eastern fly-fishers call *Ephemera guttulata* the green drake also) appears on the surface the last part of July and early August in good numbers for seven or eight days. These large mayflies emerge sporadically in the morning and with a heavy burst from 6 to 9:30 PM. The table shows the history of the hatch and estimates very, very roughly the number of mayflies I saw each evening of the hatch.

Look also at the number of 4-pound-plus brook trout caught during the green drake hatch in table 4.1. This is the total number of trout taken by anglers and recorded by the guides. It's very accurate—no cheating on the part of anglers. I said earlier that the hatch usually lasts for about eight days, and it usually takes a day or two for the trout to turn on to a hatch. Once they do, they often feed voraciously on the nymphs, emergers, duns, and spinners. (Don't worry if you don't know these terms yet. You'll find them explained later in this chapter.) The number of these heavy brook trout increased each of the first four days the hatch appeared.

On the fifth day the number of trout caught by the group declined and continued to do so until the hatch ended. Toward the end of the hatch, trout seemed to be satiated and often missed the duns on a rise. Anglers also reported that on the fifth and sixth days, some trout rose for their imitation but missed it. Here's a history of the feeding during the hatch:

1. On the first day trout seemed to acclimate themselves to the hatch. A few rose for the large mayflies.
2. On the second day the trout began feeding.
3. Over the next three or four days the trout fed heavily.
4. Toward the end of the hatch (the fifth day, in this case) trout often bumped the dun and the imitation.
5. For four or five days after the hatch the trout don't seem to feed as much.

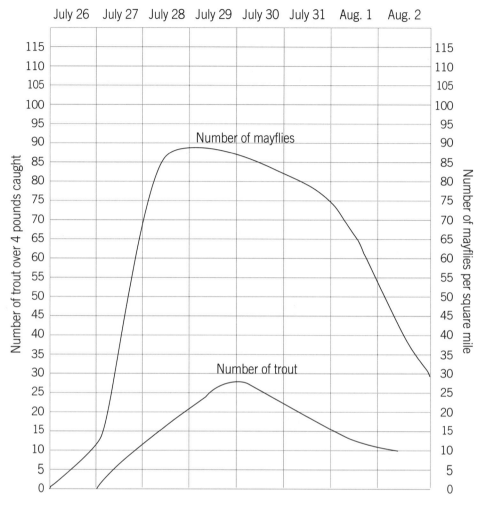

TABLE 4.1: Two charts showing the number of trout caught and a very crude estimate of the number of mayflies *(Hexagenia rigida)* emerging

Trout fed not only on the dun but also on the nymph, emerger, and spinner. This is where anglers often make a critical mistake. They assume that trout feed on the duns only during a hatch when in fact they're often feeding on the nymphs, emergers, and spinners. On several evenings during the green drake hatch, trout quickly switched to the spent-winged spinner on the water. If you're unaware of this changeover, you'll often walk away from a hatch frustrated.

On several evenings during the hatch I noticed that trout chased the nymph. Those evenings, nymphs and emerger patterns worked well. A Stimulator-type pattern called the Laid Back Hex created by Rusty Gates of Michigan seemed to suggest the green drake emerger and produced strikes—especially when I gently twitched it—when no other pattern did.

WHY A HATCH IS IMPORTANT

Why fish the hatches? Look at table 4.2, which summarizes the numbers of brook trout caught over two hatches, the green and brown drakes, at a private lodge in Labrador. In each case eight anglers fished the hatch for an entire week. These figures are quite accurate and do not include any trout caught under 4 pounds.

TABLE 4.2: Fishing a Hatch versus Fishing without a Hatch

Hatch	Number of Trout Caught	Average Number of Trout per Angler
Brown drake	134	16.7
Green drake	131	16.4
No hatch*	35	4.4

Average for four weeks without hatches

Clearly, your chances of catching big trout are much better when a major hatch appears.

Here are some of the reasons why a hatch is important to anglers:

1. Fish are easy to locate—you can sight-fish, because the trout often rise to take the emerger or dun.
2. Matching the hatch can be much more exciting.
3. Fish are feeding and looking up.
4. Fishing a hatch increases your chances of success tremendously.

Of course the most important reason to fish a hatch is that trout are easy to locate. You don't have to prospect for trout during a hatch, because it often shows you where feeding fish are. Still, hatches also have their downsides—like heavy angling crowds.

THOSE SUPERHATCHES—TO FISH OR NOT TO FISH

When easterners think of Yellow Breeches Creek in south-central Pennsylvania, they think of one hatch—the great white fly in August. When they think of Penns Creek in the same state, they immediately recall the green drake hatch. Western anglers often associate Oregon's McKenzie River with the great western March brown hatch it holds in early spring. When they think of the San Juan in New Mexico,

TABLE 4.3: Superhatches across the United States

River	Major Hatch	Other Great Hatches
Fryingpan River, Colorado	Western green drake	Blue-winged olive, PMD, chironomid
South Platte River, Colorado	Trico	PMD
Henry's Fork, Idaho	Western green drake	PMD, blue-winged olive dun, brown drake
Gunpowder River, Maryland	Sulphur	Hendrickson
AuSable River, Michigan	Hex	Brown drake, gray drake, slate drake, trico
San Juan River, New Mexico	Little blue-winged olive	PMD
Bighorn River, Montana	PMD	Trico
Kootenai River, Montana	PMD	Tan caddis
Madison River, Montana	Salmon fly	Many
Missouri River, Montana	Trico	Many
Beaverkill River, New York	Hendrickson	Too numerous to list
Delaware River, New York	Hendrickson	Sulphur, green drake, brown drake
Skaneateles Lake, New York	Green drake (Hexagenia rigida)	Brown drake
Deschutes River, Oregon	Salmon fly	PMD
McKenzie River, Oregon	Western March brown	October caddis
Falling Springs, Pennsylvania	Trico	Sulphur
Little Juniata River, Pennsylvania	Sulphur	Grannom
Penns Creek, Pennsylvania	Green drake	Sulphur, March brown, blue-winged olive, grannom
Spring Creek, Pennsylvania	Sulphur	Trico
Yellow Breeches Creek, Pennsylvania	White fly	Trico
Yakima River, Washington	Grannom	Western March brown
Brule River, Wisconsin	Hex	Brown drake

PMD=pale morning dun

they remember those great little blue-winged olive hatches that seem to emerge much of the year. Ask many midwesterners what hatch they associate with the AuSable in Michigan, and just about everyone will say, "The hex hatch."

Indeed, many of our famous rivers seem to be firmly associated with one or two major hatches. And for good reason: These hatches are often explosive and bring plenty of trout to the surface. They also bring one other important, albeit less positive ingredient—angling pressure. You'll frequently see an unbelievable number of anglers fishing the superhatches. Travel to Penns Creek during green drake time in late May and early June and you'll see conditions that remind you of opening day—almost elbow-to-elbow fly-fishing. Not my idea of a great time! The same crowds—maybe even larger ones—flock to the AuSable in Michigan. Visit one of the fly shops near Grayling, Michigan, during the hex hatch and you'll find dozens of anglers getting ready for an evening on the water. Under these circuslike conditions, trout fishing is almost secondary; the superhatches become huge annual social events.

Anglers will congregate along the river to search out fishable pools hours before the expected hatch appears, comparing notes, discussing what pattern they'll use, and coming up with other strategies. And it's not only mayfly hatches that create such angling carnivals. Stonefly hatches like the salmon fly on the Yellowstone and Madison in Montana and the Deschutes in Oregon create feeding frenzies—and angling pressure. On Washington's Yakima River and dozens of other western rivers, the Mother's Day hatch reigns supreme. This dark caddis, so called because it usually appears in the middle of May, brings out scores of early anglers.

These great hatches are often overrated. Why? First, if you enjoy angling in solitude, you won't find it during many of these well-known, well-publicized hatches. Second, trout become highly selective during these events. Ask anglers who fish over the sulphur hatch on central Pennsylvania's Spring Creek in mid-May. On some days it's almost impossible to catch trout—on *any* pattern. Third, the fishing is often complicated further when trout refuse the hatch you've come to fish (like the green drake) for a smaller fly (like the sulphur). (See "A Mixed Bag on a Summer Day" in chapter 6 for more discussion of this.)

What can you do? First, you can simply avoid these superhatches and the crowds they bring to a river. Rusty Gates often comments about the crowds on the AuSable for the hex hatch, and he adds that the same river holds a great brown drake emergence earlier in the year—yet you'll find fewer anglers there at that time. If you want to fish a certain river, then, choose a time other than during a superhatch. (Unless you want to witness this spectacle—once.)

Second, you can fish a nearby stream or river that hosts the same hatch but with fewer anglers. Rather than fish the green drake on Penns Creek or Big Fishing Creek, for instance, you could try the same hatch on a lesser-known stream. In *Pennsylvania Trout Streams and Their Hatches,* I list more than 60 streams in the commonwealth that hold the same hatch. Why not try one of those?

To Match or Not to Match the Hatch

On the first two evenings of the green drake hatch one year, Steve McDonald and I used patterns that copied the dun almost exactly. We caught trout—but we didn't do as well as we had with Stimulator patterns. When you're confronted with a hatch, here are some questions you should ask yourself.

First, you have to decide what phase or insect the trout are feeding on.

1. Are trout taking the nymph?
2. Are they taking the emerger?
3. Are they taking the dun?
4. Are they taking the spinner?
5. Are they feeding on a different hatch?
6. Are they taking the male or the female (if they're different colors)?

The type of riseform you see will give you a lot of information on what trout are taking. Sipping rises suggest that they're feeding on spentwings. A more explosive rise might suggest that they're chasing a nymph (or a caddisfly) to the surface.

Second, you have to decide what type of pattern to use. Will it be an exact copy of the dun, spinner, emerger, or nymph? Will you use a rough copy of the hatch like a yellow Stimulator pattern? Will you use a White Wulff or another popular pattern like a Light Cahill? Or will you use something completely different from the hatch—an attractor pattern? We'll examine this dilemma in more detail in chapter 10.

Matching the Hatch

I tied a parachute extended-body pattern to match the green drake. When I cast the pattern into a few duns resting on the surface, though, I had trouble distinguishing my pattern from the naturals. My close copies did catch trout, but they often didn't work as well as other patterns.

Stimulator Patterns

One evening, after I had no success with the close imitation, I tied on a pale-yellow-bellied Stimulator type called the Laid Back Hex. That evening five heavy trout took the pattern. Several of them hit it only after I moved it, then stopped and moved it again. That fly worked as well for me as any I tried over the entire week. I'm certain that it looked like an emerger to the trout—and this stage is often the most important.

Attractor Patterns

I often think that a pattern's size is more important than its general coloration. One of my favorite patterns is the Patriot attractor; I've had phenomenal success with this pattern, especially during daylight hours when occasional duns are emerging. One morning during the green drake hatch I tied on a size 10 Patriot and cast over about 15 risers taking duns off the surface. About half of them took the Patriot. Several strikes were definitely refusals, but at least six of the trout struck the pattern. So much for matching the hatch!

Common Popular Patterns

Many of the anglers fishing the hatch opted for the White Wulff. They also caught trout with this popular pattern. A size 8 Light Cahill will also work during the hatch—that is, if the trout are feeding on the duns.

So what does all of this tell you? Be prepared with several patterns for major hatches. And don't ever overlook Stimulator-type patterns during a hatch.

It seems to be more important to fish the proper phase (nymph, emerger, dun, or spinner) than it is to match the hatch. No matter how good your pattern of the dun is, if trout are taking an emerger they'll often refuse it.

NOT ALL HATCHES ARE EQUAL

The majority of hatches that you'll encounter appear for a week or less each year. Mayflies like the green drake (*Ephemera guttulata* and *Hexagenia rigida),* brown drake, and Hendrickson (*Ephemerella subvaria*) usually appear on a stream, river, or lake for about seven days. The summer blue quill (*Paraleptophlebia guttata*) and the trico emerge every morning for two to three months. But a hatch's duration is not the only consideration. The insects' size, the length of time they rest on the surface, the time of day the hatch appears, and how many insects emerge are also important. In the hatch charts you'll find in chapters 5 through 9, you'll see that I've given ratings to the dun and spinner of each important mayfly. These ratings take all of the intangibles into consideration.

HATCH CHARTS AND LIFE CYCLES
Multiple Hatches

Just how difficult is it to match the hatch? That depends on how many hatches appear at the time you're fishing. Take a look back at tables 1.3 and 1.4 in chapter 1. No, hatches don't appear consistently over the fishing season; instead they appear in spurts. All fly-fishers know that early in the season (I term it *early spring* in this book and discuss these hatches in chapter 5) there's an abundance of hatches. I've often encountered two, three, and on several occasions four hatches in one day on a stream. It's tremendously important to remember that this multiple-hatch event can occur—especially in early spring and late May.

The second peak of hatches—late May and early June for the East and Midwest—can also present problems. On any evening at this time of year you can encounter more than one hatch. Often the important hatch—the one trout are feeding on—is masked by another hatch. Look at the green drake and sulphur in the East and the western green drake and pale morning dun in the West. I've often seen trout feeding on the smaller hatches (sulphur and pale morning dun) while anglers, enthralled with the larger drake pattern, were flailing away at the risers with a Green Drake.

I like to take time during a hatch to sit back, study the surface, and see what's happening. I often see trout switch from one hatch to another one (see "A Mixed Bag on a Summer Day" in chapter 6). On one early-spring occasion that I remember vividly, trout fed on little blue-winged olives for more than an hour. I caught trout on a pattern matching that hatch. But then they switched to a second hatch within a matter of seconds. It took me more than half an hour to figure out why the fish had stopped taking my pattern. When I finally switched to a Blue Quill dry fly, I began to catch trout again.

Time of Day the Hatch Appears

As I've mentioned, mayflies generally emerge at the most comfortable time of day. In early spring that means that you'll find most hatches occurring in the afternoon—the warmest part of the day. As summer approaches and temperatures rise, many of the hatches delay their appearance until evening or early morning. Table I.1 in the introduction should help you decide what time to fish and what patterns to use. You'll see there that gray hatches appear on early-spring afternoons, whereas olives appear on late-spring and early-summer mornings. In addition, light mayflies often appear in the evening in late spring and summer.

In mid-May you'll encounter what I call transitional lights, and in fall transitional grays. After the gray hatches of early season have ended, two light hatches—the sulphur and the March brown—begin emerging. For the first few days that the sulphur appears, it often does so in the afternoon. After a couple of days the hatch moves to the evening. The March brown often appears sporadically in the afternoon, sometimes with a spurt at dusk.

In fall you'll encounter the slate drake and several little blue-winged olive duns. I've seen slate drakes appear around 7 PM in late August and as early as 3 PM in early October.

NOTES ABOUT THE EMERGENCE CHARTS

What is a *hatch chart* or an *emergence chart*? It's a list of the most common mayfly, caddisfly, and stonefly hatches that occur on rivers and streams and the time they tend to emerge or appear on the surface. A hatch chart usually contains the scien-

TABLE 4.4: Hatch Chart for Western Streams and Rivers

Dun	Spinner	Species	Date	Hook	Time of Day
Little black stonefly		*Eucapnopsis brevicauda*	February–April	16	Afternoon
Early blue or little blue-winged olive dun	Rusty spinner (early evening)	*Baetis tricaudatus**	January**–December	16–20	Afternoon
Little blue-winged olive dun	Rusty spinner (early evening)	*Baetis intercalaris**	January** –December	20–22	Afternoon
Early blue or little blue-winged olive dun	Rusty spinner	*Acentrella turbida*	January–December	22–24	Afternoon
Western March brown	Western March brown spinner	*Rhithrogena morrisoni*	February–May	14	Afternoon
Little golden stonefly		*Skawala parallela*	April 1	18	Afternoon
Blue quill	Rusty spinner	*Paraleptophlebia memorialis*	March–July	18	Morning
Quill Gordon	Quill Gordon spinner	*Epeorus longimanus*	March–May	16	Afternoon
Trico dun	Trico spinner (mid- to late morning)	*Tricorythodes minutus**	February** –December	24	Morning
Trico dun	Trico spinner (mid- to late morning)	*Tricorythodes fictus**	February** –December	20–24	Morning
Speckle-winged dun	Speckle-winged spinner	*Callibaetis americanus**	April–November	16	Morning
Little brown stonefly		*Amphinemura* spp.	April 1	16	Afternoon
Grannom (c)		*Brachycentrus occidentalis*	May 1	16	Evening
Western green drake	Dark olive spinner (afternoon)	*Drunella grandis*	May–July	12	Morning
Dark brown dun	Dark brown spinner	*Cinygmula par*	May 15	16	Noon
Salmon fly (s)		*Pteronarcys californica*	May 20	6	Morning
Pale morning dun	Pale morning spinner	*Ephemerella inermis*	May 20	16	Morning

Table continues on next page

TABLE 4.4: Continued

Dun	Spinner	Species	Date	Hook	Time of Day
Little blue-winged olive dun	Rusty spinner	*Baetis bicaudatus*	May 20	20	Afternoon
Black quill	Black quill spinner	*Leptophlebia* spp.	May 20	16	Afternoon
Little yellow stonefly		*Sweltsa coloradensis*	May 20	16	Evening
Pale morning dun	Pale morning spinner	*Ephemerella infrequens*	May 20	18	Morning
Dark red quill	Red quill spinner	*Cinygmula ramaleyi*	May 25	16	Morning
Blue-winged olive dun	Dark olive spinner	*Drunella spinifera*	June 1	16	Noon
Blue-winged olive dun	Dark olive spinner	*Drunella flavilinea*	June 15	14	Morning and evening
Pale evening dun	Pale evening spinner	*Heptagenia elegantula*	June 15	16	Evening
Green caddis		*Rhyacophila vagrita*	June 15	12–14	Evening
Yellow caddis		*Oecetis* spp.	June 15	14–16	Evening
Dark brown dun	Dark brown spinner	*Ameletus velox*	June 15	14	Late morning
Quill Gordon	Quill Gordon spinner	*Rhithrogena futilis*	June 15	12	Morning
Pale brown dun	Dark tan spinner	*Rhithrogena hageni*	July 1	14	Late morning
Dark red quill	Red quill spinner	*Rhithrogena undulata*	July 1	12	Late morning
Dark brown dun	Dark brown spinner	*Ameletus cooki*	July 1	14	Late morning
Blue quill	Dark brown spinner	*Paraleptophlebia memorialis*	July 1	18	Morning
Pink lady	Salmon spinner	*Epeorus albertae*	July 1	12	Evening
Brown drake	Dark brown spinner	*Ephemera simulans*	July 1	10	Evening
Cream dun	Cream spinner	*Leptohyphes* spp.	July 1	22–24	Evening
Little white mayfly	Little cream spinner	*Caenis* spp.	July 1	24–26	Evening
Gray drake	Gray drake spinner	*Siphlonurus occidentalis*	July 1	10	Afternoon

*More than one generation each year.
**Early dates refer to hatches in the Southwest.

TABLE 4.5: Hatch Chart for Eastern and Midwestern Streams and Rivers

Dun	Spinner	Species	Date	Hook	Time of Day
Little black stonefly		*Capnia vernalis*	February 1	14–18	Afternoon
Little blue-winged olive dun	Rusty spinner	*Baetis tricaudatus**	April 1	18	Afternoon
Early brown stonefly		*Strophopteryx faciata*	April 10	14	Afternoon
Blue quill	Dark brown spinner	*Paraleptophlebia adoptiva*	April 15	18	Afternoon
Quill Gordon	Red quill spinner	*Epeorus plreuralis*	April 15	14	Afternoon
Dark quill Gordon	Quill Gordon spinner	*Ameletus ludens*	April 18	14	Afternoon
Little black caddis		*Chimarra atterima*	April 20	16	Afternoon
Male dun: red quill Female dun: Hendrickson	Red quill	*Ephemerella subvaria*	April 20	14	Afternoon
Black quill	Early brown spinner	*Leptophlebia cupida*	April 22	14	Afternoon
Grannom (c)		*Brachycentrus fulliginosis*	April 22	12–16	Afternoon
Great speckled olive dun	Great speckled spinner	*Siphloplecton basale*	April 22	12	Afternoon
Grannom (c)		*Brachycentrus numerosis*	April 22	10–14	Afternoon
Light stonefly		*Isoperla signata*	May 8	14	Afternoon
Sulphur	Sulphur spinner	*Ephemerella rotunda*	May 8	16	Evening
Blue dun	Dark rusty spinner	*Baetis cinctutus**	May 8	22	Afternoon
Green caddis		*Rhyacophilia lobifera*	May 8	14–16	Afternoon
Little blue-winged olive dun	Rusty spinner	*Baetis brunneicolor*	May 10	20	Afternoon
Gray fox	Ginger quill	*Stenonema fuscum***	May 15	14	Afternoon and evening
Pale evening dun	Pale evening spinner	*Ephemerella septentrionalis*	May 18	16	Evening

Table continues on next page

TABLE 4.5: Continued

Dun	Spinner	Species	Date	Hook	Time of day
American March brown	Great red spinner	*Stenonema vicarium*	May 20	12	Dun: afternoon Spinner: evening
Pale evening dun	Pale evening spinner	*Leucrocuta aphrodite*	May 20	16	Evening
Sulphur	Sulphur spinner	*Ephemerella invaria*	May 20	16	Evening
Little blue-winged olive dun	Rusty spinner	*Acentrella carolina**	May 20	20–22	Afternoon
Little blue-winged olive dun	Rusty spinner	*Plauditus veteris**	May 20	22	Afternoon
Chocolate dun	Chocolate spinner	*Eurylophella bicolor*	May 22	16	Dun: afternoon Spinner: evening
Spotted sedge (c)		*Hydropsyche slossanae*	May 23	14	Afternoon
Light Cahill	Light Cahill spinner	*Stenonema ithaca*	May 25	14	Evening
Slate drake	White-gloved howdy	*Isonychia bicolor**	May 25	12	Evening
Female: pink lady Male: light Cahill	Salmon spinner	*Epeorus vitreus**	May 25	14	Evening
Light Cahill	Light Cahill spinner	*Stenacron interpunctatum*	May 25	14	Evening
Dark green drake	Brown drake	*Litobrancha recurvata*	May 25	8	Dun: afternoon Spinner: evening
Brown drake	Brown drake spinner	*Ephemera simulans*	May 25	10	Evening
Green drake	Coffin fly	*Ephemera guttulata*	May 25	8	Evening
Gray drake	Gray drake spinner	*Siphlonurus quebecensis*	May 25	10	Dun: day Spinner: evening
Blue-winged olive dun	Dark olive spinner	*Drunella cornuta*	May 25		Dun: morning Spinner: evening
Dark blue quill	Dark brown spinner	*Serratella deficiens*	May 25	16	Evening

Dun	Spinner	Species	Date	Hook	Time of Day
Blue quill	Female: dark brown spinner Male: jenny spinner	*Paraleptophlebia mollis*	May 26	18	Morning and afternoon
Male: chocolate dun Female: olive sulphur	Male: chocolate spinner Female: dark olive spinner	*Ephemerella needhami*	May 30	16	Dun: evening Spinner: evening
Pale evening dun	Pale evening spinner	*Ephemerella dorothea*	May 31	18	Evening
Dark blue sedge		*Psilotreta frontalis*	June 1	14	Evening
Blue-winged olive dun	Dark olive spinner	*Drunella cornutella*	June 10	16	Dun: morning Spinner: evening
Blue-winged olive dun	Dark olive spinner	*Timpanoga simplex*	June 15	20	Dun: morning Spinner: evening
Light Cahill	Olive Cahill spinner	*Heptagenia marginalis*	June 15	14	Evening
Cream Cahill	Cream Cahill spinner	*Stenonema pulchellum*	June 15	14	Evening
Yellow drake	Yellow drake spinner	*Ephemera varia*	June 15	12	Evening
Giant dark yellow drake	Giant dark yellow drake spinner	*Hexagenia rigida*	June 15	6–8	Evening
Pale evening dun	Pale evening spinner	*Leucrocuta hebe*	June 22	16	Evening
Blue quill	Female: dark brown spinner Male: jenny spinner	*Paraleptophlebia guttata*	June 25	18	Morning and afternoon
Golden drake	Golden drake spinner	*Anthopotamanthus distinctus*	June 25	12	Evening
Trico dun	Trico spinner	*Tricorythodes allectus (attratus)**	July 15	24	Morning
Cream Cahill	Cream spinner	*Stenonema modestum*	August 1	16	Evening
Big slate drake	Dark rusty spinner or brown drake spinner	*Hexagenia atrocaudata*	August 1	8	Dark

Table continues on next page

Dun	Spinner	Species	Date	Hook	Time of Day
White fly	White fly	*Ephoron leukon*	August 10	14	Evening
Little blue-winged olive dun	Rusty spinner	*Baetis tricaudatus** *Plauditus veteris**	September 1	20 22	Dun: afternoon Spinner: afternoon and evening
Slate drake	White-gloved howdy	*Isonychia bicolor**	September 1	14	Afternoon and evening
Autumn sedge (c)		*Neophylax* spp.	September 15	10–14	Afternoon

*More than one generation each year   ** Now combined with Stenonema vicatium
s = stonefly c = caddisfly

tific name of the insect along with a common name, the day and time of day it might appear on the surface, and the size of the pattern copying that insect. In tables 4.4 and 4.5 you'll see some of the more common mayflies, stoneflies, and caddisflies and when they appear. Often these insects appear at the same date and time every year. If you've seen brown drakes appear this year on June 10 on the AuSable in Michigan, you can expect to see that same mayfly appear on the sur-

Idaho's Henry's Fork is an insect factory with hatches appearing almost every day of the fishing season.

A sulphur hatch that occurred in midafternoon brought this trout to the surface.

face again next year on approximately the same date. These emergence dates are only approximate, of course, and vary considerably from location to location—especially in the West.

How will these hatch charts help you? They'll give you an approximate time to look for some of the more common hatches and tell you what pattern to use across the United States. All you have to do is to encounter a couple of hatches and see the way the trout feed; you'll be hooked on fly-fishing for life.

See chapter 11 for more information on emergence dates.

We've looked at a lot of information on what trout feed on in this chapter. If you want to become a complete fly-fisher, it's imperative that you learn more about the foods that trout prefer and watch what happens on the stream.

Now let's turn to look at the different times of the year and what hatch colors are most important.

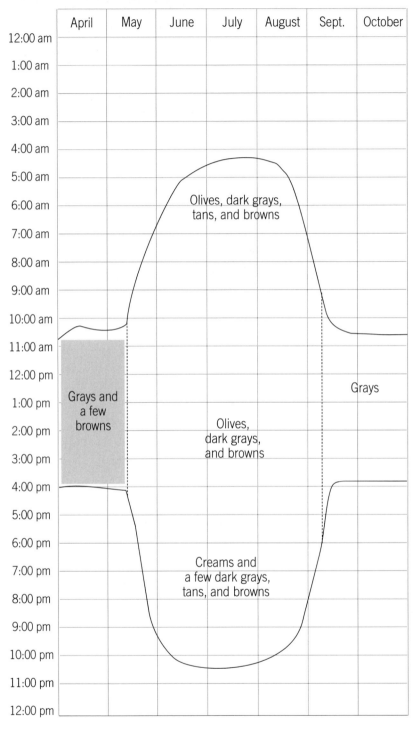

TABLE 5.1: When hatches appear and what color they are.

5. EARLY SPRING— GRAYS

Time of Year: March 1–May 15
When to Be on the Stream: 11 AM–5 PM
Predominant Color of the Hatches: Dark gray and dark brown

Serious fly-fishing season regularly begins around April 1 across much of the country. Yes, many times I fish before this, but the great hatches of spring appear in much of prime trout-fishing country in April and early May. No matter where you fish this time of year, you can encounter hatches. In the West you'll see little blue-winged olives, western March browns, blue quills, speckle-winged duns, and quill Gordons; the East boasts a bevy of heavyweights, including the Hendrickson, blue quill, and little blue-winged olive; in early May the Midwest also holds all the eastern hatches except the quill Gordon.

Even relatively unheard-of mayflies like the great speckle-winged olive (*Siphloplecton basale*) can be of local importance in spring. Just ask the editor of *Fly Fisherman* magazine, John Randolph. John and Jay Nichols, assistant editor, recently fished Clarks Creek near Harrisburg, Pennsylvania, on a mid-May evening. John caught plenty of trout during a fall of the great speckled spinners. He had one of the best fishing days of his life on Pennsylvania waters that evening.

The southwestern part of the United States—including much of Arizona, California, and part of New Mexico—holds great hatches of little blue-wings all year long. Even winter hatches of tricos are very common in this area.

All the hatches you'll encounter at this time of the year have one thing in common—they're dark gray or dark brown. Let's look at this phenomenon and some of the hatches in more detail.

GRAYS, GRAYS, GRAYS

There are two pieces of advice to remember when you fish the hatches in early spring: Fish in the afternoon and look for dark gray to brown mayflies. The vast majority of hatches that occur in late March, much of April, and early May appear in the afternoon; more than 90 percent, in fact, appear on the surface between 11 AM and 5 PM. A word of caution, however: I have seen Hendricksons on the surface as early as 9 AM and as late as 5 PM on unusually hot early-spring days.

Why are gray flies so common this time of year? In chapter 1 we reviewed the life cycle of a typical mayfly. When the dun flies from the surface, it usually lands on a tree, bush, or rock near the stream or river. And what color are the rocks and trees in early spring? Gray or dark brown—the same color as the back of all the emerging mayflies. It's protective coloration: Any yellow-colored mayfly resting on any gray branch or rock would make easy prey for birds or other predators. So over the eons any yellow mayfly that emerged at this time has been eaten. Those mayflies that have survived have dark brown or dark gray backs.

But, of course, it's not that easy. The back and abdomen of mayflies are not always the same color—and at any rate, *it's the belly, not the back, that trout most often see.* The bellies of the early-season mayflies, however, are fairly predictable. Most are dark olive, dark gray, or brown, with one exception—the Hendrickson. The male Hendrickson (called the red quill) has a reddish brown abdomen, and the female a tannish belly (see the discussion below).

Even with the knowledge that most mayflies are dark in spring there are some frustrating dilemmas and decisions you've got to make when you encounter these hatches.

One problem in early spring is multiple hatches: two or more hatches appearing at the same time. On hundreds of occasions I've witnessed not just one hatch the third or fourth week in April, but rather two, and often three hatches appearing concurrently. Dozens of streams and rivers across the Northeast and Midwest contain three April and early-May hatches. What hatches most often make up this multiple-hatch problem? Often you'll encounter little blue-winged olives, blue quills, and Hendricksons emerging at the same time. On one day in April on Big Fishing Creek in central Pennsylvania, I encountered five hatches—in the same afternoon. Around noon a caddis hatch, the grannom, appeared along with some little blue-winged olives. In a few minutes blue quills and quill Gordons emerged, while the first two continued. An hour later trout fed on a tremendous Hendrickson hatch.

On another occasion—on the same stream—I hit a spectacular little blue-winged olive hatch that lasted for more than two hours. I continued to catch trout well into the hatch. After about two hours trout abruptly refused my small dry fly. I glanced at the water's surface and grabbed one of the mayflies riding there: It was a blue quill. I then looked more closely at the surface and saw that blue quills outnumbered little blue-winged olives by 10 to 1. I quickly changed patterns and again caught trout.

When fishing the early-spring hatches—whether it's in the East, Midwest, or West—scan the surface continuously during a hatch for other mayflies. Henry's Fork in Idaho is well known for its overlapping hatches. Many anglers call this pro-

TABLE 5.2: Early-Spring Hatches of the East and Midwest

Conventional Pattern Name** Dun/Spinner	Scientific Name	Rating	Approximate Beginning Emergence Date	Time of Day Dun/ Spinner	Size	Special Pattern Suggestion** Dun/ Spinner	Restricted Pattern**
Little Blue-Winged Olive Dun	*Baetis tricaudatus*	1	March 15	Early afternoon	18–20	1	BWOD
Rusty Spinner		3		Afternoon		12	
Blue Quill	*Paraleptophlebia adoptiva*	1	April 1	Early afternoon	18	3	Adams
Dark Brown Spinner		3		Late afternoon		14	
Quill Gordon	*Epeorus pleuralis*	1	April 10	Early afternoon	14	2	Adams
Red Quill		4		Afternoon		22	
Hendrickson	*Ephemerella subvaria*	1	April 15	Early to late afternoon	14	11	March Brown
Red Quill		2		Late afternoon		22	
Dark Quill Gordon	*Ameletus ludens*	3	April 15	Early afternoon	12–14	3	Adams
Dark Brown Spinner		4		Afternoon		23	
Black Quill	*Leptophlebia cupida*	3	April 15	Early to late afternoon	12–14	3	Adams
Early Brown Spinner		3		Afternoon		23	
Great Speckled Olive Dun	*Siphloplecton basale*	3	April 15*	Early to late afternoon	12	3	Adams
Great Speckled Spinner		2		Early evening to evening		15	
Speckle-Winged Dun	*Callabaetis skokianis*	3	April 15	Afternoon	16	2	Adams
Speckle-Winged Spinner		5		Afternoon		16	

TABLE 5.3: Early-Spring Hatches in the West

Conventional Pattern Name** Dun/Spinner	Scientific Name	Rating	Approximate Beginning Emergence Date	Time of Day	Size	Special Pattern Suggestion** Dun/ Spinner	Restricted Pattern**
Western March Brown	*Rhithrogena morrisoni*	1	February 25	Mid-afternoon	14	13	March Brown
Western March Brown Spinner		4				14	
Little Blue-Winged Olive Dun	*Baetis tricaudatus*	1	Anytime	Mid-afternoon	20	1	BWOD
Rusty Spinner		2				12	
Little Blue-Winged Olive Dun	*Baetis intercalaris*	2	Anytime	Mid afternoon	20	1	BWOD
Rusty Spinner		2				12	
Speckle-Winged Dun	*Callabaetis americanus*	2	April 20	Late morning and afternoon	16	11	Adams
Speckle-Winged Spinner		4				13	
Blue Quill	*Paralepto-phlebia heteronea*	1	May 1	Late morning and afternoon	18	3	Adams
Dark Brown Spinner		3				14	
Quill Gordon	*Epeorus longimanus*	3	May 15	Late morning and afternoon	14	2	Adams
Quill Gordon Spinner		3				16	

**Patterns listed in chapter 10

lific river an insect factory. See chapter 11 for more information on multiple hatches.

There are other things to consider. For one, not all hatches are equal; some are more important than others. That's why I've included the "Rating" column in tables 5.2 and 5.3. I'd much rather fish a Hendrickson or blue quill hatch than a black quill hatch. Why? Hendricksons and blue quills emerge in heavier numbers and seem to stay on the water for a longer time. I've rated the hatches on a scale of 1 to 5 with 5 being the best. Try fishing those hatches that are rated 3 or higher.

Often in spring you're confronted with three more problems: a heavy hatch, no rising trout, and inclement weather conditions. I've been on the Delaware River and dozens of other streams during the height of an early-spring hatch of Hendricksons without seeing a single trout rise. I often switch to a nymph or emerger and try my luck with that. The same event happened one day in mid-April on the McKenzie River in Eugene, Oregon, during a western March brown hatch. Thousands of these mayflies emerged, but only a few trout showed.

Weather conditions in early spring can be downright miserable. I can't recall the number of times I've encountered a gray hatch when temperatures were in the 40s and 50s. Add to that a light drizzle and you'd think the weather couldn't get any worse. If the water temperature is near 50 degrees, however, take advantage of that lousy-weather day. A couple of days after that first float trip down the McKenzie River we hit one of those drizzly, cool early-spring days. That day we caught plenty of trout rising to the hatch.

To match the hatches, what you want is a manageable number of patterns. Tables 5.1 and 5.2 should help. The last column suggests possible patterns for the hatches. You'll find recipes in chapter 10.

There's one problem with many of the patterns you use to match early-season hatches: Most are difficult to see. Maybe this isn't a concern for you yet—but wait a few years. To overcome this problem, I often use a light gray or white wing.

A Look at Some of the Early-Spring Hatches
The Blue Quills of Early Spring

Just my luck—I selected a cold, blustery mid-April day to go fishing. Even by noon the temperature had barely risen above 40 degrees. The leaden skies spewed a few sprinkles that at times seemed to be mixed with a bit of snow. Why waste my time fishing today? Certainly no hatch would appear under these adverse conditions.

I decided to stay for a few more minutes and cast a couple of times in one more riffle. You know the procedure—*just one more cast* becomes *two more casts* and so on. In a few minutes a small mayfly appeared on the surface. Soon that one insect became a dozen, then two dozen, and then a hundred. In a riffle that I had promised myself two casts in, several trout quickly took advantage of this food supply.

I grabbed one of the duns, looked at it, and hurriedly tied on a size 18 Blue Quill to match the hatch. For two hours insects emerged; few took flight because of the cold winterlike conditions. Trout continued to feed for almost the entire emergence period. At one point I had more than 20 trout feeding freely off the surface in my view.

Wow! Was I glad I'd delayed my departure by a few minutes. That blue quill hatch turned the day from a disaster into a memorable experience.

A heavy trout that took an early-season Blue Quill.

It's extremely important to match the hatch when the early-season blue quill appears. Ask Vice President Dick Cheney if he ever matched the blue quill hatch in mid-April in Pennsylvania.

About five years ago I had a call from a Penn State University executive. Dick Cheney was to be a speaker at the university, and he wanted to fly-fish for a day or two after his talk. I had taken him to Spruce Creek the year before, but this time I wanted to show him some public water. We selected Bobs Creek in south-central Pennsylvania as our initial destination. It was the third day of the new season, and as we arrived we were confronted with more than a dozen anglers.

My son Bryan; son-in-law, Rick Nowaczek; and Craig Josephson accompanied Dick and his assistant, Andrew Goldman. Andrew had never fly-fished before, so Bryan showed him the basics while Dick and the rest of us headed upstream. About 1 PM we all met up at a relatively large pool on this small mountain stream. In the water before us at least 14 trout were rising to a hatch that had just begun. Dick looked at me; I suggested he try a size 18 Blue Quill to match the hatch. In the next hour Dick Cheney gave a fly-fishing clinic to all of us. He caught 13 of those 14 rising trout. To this day we affectionately call that pool the "Cheney Pool."

That particular blue quill species—*Paraleptophlebia adoptiva*—is very common throughout the East and Midwest. Hatches in its southern reaches appear as early as late March. In Michigan you'll often see the heaviest, most productive hatches in early May.

There are at least 30 different blue quill species (all members of the genus *Paraleptophlebia*), and most can be copied with one dark gray pattern in sizes 18 and 20. In chapter 1, I said that most mayflies appear at the most comfortable time of day. In spring the most comfortable time of day is the afternoon. In summer it's early morning and the evening; in fall the most comfortable time is, again, the afternoon.

Look how the blue quill species take advantage of the most-comfortable-time-of-day principle: Early-spring hatches (*P. adoptiva* and *P. heteronea*) appear in late morning or afternoon, whereas summer-hatching duns of other blue quill species usually appear early in the morning.

I've hit blue quills on western waters in early May. I've seen heavy hatches on the Little Colorado River by mid-May. Trout rose in the snow-fed high-altitude waters of the Little Colorado from late morning until early afternoon. Virgil Bradford fished with me at the X-Diamond Ranch near Springerville, Arizona. By 11 AM trout rose in a pool deepened by an aggressive beaver family. A parade of blue quills floated into the deeper water, and heavy trout fed on them for more than an hour. Virgil and I landed eight trout in that pool before the hatch ended. Two of them were more than 20 inches long.

Look for other blue quill hatches throughout the year. You can expect to see these mayflies from early April until late October.

The Little Blue-Winged Olive Dun

You'll find hundreds of different mayfly species emerging across North America—but only about three dozen of them are found in all areas of the United States. You can fish brown drake (*Ephemera simulans*) hatches in Idaho, Michigan, and Pennsylvania.

Another widespread species, and by far the most common across the United States, is the little blue-winged olive dun (*Baetis tricaudatus* and *B. intercalaris*). (In addition, about a dozen other members of the little blue-winged family, Baetidae, are found across the United States.) The little blue-winged olive gives you an added bonus: This mayfly bears two generations a year, thus emerging twice—in March and April and again in September and October. Fish many of the streams and rivers of the Southwest and you'll see the hatch most of the winter. I've encountered little blue-wings in December on the Red River in New Mexico and in January on the Salt River near Phoenix, Arizona; on Oak Creek just south of Flagstaff, Arizona, the hatch appears in heavy numbers in March. Local anglers on Oak Creek call the hatch the early blue.

When I compiled the information for *Arizona Trout Streams and Their Hatches,* I found little blue-wings at all altitudes and practically every one of the 40 streams I visited. Silver Creek near Showlow, Arizona, boasts one of the heaviest hatches.

I once fished this small limestone stream in mid-April just after authorities had planted trout, along with my friend Brian Williams. Snow and cold weather at that time should have precluded any hatch from appearing. Not the little blue-winged olive. Within 15 minutes after these trout had been stocked they began feeding on dozens of dazed little blue-wings resting on the surface. In front of us more than 30 trout were rising to the small dun. It was Brian's first encounter with a hatch and rising trout. Before the hatch ended that cold, blustery April afternoon he had landed 10 trout. What a way to start fly-fishing!

But dozens of different species make up what anglers call the little blue-winged olive hatch. I've seen little blue-wings from sizes 18 to 24 on hundreds of streams across North America. (Some little blue-wing hatches that were once classified under the genus *Pseudocloeon* are now in *Plauditus;* these produce great hatches.) Little blue-wings seem especially well adapted to tailwaters. Bottom-release waters like the Green River below the Flaming Gorge in Utah, the Missouri River below Holter Dam, and the Delaware River in New York all boast great little blue-wing hatches.

I call these blue-wings "lousy-day hatches." Why? If you fish in April and May or September and October, you'll often find these hatches on the water on inclement days. I can't count the number of times I've witnessed a hatch while a slight drizzle fell in cool or cold temperatures. It happened on the Metolius River in Oregon; on the Cache la Poudre in northern Colorado; on the Delaware in New York;

The Delaware River on the Pennsylvania–New York border holds some great early-season hatches.

and on the Little Juniata in Pennsylvania. Show me a lousy day and I'll show you a hatch of little blue-winged olives.

When can you expect to fish the hatch? Up to this point I've said that you can find hatches in spring and fall. I've also mentioned that there are many small mayflies anglers call little blue-winged olives. Many of these hatches continue to appear throughout the summer. I have fished over tremendous western hatches (*Baetis bicaudatus*) on Henry's Fork in Idaho in July. And I've noted that the hatch appears in the Southwest throughout much of winter. So several small mayflies that we combine to call little blue-winged olives can appear almost any time of year. I once wrote about the slate drake and called it a "Fly for All Summer." We can legitimately call the little blue-winged olive a "Fly for All Year."

What pattern works best for this hatch? The day I spent on Silver Creek taught me a thing or two about patterns. I used a comparadun pattern, while I gave Brian Williams a vernille-bodied parachute. On the first 10 casts Brian had 10 strikes, while I had only 2. Both flies had the same body color and were the same size, but Brian's pattern had the rounded extended body. You might want to tie some of the patterns with this vernille body; you'll find the recipe in chapter 10.

Hendricksons and Western March Browns

The Hendrickson (*Ephemerella subvaria*) and the western March brown (*Rhithrogena morrisoni*) have a lot in common. Both have tannish brown to light brown bodies. Both appear in midafternoon in April and early May, and both often create a feeding frenzy. A size 14 pattern copies both hatches. But that's where the similarities end. You'll find prolific western March brown hatches on coastal and near-coastal waters of the West like the McKenzie and Willamette Rivers. The Hendrickson is found throughout the East and Midwest from the Gunpowder Falls River in Maryland to the AuSable in the Michigan.

The western March brown has a long emergence time. I've seen this mayfly on some coastal rivers around the end of February. The best hatches, however, occur in late March, April, and early May. One place I enjoy fishing this hatch is on the lower 3 or 4 miles of the McKenzie River. I've seen heavy hatches there. I once floated this stretch with guide Ken Helfrich; when the hatch grew he had me get out of the boat and fish some productive riffles. I fished a tandem rig with a wet fly just a few inches under the surface and a floating Western March Brown pattern. It's not unusual to catch a dozen or more trout during the afternoon hatch of this mayfly.

The other brown-bellied mayfly is the Hendrickson, found on many trout streams of the East and Midwest. It too appears in late March to early April in its southern reaches; to early May in Michigan. Unlike the western March brown, the Hendrickson usually appears on any given stream or river for a week or less. When it does appear, though, its numbers can be overwhelming. The Beaverkill and Delaware Rivers in New York; the Housatonic River in Connecticut; the Loyalsock in Pennsylvania; and the AuSable in Michigan host tremendous hatches of this extremely important early-season mayfly.

On occasions the hatch is too heavy, and *matching the hatch* turns into *watching the hatch*. I've quit fishing on occasion during a heavy hatch for the following reasons. First, trout have too many naturals on the surface on which to feed; trying to get one to take an imitation is an exercise in futility. Second, I've seen dozens of Hendrickson hatches where thousands of duns were riding the surface, but not one trout fed on this plentiful supply of food. Why? When both the western March brown and the Hendrickson emerge, they do so in rather chilly water: Often water temperatures haven't yet reached 50 degrees. Colder water slows the activity of the trout, and they feed less. Many times trout are taking nymphs and don't come to the surface for the duns. If you experience a great hatch and see no trout rising, try fishing a tandem with a blackish brown nymph pattern tied a foot or two behind a dry fly.

One advantage of cold weather is that it slows the escape of these mayflies from the surface. Compare the hatches on warm spring days to those on cool spring days. On warm days these mayflies escape rapidly from the surface; trout get little chance to feed on them. On cool days the duns tend to rest much longer to dry their wings, and trout have a greater opportunity to feed on them.

Anglers call the male of the species (*Ephemerella subvaria*) the red quill. The belly is reddish brown compared to the female Hendrickson, whose belly is pale tannish with possibly a pink cast. I've found that one pattern (either the Hendrickson or the Red Quill) is sufficient.

Whether you fish in the West, Midwest, or East in late March, April, or early May, look for one of these great early-spring hatches and get ready for some action. You'll find the special and regular patterns for the Hendrickson, Red Quill, and Western March Brown in chapter 10.

WHERE THE HATCHES ARE FOUND—TYPICAL STREAMS AND RIVERS

Little Blue-Winged Olive Dun (*Baetis tricaudatus*)
This species appears in all regions.

Little Blue-Winged Olive Dun (*Baetis intercalaris*)
Arizona: Oak Creek, Silver Creek

Big Fishing Creek in central Pennsylvania. In spring you'll often see two or more hatches appearing at the same time.

California: Fall River, Hat Creek

Colorado: Fryingpan River, Roaring Fork, Arkansas River

Idaho: Big Wood River, Henry's Fork, St. Maries River, Silver Creek

Maryland: Gunpowder River, Big Hunting Creek

Michigan: AuSable River

Montana: Kootenai River, Missouri River

New Mexico: San Juan River, Red River

New York: Beaverkill River, Delaware River

North Carolina: South Toe River

Oregon: Metolius River

Pennsylvania: Little Juniata River, Little Lehigh

Utah: Green River

Wyoming: Bighorn River, North Platte River

Quill Gordon (*Epeorus pleuralis*) (E)

Connecticut: Farmington River, Housatonic River

Maryland: Big Hunting Creek

New Jersey: Musconetcong River

New York: Beaverkill River, Delaware River, Wiscoy Creek, Genesee River, Ischua Creek, Schoharie River, Esopus Creek, Neversink River
North Carolina: South Toe River
Pennsylvania: Big Fishing Creek, Brodhead Creek, Loyalsock Creek, Pine Creek, Bobs Creek
Virginia: Rose River
West Virginia: Elk River

Blue Quill (*Paraleptophlebia adoptiva*) (E and M);
  (*Paraleptophlebia heteroni*) (W)
Arizona: Little Colorado River
Colorado: Arkansas River
Connecticut: Farmington River, Housatonic River
Idaho: Henry's Fork
Maryland: Gunpowder River, Big Hunting Creek
Michigan: AuSable River
New York: Beaverkill River, Genesee River, Wiscoy Creek, East Koy Creek
North Carolina: South Toe River
Pennsylvania: Allegheny River, Big Fishing Creek, Little Pine Creek
Virginia: Rapidan River
West Virginia: Elk River

Hendrickson (*Ephemerella subvaria*) (E and M)
Connecticut: Housatonic River
Maryland: Big Hunting Creek, Gunpowder River
Michigan: AuSable River, Manistee River, Pere Marquette River
New Jersey: South Branch of the Raritan River
New York: Beaverkill River, Delaware River, Ischua Creek, Genesee River, Esopus Creek
Pennsylvania: Allegheny River, Lackawaxen River, Big Fishing Creek
Tennessee: South Fork of the Holston River
Virginia: Rose River
West Virginia: Elk River
Wisconsin: Namekagon River

Vice-President Dick Cheney fishes during the blue quill hatch on Bobs Creek. He caught 13 of the 14 trout rising in this pool.

Black Quill (*Leptophlebia cupida*) (**E and M**)
Michigan: Pere Marquette River, Manistee River
New York: Beaverkill River, Ischua Creek, Esopus Creek
Pennsylvania: Bald Eagle Creek, Snake Creek, Grays Run, Middle Creek
Labrador: Minipi River

Dark Quill Gordon (*Ameletus ludens*) (**E and M**)
New York: Delaware River
Pennsylvania: Bald Eagle Creek, Little Bald Eagle Creek, Loyalsock Creek, Cedar Run

Western March Brown (*Rhithrogena morrisoni*) (**W**)
Idaho: Henry's Fork
Montana: Kootenai River
Oregon: McKenzie River, Metolius River, Deschutes River, Willamette River
Washington: Yakima River

Speckle-Winged Dun (*Callibaetis* spp.) (E, M, and W)
Found in just about all alkaline lakes and ponds
Arizona: Sunrise Lake
Montana: Handkerchief Lake
Washington: Nunnally Lake
Labrador: Minipi River

Great Speckled Olive Dun (*Spihloplecton basale*) (E and M)
Maine: Narraguagus River
Massachusetts: Swift River, Gin River
Pennsylvania: Clarks Creek
Wisconsin: Black Creek, Pine River, Peshtigo River, Big Sams River
Labrador: Minipi River

Quill Gordon (*Epeorus longimanus*) (W)
Idaho: St. Maries River
Montana: Rock Creek, Bitterroot River

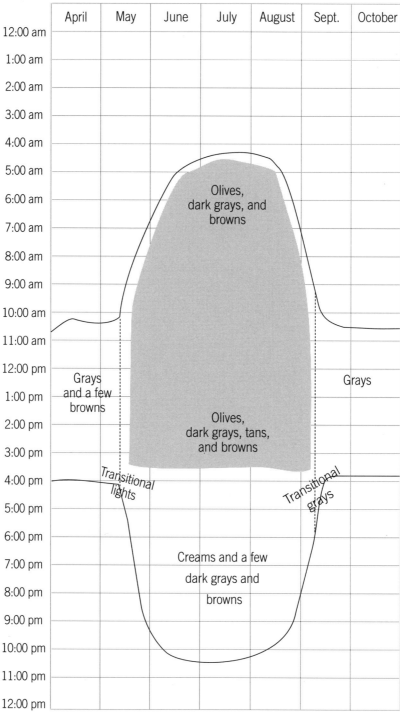

TABLE 6.1: When hatches appear and what color they are

6. SUMMER HATCHES IN THE MORNING AND AFTERNOON—OLIVES AND A FEW DARK GRAYS AND BROWNS

Time of Year: May 15–September 15
When to Be on the Stream: 6 AM–noon (occasionally in the afternoon—especially in the West)
Predominant Color of the Hatches: Olive, dark gray, and some browns

L ate May has arrived and the only time you can fish is in the morning or early afternoon. Certainly at this time of year you won't see any hatches. Right? Wrong! This is the time of the olives and grays—in the daylight hours. In the next few months you'll find blue quills (30 species of *Paraleptophlebia*), blue-winged olives (mainly *Drunella* species), little blue-winged olives (mainly *Baetis* species), gray drakes (*Siphlonurus* species), dark brown duns (mainly western *Rhithrogena* species), pale brown duns (like *Cinygmula reticulata*), and tricos (several species of *Tricorythodes*). In the next few weeks you'll see plenty of mayflies emerging. These same duns change into spinners in a day or two (see chapter 2). The spinners of tricos and blue quills—the trico spinners and dark brown spinners, respectively—fall in the morning. *Don't forget: Unusual weather conditions and tailwater fisheries make anomalies out of the theory that dark flies appear during the day and cream at night in summer.* We'll explore the weather segment of that equation in "A Mixed Bag on a Summer Day" later in this chapter.

Most of the blue-winged olive adults or spinners—called dark olive spinners by anglers (*Drunella* species)—mate and lay eggs in the evening. So do many of the western brown duns (many are *Rhithrogena* species). So if you see a particular blue-winged olive hatch or pale brown dun coming off during the day, you can expect to fish over trout rising to a spinner fall in the evening.

A LOOK AT SOME OF THE HATCHES
Tricos Coast to Coast

What a way to start a fly-fishing workshop! I arrived a day early on the Ruby River and Jake and Donna McDonald's Upper Canyon Lodge just south of Alder, Montana. I wanted to fish for a day before I conducted the workshop so I could get acquainted with the river. Besides, I wanted to fish the early-morning trico hatch this river holds. I arrived at the river behind the lodge at 8 AM; the hatch and spinner fall had already begun. A brisk wind blew thousands of these small mayflies 100 feet from the river, but they returned. Soon the same wind was blowing trico spinners into my mouth. They didn't taste very good—I don't know what trout see in them. In front of me more than 10 rainbows fed on spent-winged spinners. Just as I began casting to some of these risers, four anglers came to the river to watch. They introduced themselves as registrants for my class. They too had arrived early to get

Trico time on the Ruby River in Montana

in an extra day's fishing—but first they wanted to see how well their instructor would do with the hatch and spinner fall. My topic for the following day was "How to Catch More Trout."

Now the pressure was on. Ten casts—20 casts—30 casts—not one strike. It seemed that there were too many naturals on the water. Trout could be choosy. The foursome watching began to whisper to each other, and the pressure went even higher. What could I do? I searched through my compartmented fly box for a secret weapon—one I had tied years before and that might work here. I found it—a weighted Trico Spinner. Sacrilegious to some anglers, but I wasn't worried about that now—I had to catch a trout. My reputation depended on it.

I had tied that weighted spent-winged spinner pattern as a result of a memorable trip to Falling Springs in south-central Pennsylvania. That day more than a decade ago and 3,000 miles from the Ruby River had made an impression on me. I watched an older angler pick up half a dozen trout while I scrambled to catch one. He put me to shame. What was he doing? I finally asked, and he told me to sink the pattern. I went home that evening and tied some Trico patterns that included a few turns of lead wrapped around the body to sink them more readily. Those patterns remained in my fly box for more than a decade—never once used.

Did I say *sink the Trico pattern*? That's almost heretical, isn't it? Not when you're copying what occurs in nature. Just think of what happened to the tricos that had fallen spent 2 miles up that same Ruby River. After floating spent through two, three, or four sets of rapids, many of them sank. Trout naturally prefer to feed underwater rather than show themselves on the surface.

I hurriedly tied on the weighted spinner behind a Patriot dry fly in a tandem setup. I placed the Trico just 18 inches behind the dry fly. The Patriot acted as a strike indicator—with an attitude. If any trout hit the strike indicator, they'd get hooked. Now two more people joined the group, watching me. Six future class members stood rapt as I tied on the new pattern. They could easily see my frustration.

I had to hurry—the spinner fall would last only another hour at best, and half an hour at the worst. On my first cast the Patriot sank, and I set the hook. I quickly released a 12-inch rainbow and cast in same general direction again. A second time the Patriot went under, and again I set the hook. Soon another and another—until the hatch ended and the trout stopped rising. After about the fifth trout, my audience started applauding. What a way to turn a frustrating, disappointing event into a memorable one! That sunken Trico Spinner had done it.

Just what is this trico hatch and spinner fall? Is the hatch common? When does it appear? Where can you find it? I've fished the trico hatch from the Beaverkill and

Falling Springs is the first place I learned about the sunken Trico.

Delaware Rivers in New York to the McKenzie River in Oregon. In the southwestern waters of New Mexico and Arizona, the insect is extremely common. I've encountered the hatch on limestone and freestone streams throughout the Northeast.

When can you expect to see the hatch? Until a few years ago I thought it appeared from late June or July to early October—depending on the weather. But fishing the rivers of the Southwest changed that thinking forever. One New Year's morning several years ago I hit a trico spinner fall on the Salt River just outside of Phoenix, Arizona. No, it wasn't a heavy hatch—but a few trout rose to the spinners. On New Mexico's mostly private Rio Penasco, hatches and spinner falls occur early in spring.

Several years ago Craig Josephson and I traveled to the upper Verde River at Cottonwood, Arizona, 90 miles north of Phoenix, in mid-February to fish for trout. By 9 AM a few tiny mayflies had appeared on the surface. I suspected that they were little blue-winged olives and grabbed one to verify my thinking. Surprise of all surprises—it was a trico dun—a trico dun emerging in mid-February. Up to that point I'd felt certain that this hatch appeared only in June, July, August, and September. But here—near the Valley of the Sun—this hatch and the concomitant spinner fall occurred *five months early.* By 11 AM hundreds of these duns had emerged and a full-fledged summerlike spinner fall was taking place. I searched through my summer box of patterns and quickly grabbed a Trico Spinner. Craig and I now had more than 50 trout rising in front of us. On my first cast with that

Penns Creek in Pennsylvania—expect to see multiple hatches here.

spinner pattern I caught a trout. For the next two hours the two of us fished over pods of rising trout in the middle of February. In all that time I did not see one other fly-fisher.

I came back to that same general area in early March and saw another great trico hatch. So when somebody asks you when tricos emerge, tell him you can expect to see the hatch almost any time of year, depending on the location.

Normally you match the hatch with a size 24 or 26; on a heavily fished stream a smaller pattern sometimes works better. On the Verde River the species (*Tricorythodes fictus*) seemed a bit larger, and I used a size 22.

You'll often see trico hatches on tailwaters. On some waters, like the Missouri River in Montana, the hatch is almost too heavy. I'll never forget my first morning on the Missouri with my son Bryan. As we traveled along the waterway, we saw a vortex of tricos that I mistook for a dust devil. Thousands and thousands of those spinners soon fell, and trout began to feed in a predictable rhythm. With each rise the trout gulped in four or five or more spent spinners. We finally resorted to a bouquet of two or more Tricos tied on one larger hook. After we switched to this larger double fly and figured out the rhythm to the feeding, we caught trout.

You can find some great trico spinner falls on eastern waters, too. I mentioned earlier that Falling Springs in south-central Pennsylvania has a good trico population. I still remember that day more than 30 years ago when Dick Mills and I fished there with Barry Beck and Vince Marinaro. Barry, Dick, and I sat back while Vince cast to more than 10 trout rising to spent trico spinners. Those trout had been fished over by many anglers for more than four weeks, so they were highly selective. The more Vince cast, the more frustrated he became. Finally Barry blurted out, "Tell them who you are." Vince mumbled a few choice words and continued to fish.

You'll find some of the heaviest hatches in the East on posted water. Almost all of central Pennsylvania's Spruce Creek is private water. For a fee, however, you can fish much of the stream. Spruce Creek has a great trico spinner fall that usually begins in mid-July. Recently John Randolph, editor of *Fly Fisherman* magazine, his assistant Jay Nichols, and I accepted an invitation to fish a section of Orvis-endorsed fly-fishing water near the Six Springs Fly Shop (a division of Donny Beaver's Paradise Ranch) in the town of Spruce Creek. The shop annually guides more than 1,000 clients on several stretches of prime limestone water. Here you'll find friendly professional guides with plenty of on-the-stream experience.

By the time John and I arrived at the section of stream we planned to fish, the trico spinner fall had already started. John and I did manage to land four heavy trout—all over 15 inches long—on a size 24 imitation. If you want to not only experience the trico hatch but also catch some heavy browns and rainbows on size 24 dry flies, then this is the place to do it.

What time of day do tricos appear? When do the males emerge? A few years back Ronald Hall conducted a comprehensive study of the trico hatch and spinner fall as part of the requirements for his doctor's degree. He found that most male duns emerge from 10 PM to 2 AM, while most female duns appear on the surface in the early-morning hours, usually from 6 to 9 AM. He also discovered several other interesting facts.

Exactly 49 days after the eggs are laid by the first generation of tricos, the second generation appears (with the exception of some areas in Canada, where there's only one generation a year). There is much overlapping of generations; that's why the hatch is heavy throughout late summer. The hatch is univoltine in some parts of Canada, bivoltine in much of the northern half of the United States, and multivoltine in parts of the Southwest. That means you'll see only one generation in parts of Canada, two in much of the United States, and multiple generations in the Southwest.

Hall also learned that the trico overwinters in the egg stage. In most cases you won't find any trico nymphs from December through much of May. Of course, in those locations where you find multiple generations, you'll find nymphs much of the year. Nymphs emerge from the eggs near the end of May and emerge as duns approximately 49 days later.

Why is the information from Hall's study important? First, it gives you a total picture of the hatch and its many intricacies. After reading Hall's thesis, you certainly wouldn't use a Trico Nymph before June or July—even on streams where this is the only major hatch. Second, it should help you catch more trout.

There are several important trico species (*T. allectus* and *T. minutus* are two of the most important). One pattern to copy the male and another for the female works on most of the hatches across the North American continent. Look for the trico on your favorite water—it's extremely common from coast to coast.

Blue Wings and Olive Bodies

Jay Kapolka and I returned to the Metolius River in central Oregon for a second time. We had visited the stream just a few days before and had two trout to show for a morning's fishing. It was late May, and I wasn't certain of the weather. When we stopped in Bend, Oregon, for an early breakfast, intermittent rain and drizzle and a raw day greeted us. We decided to fish the Metolius anyway and see if we could do any better a second time. It wouldn't take long for us to find out.

We arrived on the river a couple of miles below Camp Sherman around 10 AM. As we hiked upriver, we saw dozens of trout rising in every pool and riffle. Finally we split—Jay fishing one stretch and me another. In an eddy that I selected I saw hundreds of duns floating on the surface, unable to take flight because of the weather. There were all imaginable sizes of mayflies on the surface, and trout seemed to be

Ken Rictor fishes the trico hatch on Pennsylvania's Falling Springs

feeding on all of them. I bent down and noted little blue-winged olives, pale morning duns, blue-winged olives, and western green drakes—all in good numbers. How's that for a multiple hatch?

Trout cruised in the huge eddy in front of me, picking off one mayfly after another with impunity. With this smorgasbord of food, what should I copy? I scanned the surface for just a minute and noted several trout feeding on a size 14 blue-winged olive dun (*Drunella flavilinea*). I hurriedly tied on a size 14 Blue-Winged Olive and began casting to risers in the cool drizzle. It didn't take long—in my first 10 casts, three trout hit that pattern. For the next hour trout continued to cruise the backwater taking one dazed mayfly after another—and they readily took my imitation.

Blue-winged olives are extremely common in the West. You'll find good hatches on waters ranging from the relatively small Rock Creek in Montana to the large spring-fed Henry's Fork.

But late May and early June is also the beginning of the appearance of the blue-winged olives in the East and Midwest. New York's Beaverkill and Delaware Rivers hold respectable hatches of many of these species (*Drunella* genus). I've hit some of the sacred pools on the Beaverkill in early June when a hatch has appeared. Look for the hatch in midmorning.

Preparing for the blue-winged olive hatch saved me from an embarrassing trip one day. Let me explain. I was the instructor at the Kettle Creek Lodge in north-

Ontario's Grand River holds a great trico hatch in August.

central Pennsylvania several years back. Twelve people attended that conference in late May. I discussed what hatches we might see, and then the entire class headed for Kettle Creek and some on-the-stream lectures about hatches. As I was talking along the stream bank, a heavy hatch of blue-winged olives appeared on the surface and trout rose in the riffle in front of me. Wonder of wonders—I already had a Blue-Winged Olive tied onto my tippet and began casting to show the attendees what a hatch meant in terms of success. One cast and a strike. Second cast—another rise to the pattern and a hook-up. The action continued for half an hour. I told the group to head back to their cars and get their fly-rods; they too caught trout before the hatch ended.

Usually the first two blue-winged olives to appear are the largest (*Drunella cornuta* in the East and Midwest and *D. flavilinea* in the West). The blue-winged flavs and the blue-winged corns both appear in much of their respective territories around the end of May. I've seen hatches appear on some eastern waters very sporadically into September.

A couple of weeks after the larger hatches emerge you'll find some smaller blue-wings appearing. These smaller mayflies (size 16 for *Drunella lata* and *D. cornutella*, and size 20 for *Timpanoga simplex*) appear in June and July. All are daytime emergers.

The spinners of all these species can be extremely important. Once you find a hatch of any of these species, return a day or two later in the evening and look for the spinner fall to occur. The body of many of these spinners is a very dark

TABLE 6.2: Summer Morning Hatches—East and Midwest

Conventional Pattern Name** Dun/Spinner	Scientific Name	Rating	Approximate Beginning Emergence Date	Time of Day Dun/ Spinner	Size	Special Pattern Suggestion** Dun/ Spinner	Restricted Pattern**
American March Brown	*Stenonema vicarium*	2	May 20	Afternoon	12	1 (ribbed with brown)	March Brown
Great Red Spinner		3		Evening		1 (ribbed with brown)	
Blue-Winged Olive Dun	*Acentrella turbida*	2	May 20	Afternoon	20	1	BWOD
Rusty Spinner		4		Early evening		20	
Chocolate Dun	*Eurylophella bicolor*	4	May 22	Afternoon	16	12	Willow Special
Chocolate Spinner		4		Evening		28	
Dark Green Drake	*Litobrancha recurvata*	3	May 25	Afternoon	8	8 (ribbed with olive-yellow)	Adams
Brown Drake Spinner		4		Evening		26 (ribbed with yellow)	
Gray Drake	*Siphlonurus alternatus*	4	May 25	Day	14	19	Adams
Gray Drake Spinner		1		Evening		26	
Gray Drake	*Siphlonurus quebecensis*	4	May 25	Day	14	19	Adams
Gray Drake Spinner		2		Evening		20	
Blue-Winged Olive Dun	*Drunella cornuta*	2	May 25	Morning	14	16	BWOD
Dark Olive Spinner		2		Evening		30	
Blue Quill Female: Dark Brown Spinner	*Paraleptophlebia mollis*	3	May 26	Morning and afternoon	18	8	Adams
Male: Jenny Spinner		4				26	

Table continues on next page

TABLE 6.2: Continued

Conventional Pattern Name** Dun/Spinner	Scientific Name	Rating	Approximate Beginning Emergence Date	Time of Day Dun/ Spinner	Size	Special Pattern Suggestion** Dun/ Spinner	Restricted Pattern**
Male: Chocolate Dun	*Ephemerella needhami*	3	May 30	Morning	16	13	BWOD
Female: Olive Sulphur		4		Evening		16	
Female: Dark Olive Spinner						29	
Blue-Winged Olive Dun	*Drunella cornutella*	2	June 10	Morning	16	16	BWOD
Dark Olive Spinner		1		Evening		30	
Blue-Winged Olive Dun	*Timpanoga simplex*	3	June 15	Morning	20	17	BWOD
Dark Olive Spinner		3		Evening		30	
Blue Quill Female: Dark Brown Spinner	*Paraleptophlebia guttata*	3	June 25	Morning and afternoon	18	8	Adams
Male: Jenny Spinner		4				26	
Trico Dun	*Tricorythodes allectus*	2	July 15	Morning	24	15	BWOD
Trico Spinner		1		Evening		21 (female thorax is dark brown)	

**See chapters 1 and 10 for more information

TABLE 6.3: Summer Morning Hatches—West

Conventional Pattern Name** Dun/Spinner	Scientific Name	Rating	Approximate Beginning Emergence Date	Time of Day Dun/ Spinner	Size	Special Pattern Suggestion** Dun/ Spinner	Restricted Pattern**
Speckle-Winged Dun	*Callibaetis americanus*	2	April 20*	Late morning	16	11	Adams
Speckle-Winged Spinner		4				13	
Dark Brown Dun	*Cinygmula par*	3	May 15	Noon	16	13	Willow Special
Dark Brown Spinner		4				26	
Blue-Winged Olive Dun	*Drunella spinifera*	3	June 1	Noon	16	16	BWOD
Dark Olive Spinner		3				30	
Pale Morning Dun	*Ephemerella inermis*	1	May 20	Morning	16	15, 9, and 3	BWOD
Pale Morning Spinner		1				24	
Little Blue-Winged Olive Dun	*Baetis bicaudatus*	1	May 20	Afternoon	20	15	BWOD
Rusty Spinner		2				24	
Pale Morning Dun	*Ephemerella infrequens*	2	May 20	Morning	18	3	Light Cahill
Pale Morning Spinner		3				24	
Western Green Drake	*Drunella grandis*	1	May 25	Morning	12	17	BWOD
Great Olive Spinner		4				30	
Blue-Winged Olive Dun	*Acentrella carolina*	2	May 20	Afternoon	20	1	BWOD
Rusty Spinner		4		Early evening			20

Table continues on next page

TABLE 6.3: Continued

Conventional Pattern Name** Dun/Spinner	Scientific Name	Rating	Approximate Beginning Emergence Date	Time of Day Dun/ Spinner	Size	Special Pattern Suggestion** Dun/ Spinner	Restricted Pattern**
Dark Red Quill	*Cinygmula ramaleyi*	2	May 25	Morning		11	Willow Special
Red Quill Spinner		4				26	
Blue-Winged Olive Dun	*Drunella flavilinea*	1	June 15	Morning and evening	14	17	BWOD
Dark Olive Spinner		2				30	
Dark Brown Dun	*Ameletus velox*	2	June 15	Late morning	14	13	Willow Special
Dark Brown Spinner		4				26	
Quill Gordon	*Rhithrogena futilis*	2	June 15	Morning	12	8	Adams
Quill Gordon Spinner		2				20	
Blue Quill	*Paraleptophlebia heteronea*	3	June 15	Morning	18	8	Adams
Dark Brown Spinner		3				26	
Pale Brown Dun	*Rhithrogena hageni*	2	July 1	Late morning	14	10	March Brown
Dark Tan Spinner		2				25	
Pale Brown Dun	*Cinygmula reticulata*	2	July 1	Morning	14	10	March Brown
Dark Rusty Spinner		4				25	
Blue Quill	*Paraleptophlebia memorialis*	3	July 1	Morning	18	8	Adams
Dark Brown Spinner						26	

Table continues on next page

TABLE 6.3: Continued

Conventional Pattern Name** Dun/Spinner	Scientific Name	Rating	Approximate Beginning Emergence Date	Time of Day Dun/ Spinner	Size	Special Pattern Suggestion** Dun/ Spinner	Restricted Pattern**
Gray Drake	*Siphlonurus occidentalis*	3	July 1	Afternoon	10	14	Adams
Gray Drake Spinner		4				20 28	
Dark Red Quill	*Rhithrogena undulata*	2	July 1	Late morning	12	8	Adams
Red Quill Spinner		2				28	
Dark Brown Dun	*Ameletus cooki*	2	July 1	Late morning	14	13	Willow Special
Dark Brown Spinner		4				26	
Pale Olive Dun	*Tricorythodes fictus**	2	July 1	Morning	20	15	BWOD
Trico Spinner		1				21 (female thorax is dark brown)	
Pale Olive Dun	*Tricorythodes miutus**	2	July 1	Morning	22	15	BWOD
Trico Spinner		1			26	21 (female thorax is dark brown)	

*More than one generation each year
**See chapters 1 and 10 for more information

olive. I use 9 parts of black poly mixed with 1 part of olive. That seems to be the best color.

So no matter where you fish—East, Midwest, or West—you'll see blue wings and olive bodies. Look for those great spinner falls most often in the evening—and be prepared with some dark olive spinner patterns.

A Mixed Bag on a Summer Day

Remember what I told you earlier: Weather conditions and tailwater fisheries can cause cream mayflies to appear during the day. Look at the following as a good example.

What a terrible day to plan a fly-fishing trip! As Ken and Kathy Rictor, Bryan Meck, and I prepared for a day of late-May matching-the-hatch fishing, we added extra layers of clothing. The weather reminded me of a day you might hit on the opening week of the Pennsylvania trout season—but not one in the last week in May. I had promised all three anglers that we'd hit some explosive hatches this time of the year—but with this cold, dreary weather, all bets were off.

We entered the Little Juniata River shortly after noon just above Barree in central Pennsylvania and tried to decide what pattern to select. Then it happened: A couple of huge green drakes fluttered on the surface in a desperate attempt to escape. Within half an hour hundreds of duns—on the surface and in the air—were appearing in and above the pool in front of us. Now, normally the green drake emerges just at dusk. But on this cold, blustery day these evening emergers decided to hatch during the day. Remember this when you're fishing the hatches or at least looking for them: *On cloudy, overcast, dismal days, evening emergers often appear during daylight hours.* I have witnessed this phenomenon over and over again on lousy days in the East, Midwest, and West. By the time evening approaches—the time you'd normally expect to see the hatch—it ends abruptly, around 5 or 6 PM.

By the time the four of us began casting Green Drake patterns toward rising trout, a second, smaller mayfly appeared on the surface: what anglers call a tiny blue-winged olive (*Acentrella carolina*). To match this insect you'd have to use a size 22 imitation. Few trout fed on this second supply of food. But wait! Just a few minutes later a size 16 pale yellow mayfly also appeared on the surface. Anglers match this latter hatch with a Sulphur imitation. That's three hatches occurring at the same time—two of them cream or yellow. But wait! There's even more. Within minutes respectable hatches of slate drakes and little blue-winged olive duns (*Baetis tricaudatus*) added to the parade of mayflies now floating past the four of us. By 1:30 PM we had more than two dozen trout rising within casting distance of us and five separate decent hatches appearing. Which hatch should we match?

If you count the nymph, emerger, and dun for each of the five insects that appeared that late-May day, that's a choice of 15 different patterns the trout might have been taking. Add trout taking duns with trailing nymphal shucks still attached and we now had 20 potential patterns. What do you do in a case like this—copy the most prolific hatch? Imitate the largest insect? Most fly-fishers would do what we attempted first—match the largest fly on the surface, in this case the green drake dun. Why not? Any trout could quickly satisfy its appetite with just a few of these large duns, whereas trout feeding on the smaller sulphurs or one of the tiny blue duns would take much longer to get the same amount of food. Right? But trout don't think that way.

For more than an hour the four of us attempted to cast size 10 Green Drakes into a brisk north wind. Not one of those two dozen trout even looked at the pattern. The more trout rose, the more frustrated we became.

Then I noticed that several trout in front of me were keyed in on the smaller sulphurs. I now took time out and watched some of the duns. For every trout that took an escaping green drake dun, five were feeding on sulphurs. I also noticed that the more the green drake nymph quivered as it escaped from its shuck, the more trout took this larger morsel.

A trout caught behind the Six Springs Fly shop on Spruce Creek.

After watching the procession of mayflies in front of me for what seemed like half an hour, I switched from the Green Drake pattern to a Sulphur. I then took time out to search the surface for trout feeding on the sulphur naturals. When I spotted one, I cast a few feet in front of it and waited. Within minutes I'd picked up several trout on the Sulphur imitation—whereas I'd caught none on the Green Drake pattern in a frustrating hour of fishing.

Steven Osborne of Tyrone, Pennsylvania, was fishing nearby, and he also noticed this phenomenon. He too changed from the larger Green Drake to a Sulphur. I suggested to Ken Rictor, fishing 100 feet below me, that he change to the smaller yellow pattern as well. He did, and almost immediately Ken began catching holdover brown trout.

Bryan Meck stayed with the Green Drake pattern. He scanned the surface in front of him for trout feeding on this larger dun. When he spotted one and cast above it, he usually got a strike. The multiple hatch continued for most of the afternoon. We all caught trout on our various patterns because we looked for trout feeding on the natural that our pattern copied.

By 7 PM only a few green drakes remained on the surface—all other hatches had ended. I spotted several heavy trout feeding on the few green drake naturals too cold to take flight. I switched to my Green Drake pattern and cast along a deep rock ledge at the far shore. There came a huge rise—and a trout had sucked in the pattern. Within minutes I had landed a 17-inch brown on that Drake pattern. Then even the drake hatch ended, and the surface became still.

That momentous day with five separate heavy hatches could have turned into one of those frustrating unproductive days if we hadn't taken time during the heat of the hatches to observe how and on what the trout were feeding.

Witnessing more than one hatch can be a very common occurrence on some of our better rivers nationwide, especially around the end of May. What are some of the rules you should follow if you hit one of these multiple-hatch days? First—and this goes for anytime I fly-fish—before you begin fishing, take time out to see what's happening. Look around and note whether any trout are feeding. If you see trout rise for food, try to find out what they're taking. If you see trout surface-feeding, you've got to decide whether they're taking duns or are feeding on emergers just under the surface. Look at the riseforms. Are they splashy? If they're atypical, maybe trout are feeding on caddisflies or mayfly emergers. Do you see more than one insect on the surface? See if you can find out which one most of the trout are taking. Or do as I did in the previous story and fish to those trout taking the insect you're copying. By taking just a few minutes during a frenzied-feeding episode you can make the difference between a successful and a discouraging fishing trip. (Chapter 11 looks at multiple hatches in more detail.)

WHERE THE HATCHES ARE FOUND— TYPICAL STREAMS AND RIVERS

March Brown (*Stenonema vicarium*)
See chapter 5.

Blue-Winged Olive Dun (*Drunella cornuta, D. walkeri,*
**   *D. cornutella*) (E and M)**
Connecticut: Housatonic River
Michigan: Pere Marquette River
New York: Delaware River, Beaverkill River, Wiscoy Creek,
   Willowemoc River
North Carolina: Toe River

Pennsylvania: Big Fishing Creek, Little Juniata River, Pocono Creek, Brodhead Creek, Penns Creek, Little Pine Creek
Tennessee: Little River
Vermont: Battenkill River

Blue-Winged Olive Dun *(Drunella lata)* **(E and M)**
Michigan: Little Manistee River, Sturgeon River, AuSable River, Manistee River, Pere Marquette River
Vermont: Battenkill River

Blue-Winged Olive Dun *(Drunella flavilinea, D spinifera,*
 D. coloradensis) **(W)**
California: Merced River, Trinity River, Hat Creek,
Idaho: Henry's Fork, St. Maries River
Montana: Clark Fork, Whitefish River, Rock Creek
Oregon: Metolius River, McKenzie River, Willamette River, Deschutes River
Washington: Green River, Little Spokane River
Wyoming: Yellowstone River, Firehole River

Western Green Drake *(Drunella grandis)* **(W)**
Arizona: East Fork of the Little Colorado River, Black River
Colorado: Roaring Fork, Fryingpan River, Gunnison River
Idaho: Henry's Fork, Big Wood River
Montana: Bitterroot River, St. Maries River, Rock Creek, Madison River
New Mexico: Pecos River
Oregon: Metolius River, Deschutes River, Willamette River, Santiam River
Utah: Logan River, Provo River
Washington: Little Spokane River
Wyoming: Lamar River, Wind River, Firehole River

Little Blue-Winged Olive Dun *(Acentrella turbida;* **formerly**
 Pseudocloeon carolina) **(E, M, and W)**
Connecticut: Housatonic River

New York: Delaware River
Pennsylvania: Little Juniata River

Little Blue-Winged Olive Dun (*Baetis bicaudatus*) (W)
Idaho: Henry's Fork, Silver Creek, St. Maries River, Big Wood River
Montana: Rock Creek, Bitterroot River, Clark Fork, Gallatin River
Utah: Provo River

Blue Quill (includes *Paraleptophlebia guttata, P. memorialis,*
***P. debilis, P. mollis, P. vaciva, P. bicornuta*) (E, M, and W)**
Arizona: Little Colorado River
Idaho: Henry's Fork
Michigan: AuSable River, Pere Marquette River
New York: Delaware River, Beaverkill River
Pennsylvania: Elk Creek, Spruce Creek, Big Fishing Creek, Cedar Run,
    Bobs Creek
Washington: Yakima River
Wyoming: North Platte River

Quill Gordon (*Rhithrogena futilis*) (W)
Montana: Bitterroot River, Gallatin River, Madison River, Rock Creek

Dark Red Quill (*Rhithrogena undulata*) (W)
Colorado: Roaring Fork
Idaho: Henry's Fork
Montana: Madison River, Beaverhead River, Big Hole

Gray Drake (*Siphlonurus quebecensis, S. alternatus*) (E and M)
Michigan: Manistee River, AuSable River, Grand River, Pere Marquette
    River, Muskegon River, Platte River, Little Manistee River, Betsie River
New Hampshire: Saco River
Pennsylvania: Penns Creek, Potato Creek, Bald Eagle Creek
Labrador: Minipi River

Gray Drake *(Siphlonurus occidentalis)* **(W)**
Colorado: South Platte River
Idaho: Henry's Fork, Silver Creek, Big Wood River
Montana: Bitterroot River
Washington: Yakima River
Wyoming: Yellowstone River

Dark Green Drake *(Litobrancha recurvata)* **(E and M)**
New Hampshire: Saco River
Pennsylvania: Vanscoyoc Run, Elk Creek, Big Fishing Creek
Labrador: Minipi River

Pale Brown Dun *(Rhithrogena hageni)* **(W)**
Montana: Gallatin River, Madison River

Dark Brown Dun *(Ameletus cooki)* **(W)**
Montana: Bitterroot River, Rock Creek

Little Blue-Winged Olive Dun *(Plauditus veteris)* **(size 22)**
    (E and M)
New York: Delaware River
Pennsylvania: Spruce Creek, Little Juniata River

Pale Morning Dun *(Ephemerella inermis, E. infrequens)* **(W)**
Arizona: White River, Black River
California: Merced River, Hat Creek
Colorado: South Platte River, Gunnison River, Cache la Poudre River,
    Thompson River, San Juan River
Idaho: Big Wood River, Henry's Fork, South Fork of the Snake River,
    Silver Creek
Montana: Bitterroot River, Rock Creek, Whitefish River, Kootenai River,
    Clark Fork, Bighorn River, Madison River
New Mexico: San Juan River
Oregon: McKenzie River, Deschutes River, Metolius River

Utah: Provo River, Green River
Wyoming: Laramie River, North Platte River

Trico (includes *Tricorythodes allectus, T. fictus, T. minutus*)
   (E, M, and W)
Arizona: Oak Creek, Upper Verde River
Colorado: South Platte River
Maryland: Big Hunting Creek
Michigan: AuSable River, Manistee River, Pere Marquette River
Montana: Bighorn River, Ruby River, Big Hole, Missouri River
New Jersey: Musconetcong River
New Mexico: Rio Penasco, Genesee River, Delaware River
New York: Delaware River, West Branch of the Ausable River, Genesee
   River, Wiscoy Creek
Oregon: McKenzie River
Pennsylvania: Falling Springs, Little Lehigh, Spring Creek
Utah: Green River
Vermont: Battenkill River
Virginia: Mossy Creek
Wisconsin: Namekagon River, Brule River
Wyoming: Bighorn River, North Platte River
Ontario: Grand River

Chocolate Dun *(Eurylophella bicolor)* (E and M)
New York: Delaware River
Maryland: Youghiogheny River
Pennsylvania: Pine Creek, Little Bald Eagle
Labrador: Minipi River

Dark Brown Dun *(Diphetor hageni;* formerly *Baetis parvus)*
   (E, M, and W)
Idaho: Henry's Fork
Montana: Rock Creek, Bitterroot River, Clark Fork
Wyoming: Firehole River

Dark Red Quill *(Cinygmula ramaleyi)* **(W)**
Colorado: Blue River, Colorado River
Montana: Rock Creek, Bitterroot River

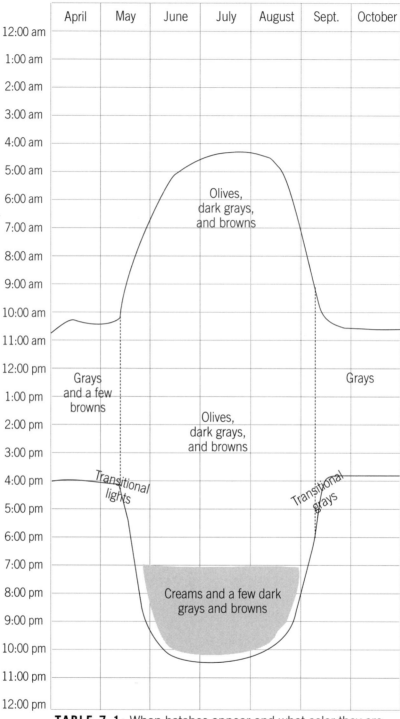

TABLE 7.1: When hatches appear and what color they are

7. SUMMER EVENINGS— THE CREAM MAYFLIES

Time of Year: May 15–September 15
When to Be on the Stream: 6–10 PM
Predominant Colors of the Hatches: Cream and yellow

A LOOK AT SOME OF THE HATCHES

Summer evenings hold plenty of mayfly hatches, and many of these are light in color. In the vast majority of cases, if a mayfly is cream or yellow, then it emerges on summer evenings. Thanks to protective coloration, these mayflies appear at the time of year when nature is full of like-colored flowers and vegetation. (Compare the trees and bushes of early spring with those of June and July.) When these brighter-colored mayflies rest on a branch of a tree before they change into a mating spinner (see chapter 2 for a full discussion of this), they don't stand out as much as they would in early spring. Still, if many of these bright-colored mayflies appeared during daylight hours, they'd be easy prey for birds and other insects. Appearing near dusk in a less-than-bright environment helps protect the brighter mayflies.

But remember that *tailwaters can change emergence times drastically.* Ask New York anglers about the sulphur hatches on the West Branch of the Delaware River in July and August. These bright yellow and cream mayflies appear in the afternoon for several weeks. Water temperatures on this tailwater are extremely cold—even in the middle of the summer. These colder temperatures affect the timing of the hatch.

What are these lights? They're the cream mayflies like the yellow drake, pale evening dun, sulphur, green drake, and cream Cahill.

Transitional Lights

What the devil does *transitional light* mean? If you've ever fished the sulphur hatch of the East and Midwest, you already know. These are mainly evening emergers that often begin hatching in the afternoon. When the sulphur first appears, it often does so in the afternoon for a few days. After those few days of daylight emerging, the hatch continues—but usually just at dusk, around 8:30 PM.

I've seen the same thing with the March brown hatch. Early in its appearance the March brown appears sporadically in the afternoon. On warm evenings and as the season progresses I've seen the hatch appear just at dusk. I still remember that evening on Bald Eagle Creek in central Pennsylvania more than 20 years ago. March browns appeared sporadically during the afternoon. Flycatchers waiting in the nearby trees grabbed just about every mayfly that escaped a trout's approach. Just at dusk thousands of these March browns decided to hatch at once, and the surface filled with newly emerged duns. The trout went absolutely crazy and fed throughout a riffle in front of me.

Justin and Fannie Leonard talked about the duns of the March brown in *Mayflies of Michigan Trout Streams*. They noted that especially on "cloudy days duns of this species often emerge in the afternoon, as well as at dusk."

Pale Morning Duns and Sulphurs

What a horrendous trip this started out to be! I had a deadline—in three weeks I had to have a manuscript in to Winchester Press for my first book, *Meeting and Fishing the Hatches*. I'd come out west to fish some of the great hatches and write about them in the upcoming book. I was scheduled that first morning to meet a local fly-fishing authority on the Bitterroot River just outside Missoula, Montana. Guess what? He didn't show for the meeting. I went back to my motel and called his home; no answer. Now I was on my own. What could I do? Where could I fish? What hatches would I see? This local expert had promised to fish with me for several days and show me the rivers and their hatches. When I look back at it now, I could hardly blame him—he probably didn't want to disclose all his secret Montana rivers. I ended up walking along the Bitterroot River that early-July morning. God must have looked over my shoulder and helped me on that trip. That first morning I hit a fantastic western green drake hatch that lasted for almost two hours. Those large mayflies began appearing around 11 AM, and even in the high waters created by snowmelt huge browns and rainbows rose to capture many of the escaping duns. My pattern imitating that hatch worked to perfection. As the green drakes continued, I had my introduction to the pale morning dun hatch. These smaller mayflies—mostly pale yellow in color—emerged along with the green drakes. At this time and on this day, however, the western green drake reigned supreme. Still, the PMDs were harbingers of things to come. For the next three weeks—on 10 different rivers in Montana and Idaho—I would fish over hatches of pale morning duns, both morning and evening.

On that three-week trip PMD body colors ranged from pale yellow to olive, reddish brown, and tan. I sent different specimens of each color to my entomologist friend, Will Flowers, to identify. He keyed each of the four to one mayfly: *Ephemerella inermis*. That species—possibly more than any other—varies tremendously in coloration from river to river. I've even seen different colors of this mayfly on the same river.

Not only does the pale morning dun vary tremendously in color, but it also

Tom Rogers of Brule, Wisconsin, is ready for Labrador's green drake with plenty of patterns.

appears at different times of the day. *This mayfly is one of the very few exceptions to my rule that cream mayflies appear in the evening.* You'll encounter many hatches of this insect in the morning, but it also emerges in the evening.

The PMD hatch is found on just about every good stream and river in the West. It's common even on Alaskan waters. In the lists below you'll see some of the rivers that host the hatch.

The pale morning spinner can also be important. My own first good spinner fall occurred while I was working on the book *Great Rivers—Great Hatches.* My son Bryan accompanied Richie Montella and me on a late-July float trip on Montana's Bighorn River. Richie drifted his McKenzie boat through a series of runs and pools and guided the boat to shore. He asked the two of us to get out and start casting to a pod of risers just 100 feet upriver. We decided to take turns so we wouldn't scare the 15 or so rising trout. A few pale morning spinners fell, and trout continued to feed. I tied on a tannish brown spinner pattern and began casting. On my first good drift with that spinner pattern, I saw a heavy swirl. I landed a 20-inch brown trout. Now Bryan cast into the feeding pod. He too landed a heavy brown in no time at all. For the next hour or more—we were so focused on the rising pod that we lost track of time—we caught trout. We ended up estimating that we'd landed 14 of those risers before the spinner fall ended.

I tie up several patterns to match the dun (see the suggestions below). I often

Anglers wait for the famous white fly hatch in August on Yellow Breeches Creek in south central Pennsylvania.

use a Sulphur pattern to match this western hatch. Both the PMD and the sulphur are pale yellow in color and about the same size, so one pattern can copy both. (You'll need other patterns to match other color phases.)

The sulphurs (*Ephemerella invaria* and *E. rotunda*) found in the East and Midwest sometimes appear during the day as well. Some of the best hatches I've ever experienced came in midafternoon in early to mid-May. For the first few days that the sulphur appears each year, it often does so in the afternoon. Toss in an overcast sky, cool temperatures, and some drizzle and you'll see the sulphur on the surface for four or five hours in mid-May. Some of my most memorable trips have occurred when I confronted bad weather.

Elk Creek in central Pennsylvania is a fertile limestone stream with myriad great hatches. One of its finest is the sulphur. Vince Gigliotti, Bryan Meck, and I arrived at Elk one midmorning in the third week of May. Drizzle fell as we assembled our gear. I decided to take photos while Bryan and Vince headed toward the water. When we arrived at the stream bank we saw dozens of trout rising and a good hatch of sulphurs already under way. For the next five hours those duns continued to appear on the surface. They were slow to take off, so trout fed on them continuously. Conservatively, I estimated that Bryan and Vince caught more than 40 trout that day on Elk Creek.

Several species (*Ephemerella rotunda, E. invaria, E. dorothea,* and *E septentrion-*

TABLE 7.2: Hatch Chart for Western Streams and Rivers

Conventional Pattern Name** Dun/Spinner	Scientific Name	Rating	Approximate Beginning Emergence Date	Time of Day Dun/Spinner	Size	Special Pattern Suggestion** Dun/Spinner	Restricted Pattern**
Pale Morning Dun	Ephemerella inermis	1	May 20	Morning and evening	16	3, 5, and 11	Light Cahill, BWOD
Pale Morning Spinner		1			24		
Pale Morning Dun	Ephemerella infrequens	2	May 20	Morning and evening	18	2	Light Cahill
Pale Morning Spinner		2				24	
Pale Evening Dun	Heptagenia elegantula	4	June 15	Evening	16	6	Light Cahill
Pale Evening Spinner		4				19	
Pink Lady	Epeorus albertae	3	July 1	Evening	12	4 (with pink)	Light Cahill
Salmon Spinner		4				23	
Little White Mayfly	Caenis spp.	5	July 1	Evening	24–26	1	Light Cahill
Little White Spinner		5				21	
Light Cahill	Cinygma dimicki	4	July 1	Evening		2	Light Cahill
Light Cahill Spinner		3				22	
Gray Fox	Heptagenia solitaria	4	August 1	Evening		2	Light Cahill
Gray Fox Spinner		2				24	
White Fly	Ephoron album	4	August 15	Evening		1	Light Cahill
White Fly Spinner		3				21	

**Refer to chapters 1 and 10 for more information.

TABLE 7.3: Hatch Chart for Eastern and Midwestern Streams and Rivers

Conventional Pattern Name** Dun/Spinner	Scientific Name	Rating	Approximate Beginning Emergence Date	Time of Day Dun/ Spinner	Size	Special Pattern Suggestion** Dun/ Spinner	Restricted Pattern*
Sulphur	*Ephemerella rotunda*	1	May 8	Evening	16	3	Light Cahill
Sulphur Spinner		1				24	
Pale Evening Dun	*Ephemerella septentrionalis*	3	May 18	Evening	16	2	Light Cahill
Pale Evening Spinner		4				23	
March Brown	*Stenonema vicarium*	2	May 20	Afternoon	12	2	March Brown
Great Red Spinner		3		Evening		24	
Pale Evening Dun	*Leucrocuta aphrodite*	4	May 20	Evening	16	2	Light Cahill
Pale Evening Spinner		4				24	
Sulphur	*Ephemerella invaria*	2	May 20	Evening	16	3	Light Cahill
Sulphur Spinner		2				24	
Light Cahill	*Stenonema ithaca*	3	May 25	Evening	14	2	Light Cahill
Light Cahill Spinner		3				24	
Female: Pink Lady	*Epeorus vitreus**	2	May 25	Evening	14	4 (add pink)	Light Cahill
Male: Light Cahill Salmon Spinner		4				22	
Light Cahill	*Stenacron interpunctatum*	2	May 25	Evening	14	4	Light Cahill
Light Cahill Spinner		3				23 (add orange)	

Conventional Pattern Name** Dun/Spinner	Scientific Name	Rating	Approximate Beginning Emergence Date	Time of Day Dun/ Spinner	Size	Special Pattern Suggestion** Dun/ Spinner	Restricted Pattern**
Green Drake	*Ephemera guttulata*	1	May 25	Evening	8	2	Light Cahill
Coffin Fly		1				1	
Pale Evening Dun	*Ephemerella dorothea*	2	May 31	Evening	18	23	Light Cahill
Pale Evening Spinner		2				24	
Michigan Caddis	*Hexagenia limbata*	1	June 5	Evening	6	2	Light Cahill
Hex Spinner		1				23	
Giant Yellow Drake or Green Drake	*Hexagenia rigida*	2	June 10	Evening	8	2	Light Cahill
Giant Dark Yellow Drake Spinner		2				23	
Light Cahill	*Heptagenia marginalis*	3	June 15	Evening	14	2 (olive reflections)	Light Cahill
Olive Cahill Spinner		2				22	
Cream Cahill	*Stenonema pulchellum*	3	June 15	Evening	14	1	Light Cahill
Cream Cahill Spinner		3				22	
Yellow Drake	*Ephemera varia*	3	June 15	Evening	12	2	Light Cahill
Yellow Drake Spinner		3				23	
Pale Evening Dun	*Leucrocuta hebe*	4	June 22	Evening	16	2	Light Cahill
Pale Evening Spinner		4				23	

Table continues on next page

Conventional Pattern Name** Dun/Spinner	Scientific Name	Rating	Approximate Beginning Emergence Date	Time of Day Dun/ Spinner	Size	Special Pattern Suggestion** Dun/ Spinner	Restricted Pattern*
Golden Drake	*Anthopotamus distinctus*	4	June 25	Evening	12	4	Light Cahill
Golden Drake Spinner		4				23 (with orange)	
Cream Cahill	*Stenonema modestum*	3	August 1	Evening	16	1	Light Cahill
Cream Spinner		3				21	
White Fly	*Ephoron leukon*	1	August 12	Evening	14	1	Light Cahill
White Fly		1				21	

*More than one generation each year.
**Refer to chapters 1 and 10 for more information.

alis) make up what we call the sulphur hatch. Most appear from mid-May through much of June. In the West anglers call two species—*Ephemerella inermis* and *E. infrequens*—pale morning duns. By far the more common, more important, and more widespread is the former.

If you want to fish a rewarding, sometimes explosive, hatch, try fishing the pale morning dun hatch of the West or the sulphur in the Midwest and East.

The Green Drake—A World of Difference

So you want to see a great hatch and fish over trout rising to it. The trout have to be native brookies of better than 4 pounds, and hopefully up to 8 pounds. You prefer to fish when a large, easy-to-see mayfly emerges—light colored—and you'd like to fish on pleasantly cool summer evenings. You want the mayfly to appear on the surface then rest there for several seconds—or maybe up to a minute or more—so the trout get a chance to take it. The mayfly should appear while it's still light and you're not fumbling with a pattern that you can't see.

In my more than 50 years of fly-fishing, I've seen only one place in the world that has all these ingredients—Labrador.

Recently I accompanied Steve McDonald—an anesthesiologist from Doylestown,

EARLY SPRING—GRAYS (DUNS)

Female Hendrickson dun
(Ephemerella subvaria)

Male little blue-winged olive dun
(Baetis tricaudatus)

Female speckle-winged dun
(Callibaetis spp.)

Female dark quill Gordon dun
(Ameletus ludens)

Female quill Gordon dun
(Epeorus pleuralis)

EARLY SPRING—DARK BROWNS
(SPINNERS)

Female quill Gordon spinner
(Paraleptophlebia adoptiva)

Female quill Gordon spinner
(Epeorus pleuralis)

Male red quill spinner
(Ephemerella subvaria)

SUMMER MORNINGS AND AFTERNOONS—
GRAYS, OLIVES, AND TANS (DUNS)

Male pale morning dun
(Ephemerella infrequens)

Western green drake
(Drunella grandis)

Female blue-winged olive dun
(Drunella cornuta)

SUMMER MORNINGS AND AFTERNOONS—
BROWNS (SPINNERS)

Male gray drake spinner
(Siphlonurus mirus)

Brown drake spinner
(Litobrancha recurvata)

Female gray drake spinner
(Siphlonurus spp.)

Female western green drake spinner
(Drunella grandis)

SUMMER EVENINGS—CREAMS (DUNS)

Female green drake dun
(Hexagenia rigida)

Female yellow drake dun
(Ephemera varia)

Female light Cahill dun
(Stenacron interpunctatum)

Female pink lady dun
(Epeorus vitreus)

Female sulphur dun
(Ephemerella rotunda)

Female pale evening dun
(Ephemerella septentrionalis)

SUMMER EVENINGS—CREAMS (SPINNERS)

Male coffin fly spinner
(Ephemera guttulata)

Male pale evening spinner
(Leucrocuta aphrodite)

SUMMER EVENINGS—BROWNS (DUNS)

Female brown drake dun
(Ephemera simulans)

Female slate drake dun
(Isonychia bicolor)

Female blue-winged olive dun
(Drunella flavilinea)

SUMMER EVENINGS—BROWNS (SPINNERS)

Female hex spinner
(Hexagenia limbata)

Female rusty spinner
(Hexagenia atrocaudata)

White-gloved howdy spinner
(Isonychia bicolor)

FALL AND WINTER—GRAYS AND OLIVES (DUNS)

Female little blue-winged olive dun
(*Baetis tricaudatus*)

Female little blue-winged olive dun
(*Plauditus veteris*)

FALL AND WINTER—BROWNS (SPINNERS)

Female rusty spinner
(*Baetis tricaudatus*)

Male jenny spinner
(*Paraleptophlebia guttata*)

White-gloved howdy spinner
(*Isonychia bicolor*)

Light Gray with Olive Reflections

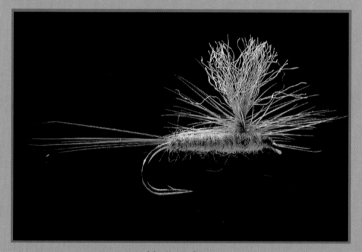

Medium Gray

Dark Gray

Tannish Brown

Reddish Tan

Blue-Winged Olive

Blue Quill

CHAPTER 5—EARLY SPRING (SPINNERS)

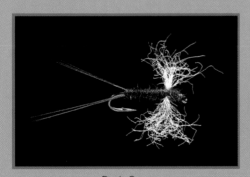

Dark Gray

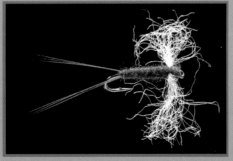

Reddish Brown

Medium Gray

Tannish Brown

Chocolate Brown

Medium Olive

Blue-Winged Olive

Blue Quill

Tan

Dark Brown

Light Olive

Dark Olive

CHAPTER 6—SUMMER MORNINGS AND AFTERNOONS (SPINNERS)

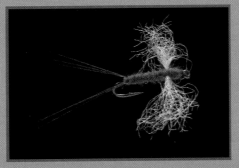

Light Gray

Medium Gray

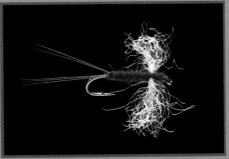

Dark Brownish Black

CHAPTER 7:
SUMMER EVENINGS—CREAMS (DUNS)

Creamish White

Yellowish Cream

Pale Olive with Yellow Reflections

Pale Orange

CHAPTER 7:
SUMMER EVENINGS—CREAMS (SPINNERS)

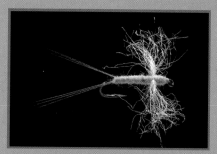

White

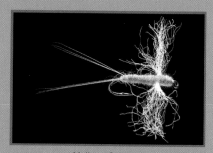

Yellow-Orange

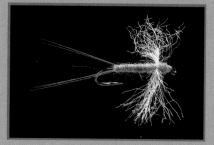

Cream

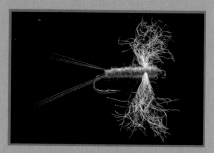

Cream-Pink

CHAPTER 8—SUMMER EVENINGS: DARK HATCHES (DUNS)

Yellow-Tan

Dark Gray

Tannish Brown

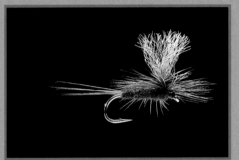

Brownish Black

CHAPTER 8—SUMMER EVENINGS: DARK HATCHES (SPINNERS)

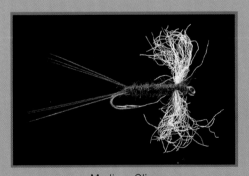

Medium Olive

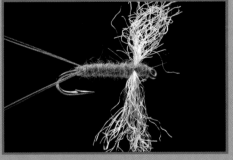

Dark Olive Black

CHAPTER 9—
EARLY FALL AND WINTER (DUNS)

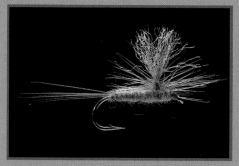

Medium Gray

Dark Gray

Blue Quill

Blue-Winged Olive

CHAPTER 9—
EARLY FALL AND WINTER (SPINNER)

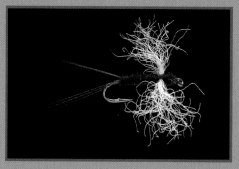

Maroon

Brook trout caught during a green drake hatch in Labrador

Pennsylvania—on a trip to fish that great hatch and in search of behemoth brookies. Steve had excitedly told me unbelievable stories about one of the last true wilderness areas left in North America.

We flew into Goose Bay, Labrador, then took a floatplane to the Anne Marie Lodge, 70 miles south. Jack and Lorraine Cooper of Goose Bay have operated Anne Marie, Minonipi, and Minipi Lodges since 1979. All are located on a large stretch of the Minipi River system in southern Labrador. The vast majority of the fly-fishing here is catch-and-release.

We arrived at camp minus our luggage. The airline said the plane was overweight, so they left our luggage back in Halifax, Nova Scotia. No fishing gear for the first day and a half—all dressed up and nowhere to go. Fortunately, some of the other guests at the lodge loaned us fishing gear that first evening. All total, nine anglers spent a week at the camp.

But would this place live up to my high expectations? Would I see this hatch that the guides called the green drake? The expert guides at the camp—Raymond Best, Ralph Coles, Chad Snow, Patrick Broomfield, and Howard Guptill—told us that the green drake had begun just the night before. Wow! Things seem to be going just right. Still, would I see the huge brook trout taking dry flies on the surface that Steve had bragged about? I didn't have to wait long to find out. Steve and I headed out by motorized canoe for an evening of exploring and fishing just an hour after our floatplane landed at the camp.

Elk Creek in West Virginia boasts a green drake hatch in late May.

The Minipi River system is a series of lakes, ponds, and flowing rivers. You can travel for a couple of miles on a lake and all of a sudden see a flowing river emptying into or out of it. Steve McDonald, our guide Ralph Coles, and I headed to an area near Smoke Island. As we rode to our destination, I looked in awe at the number of green drakes already on the surface. The weather had dealt a severe blow to the hatch that evening. Literally millions of these huge duns—stunned and dazed by the unusually cool evening temperatures—covered the surface of the lake. These mayflies (*Hexagenia rigida*) emerged in two color forms. The larger female did in fact resemble the famous green drake (*Ephemera guttulata*) of the eastern United States and Canada with its yellowish cream abdomen and olive-green wings. The male was smaller, with an abdomen of tannish brown. Too many mayflies and too few trout rising that first evening (see "Why a Hatch Is Important" in chapter 4). As we rode back to camp in the cool late-July evening, I continued to be amazed at the duns on the surface struggling to set themselves completely free from their aquatic environs. They failed; very few duns would be tomorrow night's spinners.

The green drake is the only cream emerger in Labrador, and it's fairly predictable in the time of the year that it emerges. Labrador temperatures reach their peak in late July; you'll thus find the warmest evening temperatures of the year there right at the time the green drake appears. If the duns were to appear on the surface any earlier or later in the year they would encounter cooler evening temperatures (like what we experienced that evening), and they wouldn't be able to escape. Duns are unable to cope with cool weather. Spinners, on the other hand, can delay their flight for an evening or two if they encounter cool temperatures.

So that first night of meeting the green drake on the Minipi River was pretty much a bust—though Steve did manage to coax a 4½-pound brook trout to take a Green Drake dry fly.

This would change in the next few days. Two evenings later we motored out to the same general area, near Smoke Island. That evening the hatch and the weather cooperated. Huge cream mayflies began appearing on the surface sporadically around 6 PM and continued until well after 9 PM. The number of duns hatching that evening was much smaller than we'd seen a couple of days before. The hatch was still heavy, however; within a short distance we saw hundreds of duns resting on the surface for minutes before they were able to escape. Loud slurping noises echoed from one side of the lake to the other. The calm waters unmistakably exposed the huge rising brook trout. Steve McDonald cast a size 8 Twisted Dun pattern (see chapter 10) to what seemed like a large fish. The trout inhaled a dun or two and moved on rapidly to another feast. It was extremely difficult to predict the direction these trout would swim. We had to guess where they'd pop up again and cast in that direction. On the third or fourth cast Steve predicted correctly where the trout would make its next rise, made a perfect cast, and landed a feisty 4½-pound brook trout.

We continued to follow rising trout for the next two hours. They'd feed on a

West Canada Creek in northern New York holds white flies and golden drakes.

dun or two and then move rapidly on to another location 15 to 30 feet away. I'm convinced that they followed this unusual feeding procedure because of the northern pike and ospreys on the area. If they fed in the same area continuously, they'd suffer some predation—or at least they did when they were younger. We were ready to call it a day and quit, but our guide that evening, Pat Broomfield, spotted one last feeder. Steve cast a Twisted Poly Spinner pattern over the moving riser and correctly guessed the lunker's movement on the first cast. It happened quickly—a huge gulp and the fish went deep. Finally Steve landed the 7-pound spinner feeder. We headed back to the lodge full of tales to tell the other anglers.

This same action—casting over feeding trout—lasted for the entire week we were at the lodge. Later in the week a pale yellow Stimulator-type pattern, the Laid Back Hex, first tied by Rusty Gates of Michigan, worked extremely well. I'm convinced that trout think of the Laid Back Hex as an emerging nymph. They certainly sucked it in readily.

A few evenings later I tied a few Laid Back Hex type patterns for the rest of the anglers at the lodge. I gave one of these to Steve McDonald to test one evening; he landed an 8-pound brookie and I landed a 6¾-pounder on that same pattern. Two huge brook trout on the same pattern—wow! I went back that evening and tied even more of them. I've listed the tying directions for the Laid Back Hex pattern in chapter 10.

How do the Minipi brook trout get so big? Why do they look like footballs? They gorge themselves on a constant supply of food in June, July, and August. Much of this food consists of mayflies, caddisflies, and stoneflies. Surprisingly, many of the mayflies found in Labrador are the same ones found in the United States.

The green drake (*Hexagenia rigida*) also inhabits Skaneateles Lake near Syracuse, New York. Locals there call it the hex hatch. Mike DeTomasco of the Royal Coachman Fly Shop in Skaneateles says that an angler in the past year landed a 6-pound rainbow in the lake during the hex hatch. Visit that water around July 4 and you'll see the same great hatch we witnessed in Labrador. Both Skaneateles Lake in New York and the Minipi River system have another great hatch—the brown drake. (See the story on the brown drake in chapter 8.) Which is the better hatch in Labrador? Dave Fillmore of Nova Scotia is one of the finest fly-fishers I encountered at the Minipi lodges. He has trouble deciding which of the two is the better hatch.

What great matching-the-hatch opportunities I experienced on the Minipi River system—especially at night! What heavy native brook trout. I had never seen trout like these before in the 50 years I fly-fished. The one-week trip to the Coopers' Minipi Lodge turned out to be much more than I had anticipated. It's a once-in-a-lifetime experience. But it was more than just great fly-fishing over huge trout for a week—it was also meeting new friends. Staying at the camp with Steve and me were Dave and John A. Fillmore, Tom Rogers, Henry Taylor, John Clarke, Ed Quigley, and George Boder. Henry from Green Valley, Arizona, and Tom Rogers from Brule, Wisconsin, traveled to the camp to complete a Labrador video they've been working on for several years. Dave, John A., and John Clarke were Canadians and some of the finest fly-fishers I have ever encountered. We all became friends after a week of sharing fly-fishing experiences on the Minipi River.

Dave Fillmore taught me several lessons when fishing for brook trout at the Minipi camps. Afternoon fishing was usually slow—few mayflies emerging and few trout rising. Dave and his guide thus used the afternoon hours to decide where they'd spend the productive evening. They'd look for feeding fish, for insects appearing, and then decide on a strategy for the evening.

You can't lie about the number of trout you catch at the Coopers' Minipi camp. The guides keep a record of every trout over 3 pounds. They even tag some of the fish so they know their movement. For the week the group caught 131 trout of 3 pounds or more.

When somebody mentions the green drake I'll never again think only of the large eastern U.S. mayfly that appears in late May and early June. From now on I'll fondly remember the Coopers' Minipi camps and that other green drake—a world of difference.

WHERE THE HATCHES ARE FOUND—TYPICAL STREAMS AND RIVERS

Sulphur (*Ephemerella rotunda, E. invaria*) (E and M)
Connecticut: Housatonic River, Farmington River
Maryland: Gunpowder River
Massachusetts: Deerfield River
Michigan: AuSable River, Rifle River, Manistee River, Little Manistee River, Pere Marquette River, Boardman River
New Jersey: South Branch of the Raritan River, Musconetcong River
New York: Oatka Creek, Spring Brook, Delaware River, Beaverkill River, Limestone Creek
Pennsylvania: Big Fishing Creek, Little Juniata River, Spring Creek, First Fork of the Sinnemahoning, Savage River, Codorus Creek
Virginia: Rapidan River, Mossy Creek
Wisconsin: Namekagon River

Pale Morning Dun (*Ephemerella inermis, E. infrequens*)
  (appears morning, afternoon, and evening) (W)
Arizona: White River, Black River
California: Merced River, Hat Creek
Colorado: South Platte River, Gunnison River, Cache la Poudre River,
  Thompson River, San Juan River
Idaho: Big Wood River, Henry's Fork, South Fork of the Snake River,
  Silver Creek
Montana: Bitterroot River, Rock Creek, Whitefish River, Kootenai River,
  Clark Fork, Bighorn River, Madison River
New Mexico: San Juan River
Oregon: McKenzie River, Deschutes River, Metolius River
Utah: Provo River, Green River
Wyoming: Laramie River, North Platte River

Giant Yellow Drake or Green Drake (*Hexagenia rigida*) (E and M)
New York: Skaneateles Lake, numerous Adirondack lakes
Michigan: Muskegon River
Labrador: Minipi River, Park Lake, Osprey Lake

Michigan Caddis (*Hexagenia limbata*) (E, M, and W)
See chapter 8.
Pale Evening Dun (*Ephemerella dorothea, E. septentrionalis*) (E and M)
Michigan: Little Manistee River, Pere Marquette River
New York: Ausable River, Schoharie Creek, Beaverkill River
Pennsylvania: Pine Creek, Little Bald Eagle Creek, Elk Creek, Sixmile Run
Tennessee: Little River
Virginia: Rapidan River, Rose River

Light Cahill (*Stenacron interpunctatum canadense, Stenonema ithaca*)
  (E and M)
Connecticut: Housatonic River
Massachusetts: Deerfield River
Michigan: AuSable River

New York: Delaware River, East Koy Creek, Ischua Creek, West Branch of Oswego Creek, West Branch of the Ausable River

Pennsylvania: Spring Creek, Little Juniata River, Penns Creek, Big Fishing Creek, Oswego Creek, Pine Creek

Vermont: Battenkill River

Virginia: Rose River, Rapidan River, Little River

Yellow Drake *(Ephemera varia)* **(E and M)**

Connecticut: Housatonic River

New York: East Canada Creek

Maryland: Big Hunting Creek, Gunpowder River, Youghiogheny River

Pennsylvania: Bald Eagle Creek, Woodcock Creek, Clarion River, Youghiogheny River, Little Juniata River

Vermont: Battenkill River

Cream Cahill *(Stenonema modestum)* **(E and M)**

Michigan: AuSable River, Pere Marquette River

Pennsylvania: Little Juniata River, West Branch of the Susquehanna River (Clearfield area)

Green Drake *(Ephemera guttulata)* **(E)**

Connecticut: Housatonic River

Maryland: Big Hunting Creek, Savage River

New York: Delaware River, Beaverkill River, Gennyganslett Creek, East Koy Creek, Wiscoy Creek, Ischua Creek, West Canada Creek, East Branch of the Delaware River, West Branch of the Ausable River

Pennsylvania: Penns Creek, Yellow Creek, Little Juniata River, Big Fishing Creek, Little Pine Creek, West Hemlock Creek, Kettle Creek

West Virginia: Elk River, Cheat River system

White Fly *(Ephoron leukon, E. album)* **(E, M, and W)**

Connecticut: Housatonic River

Idaho: Snake River

New York: West Canada Creek, Delaware River

Pennsylvania: Yellow Breeches Creek, Little Juniata River, Kishaquokillas Creek
Wisconsin: Namekagon River
Wyoming: North Platte River

Pink Lady (*Epeorus vitreus*) **(E)**
Michigan: Pere Marquette River
New York: Delaware River, Beaverkill River
Pennsylvania: Brodhead Creek, Big Fishing Creek, Sixmile Run

Pink Lady (*Epeorus albertae, E. deceptivus*) **(W)**
Colorado: Fryingpan River, Roaring Fork
Idaho: Henry's Fork
Montana: Madison River

Gray Fox (*Heptagenia solitaria*) **(W)**
Colorado: Colorado River

Light Cahill (*Cinygma dimicki*) **(W)**
Montana: Bitterroot River, Clark Fork

Pale Evening Dun (*Heptagenia elegantula*) **(W)**
Colorado: Colorado River
Idaho: Silver Creek
Montana: Big Hole

Golden Drake (*Anthopotamus distinctus*) **(E and M)**
Connecticut: Housatonic River
New York: Delaware River, West Canada Creek, Genesee River, Willowemoc River
Wisconsin: Namekagon River

March Brown (*Stenonema vicarium*) (afternoon and evening
emerger) (E and M) (includes the gray fox,
which is now part of the same species)

Connecticut: Housatonic River, Farmington River

Maryland: Gunpowder River

Massachusetts: Deerfield River

Michigan: Pere Marquette River, Rapid River

New Hampshire Connecticut River, Saco River

New York: Delaware River, Beaverkill River, Willowemoc River

North Carolina: South Toe River

Pennsylvania: Middle Creek, Elk Creek, Pine Creek, Bald Eagle Creek

Vermont: Battenkill River

Virginia: Rapidan River

West Virginia: Elk River

Wisconsin: Namekagon River

Pale Evening Dun (*Leucrocuta aprhrodite, L. hebe*) (E and M)

New York: Delaware River, Beaverkill River

Michigan: Pere Marquette River

Pennsylvania: Bald Eagle Creek, Penns Creek

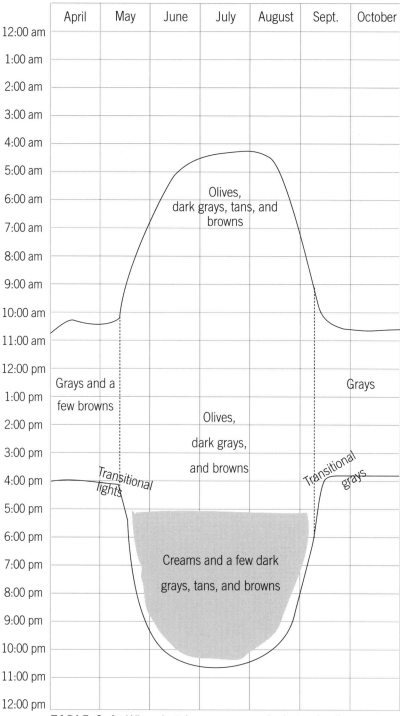

TABLE 8.1: When hatches appear and what color they are

8. SUMMER EVENINGS— THOSE DARK HATCHES

Time of Year: May 15–September 15
When to Be on the Stream: 6 PM–midnight
Predominant Color of the Hatches: Dark brown and gray (remember, the majority of duns appearing in the evening are cream; see chapter 7)

While the preponderance of mayflies that appear during summer evenings are cream and yellow, you'll still find some very important tan, brown, and dark gray mayflies appearing at that time. These tan and gray mayflies can produce some important matching-the-hatch opportunities and shouldn't be overlooked. Who hasn't heard of the great hex hatches that appear mainly on midwestern and western waters? The slate drake is also important at this time of the year. (We'll look at this two-generations-a-year mayfly in more detail in chapter 9.) Another important, albeit short-lived, hatch is the brown drake.

Isn't it interesting that the only two major dark hatches in the West are two mayflies that also appear in the East and Midwest?

THE BROWN DRAKE OF LATE SPRING AND EARLY SUMMER

Within the past 30 years I can count on one hand the number of times I haven't had a good imitation to match a hatch. I quickly forget about most of these frustrating poor matching-the-hatch events, but one of those failed attempts still haunts me 30 years later. I talked about it in chapter 1, but let's look at the same incident in more detail here.

I'll never forget that evening on Pine Creek at Cedar Run in north-central Pennsylvania. Jim Heltzel had just taken up fly-fishing, and we decided to fish one evening early in June. Around 7 PM we headed up the lower end of Cedar Run and hit the first couple of riffles on that excellent small stream. Around 8 PM we decided to head downstream and end the evening on Pine Creek. As we retraced our steps, we noticed some large mayfly spinners in the air. When we arrived back on Pine Creek we saw hundreds and then thousands of these same large dark mayflies. I assumed they were March browns, so both of us tied on March Brown Spinners and began casting to dozens of feeding trout.

TABLE 8.2: Dark Evening Hatches in the East and Midwest

Conventional Pattern Name** Dun/Spinner	Scientific Name	Rating	Approximate Beginning Emergence Date	Time of Day Dun/Spinner	Size	Special Pattern Suggestion** Dun/Spinner	Restricted Pattern**
Brown Drake	*Ephemera simulans*	1	May 25	Evening	10	10	March Brown
Brown Drake Spinner		1				24	
Male: Chocolate Dun Female: Olive Sulphur	*Ephemerella needhami*	3	May 25	Evening	16	12 / 16	Willow Special / BWOD
Male: Chocolate Spinner Female: Dark Olive Spinner		4				26 / 29	
Dark Blue Quill	*Serratella deficiens*	3	May 25	early evening	16	8	Adams
Dark Blue Quill Spinner		4				20	
Big Yellow May Michigan Caddis	*Hexagenia limbata*	2	June 10	Evening	6–8	5	Light Cahill
Great Lead-Winged Drake		1				23	
Big Slate Drake	*Hexagenia atrocaudata*	4	August 1	Evening	8	8	Adams
Dark Rusty Spinner or Brown Drake Spinner		3				26 (ribbed with yellow)	

Trout fed everywhere, mostly on large dark spinners returning to lay eggs and die. There were so many spinners in the air that you could hear the humming of their wings. Within reach of my cast I saw no less than 100 trout eagerly taking this seemingly unending supply of food. What a terrific way to match the hatch. Jim and I began casting—and casting—and casting—with very little success. After more than half an hour of fruitless casting, I finally switched to a Black Quill pattern and caught one trout. Can you believe it? One trout, when I had more than 100 feeding freely within casting distance.

TABLE 8.3: Dark Evening Hatches in the West

Conventional Pattern Name** Dun/Spinner	Scientific Name	Rating	Approximate Beginning Emergence Date	Time of Day	Size	Special Pattern Suggestion** Dun/Spinner	Restricted Pattern*
Blue-Winged Olive Dun	*Drunella flavilinea*	2	May 20	Morning and evening	14	16	BWOD
Dark Olive Spinner		3				30	
Brown Drake	*Ephemera simulans*	1	May 25	Evening	10	10	March Brown
Brown Drake Spinner		1				24	
Michigan Caddis	*Hexagenia limbata*	1	June 10	Evening	6–8	5	March Brown
Great Lead-Winged Drake		1				23	

**Refer to chapters 1 and 10 for more information.

When dusk arrived the spinner fall began to wane, but a few large duns appeared on the surface. Jim and I walked away from that event frustrated, confounded, disgusted, and shaken. I grabbed a couple of the large duns and spinners, looked at them carefully, and decided they were brown drakes—a very close relative of the green and yellow drakes. Guess what? I had no fly that adequately copied the dun or spinner of that mayfly. Sure, I had heard about the great hatches that Michigan and Wisconsin waters like the AuSable, Namekagon, and Brule held, but not the Northeast. And yes, I had experienced the very same hatch and spinner fall on Henry's Fork and Silver Creek, both in Idaho—but no one ever wrote about the great hatches in the Northeast. In fact, until that day on Pine Creek I had not realized that this hatch appeared in any numbers in Pennsylvania or New York. Yes, before that frustrating first encounter I had seen a few of these brown drakes on the Beaverkill, but not enough to create a feeding frenzy.

Since that confrontation with the brown drake on Big Pine Creek, I have not been without a good pattern to match the hatch and spinner fall.

The brown drake (*Ephemera simulans*) is a burrowing mayfly (the nymph burrows in fine to medium gravel); its close relatives the green and yellow drakes are also burrowers. If you look at the barred (spotted) wings of all three, you'll see the similarity.

The brown drake is one of only a few dozen mayflies that are found on eastern, midwestern, *and* western trout streams of the United States, as well as many in Canada. Hatches of this species are found from Idaho to Connecticut to Labrador. Most of the better-known Michigan and Wisconsin trout waters harbor great brown drake hatches.

New York trout streams and lakes hold plenty of these mayflies. You'll find a great hatch on the Delaware River and even a few on the Beaverkill. Skaneateles Lake near Syracuse is an unbelievably clear, deep lake. About June 18 this water explodes with a great brown drake hatch. Fish this lake at that time and it comes alive with trout rising to these mayflies. Mike DeTomasco, owner of the Royal Coachman in Skaneateles, says that local anglers call the hatch the "Father's Day" hatch because it appears near that Sunday. The Housatonic in Connecticut also boasts a great hatch of brown drakes. Hatches in the Northeast most often appear the latter part of May and early June (see table 8.1). On streams and rivers that hold both green and brown drake hatches you might encounter the two species on the water at the same time. In the Midwest expect to see the brown drake a couple of weeks after the hatch has ended in the East; in the West the hatch appears on Henry's Fork and Silver Creek near the end of June. Hatches in Labrador, Canada, appear on the Minipi River system around the end of the first week in July.

I first met the hatch on Henry's Fork in Idaho in late June more than 25 years ago. What a spectacular sight! All other anglers had left the Railroad Ranch section of these fantastic trout waters hours before. Then about 9 PM brown drakes appeared and continued for the next two hours. Huge rainbows fed throughout the section we fished. Al Gretz and I cast over rising trout until 11 PM. That wasn't the heaviest hatch I've ever seen, but it was one of the most productive.

The brown drake is one of the shortest hatches of the season. Depending on the weather, the brown drake can appear out of water for as few as three days and as many as eight days. I've seen occasions, especially hot evenings, when the hatch occurs and most of the mayflies appear within a couple of hours. The hatch is a fairly large one—to match it I use a size 12 long-shank dry-fly hook.

If you're tying a conventional pattern, the most important part of the natural to copy—and also the most difficult—is the yellowish brown underbelly body. I use poly dubbing because it comes in dozens of shades. Check out the new method of copying the dun (Twisted Dun) and spinner in chapter 10. I twist poly yarn, and it forms a perfect body. I still prefer to use mallard flank feathers or tan elk hair to copy the wing of the dun. Otherwise you can copy the dun with the recommended pattern listed in chapter 10.

As I've noted before, mayflies appear at the most comfortable times of day. In summer these times are morning and evening. Go farther north—say, Labrador—

and see how this theory pans out. In the United States the brown drake appears in the evening, just at dusk, from late May through late June. In Labrador the brown drake emerges in early to mid-July. Evenings at that time of year can be cool—too cool for a mayfly to successfully escape from the water's surface. So in Labrador the brown drake emerges from 2 to 5:30 PM (table 8.1). The Labrador brown drake spinner, however, mates in the evening. It has more choices than the dun. If conditions are too cool, it can wait until another evening to mate. Duns don't have that choice. If they emerge when temperatures are too cool, they die.

Have you ever been frustrated by your inability to match a hatch? Be prepared to match the brown drakes that are so common in the Northeast and Midwest—and explosive on a few rivers of the West. Tie a few of these patterns and save them for those frustrating days in late May or June—even into July in Labrador. When this hatch appears, it can be one of the most aggravating—or rewarding—of the entire season.

IS THE HEX OVERRATED?
BY BRYAN C. MECK

It was June 22, 2001, and I was on my way to fish the world-renowned AuSable River, just east of Grayling, Michigan. I had a lot of thoughts running through my

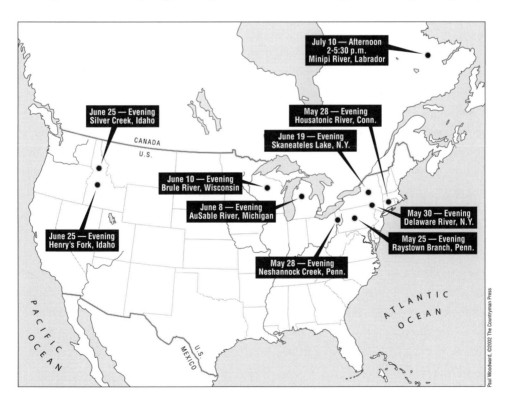

TABLE 8.4: Approximate hatch times and dates for the brown drake (Ephemera simulans) across North America.

Hex spinners on the AuSable.

head . . . would I see the famous *Hexagenia limbata* that I and countless others traveling to northern Michigan were chasing? Would the giant trout lose their inhibitions when a mayfly so large that it takes two years and about 24 moltings to emerge blanketed the waters? Finally, and probably most importantly, how many others would also travel to see the hatch, and could I even get a spot to fish on the river? I arrived in Grayling and quickly made my way east on Michigan Route 72, turning left at Stephan Bridge Road and stopping at Rusty Gates's AuSable fly shop and lodge. There were probably 50 cars in the lot with a sign welcoming us to the hex hatch. It read GET INTO A TRANCE, DO THE LIMBATA DANCE . . . I had arrived! Rusty quickly told me to head down to McCormick Bridge later that evening, about 10 miles downstream. I was not interested in catching trout this evening, just hexes! I arrived on the water at 7:30 PM and for almost two hours watched a great *Isonychia* spinner fall as well as sulphurs, caddis—just about everything but what I had come so far to see. Then at about 9:30 I started to see what looked like miniature helicopters in the air. From about 9:45 until midnight there were literally thousands of hexes in the air and on the water. The spinner fall was heavier than anything I had ever seen. The closest previous to that was the green drake on Penns Creek in central Pennsylvania in late May. The air literally buzzed from the wings of all the hex spinners.

That night, because of heavy fishing pressure at the access point (I saw three wading fishermen, 26 canoes, three motorized rowboats, belly boats, rafts . . . if it floated, I saw it), I made only a few casts. I could see that the fish were taking hex spinners.

The next morning I was curious to learn more about the hex and stopped by guide Dave Wyss's location on the AuSable at Waverly Bridge (downstream from Stephan Bridge). Dave spends his summers guiding anglers on the AuSable and his winters guiding in Florida for redfish, bonefish, and snook. With an average snowfall of 200 inches in Grayling, who could blame him! Dave explained that the hex is also often referred to as the Michigan caddis. He told me about a heavy, large caddis hatch that had been on the river when a sewage plant was open upstream at Grayling. After the water was cleaned up, it started to produce more hexes and lost the large caddisflies that it once held. Others in the area say that was what everyone had called it for years. Throughout my trip I heard the hex hatch referred to as the drake, the sandfly, the mayfly, and, in Joe Heywood's book, "the snowfly." Since the AuSable is made up of several branches, and has several dams on the main branch, the hatch is complex to understand and follow. It can usually be found at McMasters Bridge around June 20. A sure bet, however, is to check out two web sites: http://www.TroutBums.com, operated by Steve Southard from the Fly Factory in Grayling, and http://www.Gateslodge.com, which Rusty Gates updates every Wednesday. These two sites will give you up-to-date information based on the current weather conditions. This could make the difference between a productive fishing trip and just a long drive to northern Michigan.

Henry's Fork in Idaho holds a great brown drake hatch in late June.

I stopped by Ray's Canoe Center and the Fly Factory and spoke to Steve Southard. Steve has fished the AuSable for years, and he had plenty of stories of nights when he made only two or three casts the entire evening and landed two trout over 20 inches long. His largest was a 29-inch 8-pound rainbow that succumbed to a Hex pattern. He remembers as a child sleeping in an Alumicraft canoe and being awakened by a battle that his father was having with a 30-inch rainbow. It was well after midnight; Steve thought he was dreaming until the next day, when his father thanked him for netting the monster.

Steve, Dave, and Rusty pointed out that the number one mistake most visiting anglers make is that they're unfamiliar with the waters they're fishing. The fishing is best late at night, and even though Grayling is on the western edge of the eastern time zone, by 11 PM it gets pretty dark. Many new anglers wade right through rising fish. When planning a trip, arrive early and scout out productive water during the day. Know where the drop-offs and fast waters are located. Steve also recalls many anglers motoring up the river in darkness with a spotlight to look for rising fish—totally shutting off the fish. If this sounds more like a carnival scene than a peaceful evening of fly-fishing, it is, but if you're drawn to the lore of the hex hatch it seems to be a necessary evil.

Steve Southard also recommends looking in the backwaters to see if there are any pods of dead hexes; or look in the shallow mud bottoms for aquatic life. Hexes

Michigan's Pere Marquette River holds a heavy hex hatch in mid- to late June.

become more active before they emerge. This is how the locals determine whether the hatch will be on in a particular area that night.

That first evening I watched and observed more than I fished. The next evening I was intent on trying to catch some of those large trout that have made the hex hatch and the AuSable so famous. I fished part of the 14-mile Mason Tract section on the South Branch of the AuSable early in the evening. I then fished the lower section of the South Branch at the Smith Bridge access point, where Michigan Route 72 crosses the river. The evening started with temperatures in the mid-60s, but with cloudless skies the mercury dropped quickly to the mid-40s. No hexes emerged that evening due to the cold air temperatures. Still, the trout were so programmed to feed on hexes that I managed to hook and release more than a dozen fish. The last was over 20 inches and caught on one of Rusty Gates's Spinner patterns.

There are truly some big fish in the AuSable. It is unfortunate that only some of the stream is designated for special regulations. If Rusty Gates could, he would impose a one-fish limit on the entire AuSable to cut down on the generous limits in certain sections. It is estimated that more than 80 percent of the fish that are killed during the entire season on the AuSable are taken during the three-week stretch from mid-June to early July—during the hex hatch. One local guide report- edly killed 16 native trout over 15 inches long in a several-day stretch. What a shame to have killed such beautiful, large, native trout.

Rusty also points out that too much emphasis has been placed on the hex. There are also gray drake (*Siphlonurus*) and heavy brown drake (*Ephemera simulans*) hatches a few weeks earlier that bring up the same big fish. But these hatches and spinner falls bring only about one-quarter of the fishermen. I saw one of the heaviest white-gloved howdy (*Isonychia*) spinner falls of my life during both evenings.

The hex can be fickle. If temperatures are low, as they were during my second evening on the AuSable, the duns won't hatch and the spinners won't mate. An overcast day, however, can produce some excellent fly-fishing, especially when the air temperature is too cold for the insects to fly (look what happened in chapter 7 with the hex hatch in Labrador). Often the hex emerges in the morning after a pro- longed cold snap. This is why it's so important to check Steve's and Rusty's web sites for up-to-date information.

Rusty also points out that streams like the Manistee (Michigan Route 72 at CC Bridge) fish well for a week to 10 days after the AuSable. If you go north from the AuSable, you can fish hexes well into July. You'll also see fewer fishermen.

Was the trip to Michigan worth it? You bet! I saw one of the most intense mayfly hatches of my lifetime. I also, however, saw hundreds of fishermen. I caught sev- eral large stream-bred brown trout and experienced the spectacle of what has become an event in itself. I recommend hiring a guide to fish the area first, because it's an

Pine Creek in Pennsylvania is home of the brown drake.

extremely difficult river to understand, and access is rough on many stretches. Give Steve Southard, Dave Wyss, or Rusty Gates a call for more information. I also recommend—unless you enjoy crowds or you are intent on seeing the *Hexagenia limbata* hatch, as I was—that you plan your trip to the AuSable in late May or early June. You'll see hatches at that time and fewer anglers.

Another option is to fish the trico hatch in July and August after the hex hatch has ended. The AuSable has so much to offer that it's a shame it often gets credit only for the hex hatch. After all, when I asked Rusty where he fished when he went on fly-fishing trips, he said, "I used to go out west, and then I realized that the best fly-fishing in the country is literally out my back door. Why go anywhere else?" I could not have said it better myself.

The hex hatch appears June 10 through June 30; June 18–23 is usually the heaviest period. Try the Manistee River (Michigan Route 72 at the CC Bridge) from June 25 through July 8. And in mid-July, fish the streams and rivers an hour north of Grayling.

WHERE THE HATCHES ARE FOUND— TYPICAL STREAMS AND RIVERS

Brown Drake (*Ephemera simulans*) (E, M, and W)
Connecticut: Housatonic River

Idaho: Silver Creek, Henry's Fork

Michigan: AuSable River, Pigeon River, Manistee River, Pere Marquette River, Muskegon River, Platte River

New York: Delaware River, East Branch of the Delaware River, Skaneateles Lake

Pennsylvania: Pine Creek, Neshannic Creek, Raystown Branch of the Juniata River, Kettle Creek, Honey Creek, First Fork of Sinnemahoning Creek

Wisconsin: Brule River

Wyoming: Firehole River, Namekagon River

Labrador: Minipi River (appears in the afternoon)

Big Yellow May, Michigan Caddis, Green Drake (*Hexagenia limbata*) (can be grouped with light or dark mayflies) (E, M, and W)

California: Fall River

Michigan: Manistee River, Pere Marquette River, AuSable River, Boardman River, Platte River, Little Manistee River

Montana: Flathead Lake

New Hampshire: Back Lake

Oregon: Williamson River

Wisconsin: Brule River, Namekagon River, Clam River, Flag River

Slate Drake (*Isonychia bicolor*) (E and M)

Maryland: Big Hunting Creek

Michigan: AuSable River, Manistee River

New Jersey: South Branch of the Raritan River, Musconetcong River, Paulinskill River, Big Flat Brook

New York: Ausable River, Delaware River, Beaverkill River, Wiscoy Creek, Esopus Creek

Pennsylvania: Loyalsock Creek, Penns Creek, Lehigh River, Big Fishing Creek, Little Juniata River

Tennessee: Little River

Virginia: Rapidan River, Rose River, North Fork of the Moormans River

Dark Brown Dun (Male); Olive Sulphur (Female)
(*Ephemerella needhami*) (E and M)
Michigan: AuSable River, Pere Marquette River, Platte River, Manistee
   River
New York: Delaware River
Pennsylvania: Spruce Creek, Brodhead Creek

Dark Blue Quill (*Serratella deficiens*) (All)
Michigan: Pere Marquette River, Little Manistee River, Platte River
Pennsylvania: Little Juniata River

Big Slate Drake or Brown Drake (*Hexagenia atrocaudata*) (E and M)
Maryland: Big Hunting Creek, Antietam Creek
New Jersey: South Branch of the Raritan River
New York: Delaware River
Pennsylvania: Little Lehigh, Penns Creek, Loyalsock Creek, Manatawny
   Creek, Yellow Breeches Creek, Falling Springs Branch
Virginia: Mossy Creek
Wisconsin: Namekagon River

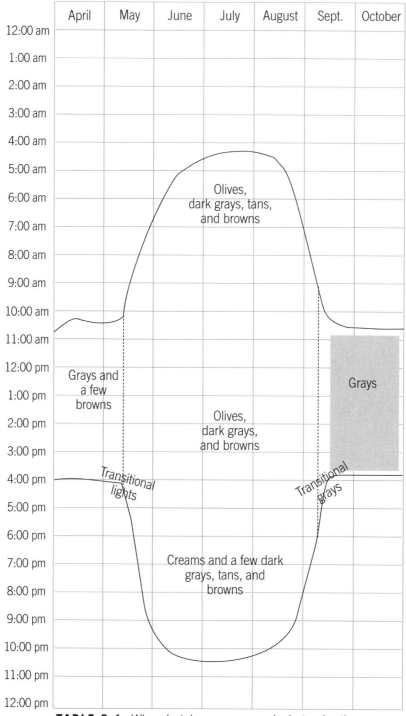

TABLE 9.1: When hatches appear and what color they are

9. EARLY FALL AND WINTER—THE GRAYS (AND OLIVES) RETURN—

Time of Year: September 15–November 30 (even later in the Southwest)
When to Be on the Stream: 9 AM–6 PM
Predominant Color of the Hatches: Gray

It's mid-September and the gray mayflies of fall have appeared. You'll find little blue-winged olives appearing again, and blue quills and tricos still emerging in the late morning. Fish on a cool, overcast morning in September or October and you'll probably see plenty of blue quills. Look for hatches of little blue-winged olives to appear in the afternoon. A second generation of a great spring drake, the slate drake, also appears again. This fall slate drake can be one of the best hatches of the season.

THE DRAKES OF FALL

Mention the slate drake and I get sentimental. The first fly-fishing article I ever wrote, in 1968, was titled "A Fly for All Summer." It appeared in a local northeastern Pennsylvania publication, *Ka Hagen,* that no longer exists. That article was the first of thousands I was to write—but I remember it as if I had written it yesterday.

In that article I mentioned that there were four important species (*Isonychia bicolor, I. matilda, I. harperi, I. saderli*) that all looked alike and all could be effectively copied by one pattern—the Slate Drake. I noted that you could find slate drake hatches almost every evening throughout late spring and early summer. Furthermore, I mentioned that one of the species waited until September and early October to appear on waters.

Surprise of surprises—entomologists have now grouped most of these large dark gray mayflies into one species: *Isonychia bicolor.* The scientists who combined these mayflies—Boris Kondratieff and J. Reese Voshell—discovered that this particular hatch has two generations each year. That means that the same mayfly appears more than once a year. You'll find slate drakes emerging from late May through much of June. The next generation or group of the same mayflies emerges again in September and early October. The generations also overlap to some extent: Some members of the second generation (the fall generation) appear in late summer at the same time that the last members of the first generation (spring generation) are appearing. Mating adults or spinners of the first generation most often lay their eggs in June, and the nymphs emerge as duns in August, September, and October.

Few anglers get a chance to fish this second hatch of slate drakes, but it can be much more important than the first hatch, because it often appears in cool weather and long after many anglers have hung up their fly-rods for the season. That second generation—the fall one—can bring trout to the surface for one last time before winter arrives. Trout seem to sense this fact and often gorge themselves on one last large source of food.

There are some differences between the two generations of mayflies. The spring generation is larger, and when it's ready to change into a dun, the nymph often crawls farther onto a rock or log to emerge than does its fall counterpart. What does this mean? Hypothetically, the dun of the spring generation is less available as a source of food than is the fall-generation dun. Entomologist A. H. Morgan, however, found that these large nymphs exhibit dual emergence behavior: Nymphs tend to crawl out of shallow, calmer water and emerge in deep and swift water. Therefore, *if you want to fish over more rising trout, then fish this hatch in deep, swift water.* Theoretically, deeper and swifter water will hold more rising trout. Also, because the nymph of the spring generation lives for a longer period of time, the dun is larger. It's often copied by a size 12 pattern, whereas a size 14 copies the fall natural.

In chapter 11 we'll look at special considerations about the hatches. One of these is mayfly body color. From stream to stream the same mayfly species can vary tremendously in color. Paul Weamer, an excellent fly-tyer and fly-fisher of Border Water Outfitters just outside of Hancock, New York, reports that when the slate drake dun first emerges on the Delaware River, its dark gray body has a definite olive cast. After a short while the body becomes more gray. He adds that olive-gray patterns—even copying the nymph—work well on the Delaware.

What are the best conditions to meet and fish the hatch? Give me an overcast, raw day in late May or late September on a stream that holds this hatch and I'll show you some great fly-fishing. I've seen these conditions over the years on Penns Creek and the Little Juniata River in central Pennsylvania, and on the Delaware River in New York. One particular late-September hatch on Penns Creek stands out even though it occurred more than 20 years ago. It was one of those lousy early-fall days with a slight drizzle and air temperatures not rising out of the 50s. For the entire afternoon slate drakes attempted to swim to nearby rocks to emerge. Few of them made it; most appeared in midstream. Trout rose continuously to the dazed duns all afternoon long. That event was possibly the most dynamic and latest-in-the-season matching-the-hatch episode I've ever experienced.

Where *can't* you find the slate drake? That's probably a better question than where you can find the hatch. Practically every stream in the northern half of Pennsylvania (and many in southern and central counties) hosts slate drake hatches.

Tennessee's Little River holds a good population of slate drakes.

Streams like the Delaware River, Loyalsock Creek, Penns Creek, Little Juniata River, and Little Pine Creek hold heavy hatches of slate drakes.

There's another reason why the slate drake is so common in Pennsylvania. This mayfly is one of the first to appear on a stream after it returns from a bout with pollution, especially acid mine drainage. Streams like the Stonycreek River in the southwestern part of Pennsylvania hold heavy hatches of stoneflies and slate drakes. So if you plan to fish a recovering stream, or one that has plenty of fast water, you'll probably find plenty of these mayflies. The Lehigh River near Lehighton in eastern Pennsylvania has recently gotten some well-deserved acclaim for its trout fishing. One of the best hatches to match on that scenic river is the slate drake in September and October.

Up to this point you might think that the slate drake is a local phenomenon occurring only in New York and Pennsylvania. It isn't. Slate drakes are extremely common across the East and Midwest. If you've experienced a good spring hatch, visit that same water in fall for a spectacular day of matching the hatch. Many of the great Michigan rivers, including the AuSable and Manistee, boast productive slate drake hatches. Here the white-gloved howdy spinner can take on special importance. Often anglers find the slate drakes emerging and the spinners falling at the same time that the Michigan caddis (*Hexagenia limbata*) appears (see chapter 8).

Rick Nowaczek fishes the Ken Lockwood Gorge of the South Branch of the Raritan in New Jersey in late August during a hatch of slate drakes.

Anglers find heavy hatches on many of the better Michigan waters. Eastern anglers can fish the hatch on the West Branch of the Ausable River in New York, the Delaware River in New York, and the Little River near Knoxville, Tennessee.

New Jersey gets a bum rap when it comes to trout waters. I'll never forget the first evening I fished the Pequest River in the north-central part of the state. As I assembled my fishing gear, another angler came over to me and asked why I was fishing here. He'd noticed the Pennsylvania license plate on my car and was curious why I didn't stay in a state that had a less dense population and better fly-fishing opportunities. But New Jersey has some great trout waters—and some respectable hatches. Take a ride along the South Branch of the Raritan River in the Ken Lockwood Gorge area. If you didn't know any better, you'd think you were lost in the wilderness of the West—but it's New Jersey, just 50 miles from New York City. I recently fished this area in early September with my son-in-law, Rick Nowaczek. I didn't expect to see any hatches, but I did want to see how the river held up after a cool summer. As I approached a heavy riffle, I noticed a couple of rising trout. I sat back and watched for a few minutes. A large dark gray mayfly was emerging. I grabbed one of the mayflies, looked at the body, and immediately changed my fly pattern to a Slate Drake. That evening Rick and I landed half a dozen trout on that size 14 pattern. Not bad for an early-fall trip to a heavily fished river!

I mentioned earlier that slate drakes emerge in an unusual manner. The nymph often swims to shore or to an exposed rock or bit of debris, then crawls out of the water and changes into a dun. By crawling out of the water, slate drakes lessen the threat of being eaten by trout. On many occasions, therefore, few of the duns are available to trout. But add an overcast day or high water to the mix, and more of the duns will emerge on the surface; the same holds true for the fall hatch. Remember, too, that slate drakes tend to crawl out of the water in shallower, calmer areas but emerge *in* the water in deeper, swifter areas. Armed with this information, if you expect a hatch you should position yourself at a deeper, swifter part of the river to see more rising trout.

Don't overlook the spinner, known as the white-gloved howdy. Bryan Meck relates that one evening in late June while he was on the AuSable near Grayling, Michigan, the temperature dropped into the higher 40s. That evening no Michigan caddis spinners appeared over the water. The white-gloved howdy mated, however, and trout fed on them freely.

The slate drake is relatively easy to identify on the stream. It's a fairly large dark slate gray mayfly with two tails. The two hind pairs of legs are cream, whereas the front pair are dark brown. If you find a stream or river with a hatch in late May and

TABLE 9.2: Fall Hatches in the East and Midwest

Conventional Pattern Name** Dun/Spinner	Scientific Name	Rating	Approximate Beginning Emergence Date	Time of Day Dun/ Spinner	Size	Special Pattern Suggestion** Dun/ Spinner	Restricted Pattern**
Little Blue-Winged Olive Dun	*Baetis tricaudatus**	2	September 1	Afternoon	20	6	BWOD
Rusty Spinner		3		Afternoon and evening		24	
Little Blue-Winged Olive Dun	*Plauditus veteris*	2	September 1	Afternoon	22	6	BWOD
Rusty Spinner		3		Afternoon and evening		24	
Blue Quill	*Paraleptophlebia guttata*	4	September 1	Late morning	8	18	Adams
Dark Brown Spinner		4				26	
Slate Drake	*Isonychia bicolor**	2	September 1	Afternoon and evening	14	8	Adams
White-Gloved Howdy		3				27	

*More than one generation per year
**See chapters 1 and 10 for more information

TABLE 9.3: Fall Hatches in the West

Conventional Pattern Name** Dun/Spinner	Scientific Name	Rating	Approximate Beginning Emergence Date	Time of Day Dun/ Spinner	Size	Special Pattern Suggestion** Dun/ Spinner	Restricted Pattern**
Little Blue-Winged Olive Dun	*Baetis tricaudatus**	2	September 1	Afternoon	20	6	BWOD
Rusty Spinner		3		Afternoon and evening		24	
Little Blue-Winged Olive Dun	*Baetis intercalris*	2	September 1	Afternoon	22	6	BWOD
Rusty Spinner		3		Afternoon and evening		24	
Blue Quill	*Paraleptophlebia bicornuta*	3	September 1	Late morning	18	8	Adams
Dark Brown Spinner		4				26	

*More than one generation per year
**See chapters 1 and 10 for more information

June, try returning that same water in fall for a great treat—fishing the "drakes of fall."

FALL AND WINTER FISHING IN THE SOUTHWEST

Until a few years ago I hung up my fly-rod up in November. That meant five months of fly-fishing inactivity. Sure, I made the occasional sojourn to the rivers of the Northeast in December, January, and February. And yes, I've hit hatches of chironomids and little black stoneflies in winter. For all intents and purposes, though, I quit any serious fly-fishing—and matching the hatch—until April.

Then two disastrous winters occurred in the Northeast in 1994 and 1995. One of the storms dumped almost 30 inches of snow; meteorologists called it the storm of the century. All I know is that I shoveled snow for two days just to get out of my house. Enough's enough, already. We headed to Phoenix, Arizona, in 1995 to escape from the harsh climes of the Northeast. I became a snowbird. Why did I choose Arizona? It was for one reason: Arizona has trout fishing—all year long. The state also features great winter weather and some good winter mayfly hatches. And Arizona and neighboring New Mexico have some great late-fall and winter fishing. Together

The San Juan River in New Mexico has good fishing much of the winter.

with John Rohmer, I wrote about all of this in *Arizona Trout Streams and Their Hatches*.

Just a few years ago, in mid-December, I gave a talk at the the Reel Life—a shop owned by Manuel Monasterio in Santa Fe, New Mexico. The next day Manuel, Virgil Bradford, Ed Adams, and I headed north to fish the lower end of the Red River north of Taos. The temperature barely rose above 40 degrees, but that didn't stop a hatch of little blue-winged olives from appearing at midday. All of us landed some heavy cutbows over 20 inches long that day.

Visit the San Juan to the west of the Red River and you'll see the same little blue-winged olive hatch throughout much of the winter. I've seen this river come alive in February with chironomids and little BWOs.

And there are still other hatches you can see in midwinter in the Southwest. You can fish over trout rising to the trico—yes, the trico—in January, February, and March. I'll never forget my first fly-fishing trip to the Cottonwood area of Arizona with Craig Josephson one mid-February day. I unexpectedly hit one of the finest trico spinner falls I had ever witnessed—in the middle of winter!

I've seen trico spinners in small numbers on the Salt River near Phoenix on Christmas and New Year's mornings. I wrote about this phenomenon and other great winter fishing on the Salt River and other nearby streams in *Fly Fisherman* magazine several years back. Guess what? The week after the article appeared, the Salt River Project cut the river's flow to 9 cubic feet per second—just a trickle.

The White River in Michigan holds some great fall hatches.

Anglers appeared on the Salt River, but there was little water and very few trout to catch. Prior to the article the river often flowed with more than 100 cubic feet per second, and the state planted trout in it all winter long. Ten-inch trout stocked in October grew several inches by April—water temperatures in the Salt rarely ever dip below 50 degrees, even in the middle of "winter." Now only the lower half, from Phon de Sutton to Granite Reef, is stocked with trout in winter. (Of course, that's still more than 5 miles of trout fishing.) Water is king in the Southwest—not trout fishing. So until the heavens pour more rain, the upper end of the Salt River— by the way, a tailwater—will remain an iffy situation.

Despite such poor trout management in the Salt—and, for that matter, most southwestern trout waters—many of them have good hatches. In addition to the occasional trico, you'll see little blue-wings almost every afternoon. The hatch grows heavy in March and April on Oak Creek near Sedona, Arizona; locals call it the early blue (*Baetis tricaudatus*). That hatch can produce some heavy browns. I've landed several in the 17-inch category during the *Baetis* and little black stonefly hatches in late winter.

The Salt River holds a great midwinter hatch and spinner fall of little blue-winged olives (*Baetis intercalaris*). On many January evenings from 5 to 6 PM I've seen pods of trout rising to spent rusty spinners. Spinner falls occur every evening throughout the winter—that is, if there's enough water for trout.

Tricos appear on many streams throughout the Southwest at unusual times. In addition to the upper Verde and the Salt Rivers in Arizona you'll find some appearing on the Rio Penasco in southeastern New Mexico in March.

So, what are you doing this winter? Hanging up your fly-rod and griping about the cold weather? Or would you rather visit (or move to!) an area where hatches appear and trout rise year-round? Look to the Southwest.

WHERE THE HATCHES ARE FOUND—TYPICAL STREAMS AND RIVERS

Slate Drake (*Isonychia bicolor*)
Michigan: AuSable River, Manistee River
New Jersey: South Branch of the Raritan River
New York: Delaware River, West Branch of the Ausable River, Beaverkill River, Willowemoc River
Pennsylvania: Lehigh River, Penns Creek, Big Fishing Creek
See chapter 8 for more locations.

Little Blue-Winged Olive Dun (*Baetis tricaudatus, Plauditus veteris*)
See chapter 6.

Blue Quill (*Paraleptophlebia guttata*) (E and M); (*P. bicornuta*) (W)
Colorado: Colorado River
Idaho: Henry's Fork
New York: Delaware River, Beaverkill River
Pennsylvania: Elk Creek, Spruce Creek, Lehigh River
Wyoming: North Platte River

Trico (*Tricorythodes attratus, T. minutus, T. fictus*)
See chapter 6.

Canyon Creek in Arizona holds great trout and some hatches in midwinter.

10. PATTERNS FOR THE HATCHES —————————

What are the predominant colors of mayflies? In spring you'll find grays; in summer olives, grays, browns, and creams; and in fall you'll again see grays. So the four important colors to copy are various shades of gray, olive, cream, and brown. Spinners or the mating adults of mayflies also have the same four dominant colors: gray, brown, cream, and olive. Spinners are often darker than duns—but there are many exceptions.

I discussed pattern selection in the introduction, noting that there are four possible methods of matching the hatches: using *conventional, special, suggestive,* and *restricted patterns.* In "To Match or Not to Match the Hatch," in chapter 4, we looked at patterns used in a specific hatch, the green drake. During that hatch I used conventional patterns, restricted patterns, suggestive patterns like a Stimulator type, and attractor patterns. The Stimulator and attractor patterns worked extremely well during the hatch. I got into a routine of using the Patriot during the day and a Stimulator pattern in the evening.

By *special patterns* I mean a list of body colors that will match most hatches across the United States—no, the world. Under each color category I include three or four shades of four basic mayfly colors to cover most duns and spinners. All total there are 31 body shades for all mayflies—17 for the duns and 14 for the spinners. That's it—it's that simple. Using several shades of four colors you can match the vast majority of hatches and spinner falls.

You'll notice that I've given a number to each pattern. That number corresponds with the hatch charts in chapters 5 through 9. If the body or wing requires something special, it's noted in the chart.

A second method, albeit more primitive, is to make a selection of just a few patterns and carry these in several sizes to match most hatches. These are the *restricted patterns*—five patterns that copy most mayfly hatches, with their predominant body colors of olive, cream, brown, and gray. These patterns are the Blue-Winged Olive (olive), Light Cahill (cream), Adams (gray), Willow Special (dark reddish brown), and March Brown (tannish brown). Talk about simple—it doesn't get easier than that. If you experience special hatches that one of these five doesn't copy closely enough, then tie a special pattern for that hatch. You need six spinner patterns—the Cream Spinner, Tan Spinner, Dark Brown Spinner, Red Quill Spinner, Rusty Spinner, and Dark Olive Spinner—to complete your list.

A third method of matching the hatch—and one many of us still adhere to—is to use *conventional patterns*. This method copies each and every mayfly as closely as possible. At the end of this chapter I'll list all of the conventional patterns so near and dear to many hatch matchers.

TABLE 10.1: How Many Patterns Do You Need to Match the Hatches?

Type of Pattern	Number Needed to Match Most Hatches
Conventional	70 separate patterns just to match the hatches listed
Special encounter	31 patterns will probably match every hatch you ever encounter
Restricted	11 patterns will match most hatches you ever encounter

Until recently I have not been much of a fan of *suggestive patterns* like the Stimulator. During that green drake hatch in Labrador, however (see chapter 7), a Stimulator-type pattern proved to be the top producer of huge brook trout the entire week of the hatch. Randall Kaufmann in *Tying Dry Flies* stated that the pattern works well for caddis and stonefly hatches. I'm convinced that a refined version of the pattern works well during the hatches because it suggests a natural emerger to trout. Whatever it is, it works.

What makes trout hit one pattern and refuse another? Look at table 10.1. The most precise hatch matchers are the conventional patterns. I've often matched the green drake of the East (*Ephemera guttulata*) with a pattern that's hard to tell from the natural. I often come away from the hatch frustrated. On several occasions I've tied on a pattern first developed by George Harvey with a bright yellow wing and a bright pale yellow body. I've caught trout on the Harvey pattern when I didn't on the more precise copy. Why? I'm convinced that on heavily fished waters, trout will take a pattern that is different—at least to some extent.

The long-winded point I'm trying to make is that even the closest copy of the natural doesn't work all the time; sometimes one that's not nearly as similar will catch trout. *I'm convinced that the size and the shape of the pattern is often more important than is the color.*

In *How to Catch More Trout* I noted that pattern selection is extremely important. How many times have you seen a nearby angler catching scores of trout while you caught only a few? How many times have I been poised for a specific hatch at dusk, tied on a Sulphur Dun pattern—and found that the Sulphur Spinner was what the trout were taking? On some frustrating occasions I've sworn that I'd start carrying two fly-rods—one with a Sulphur Dun and the other with a Sulphur Spinner tied on. The hatch and spinner fall occur just at dusk, so changing the pattern

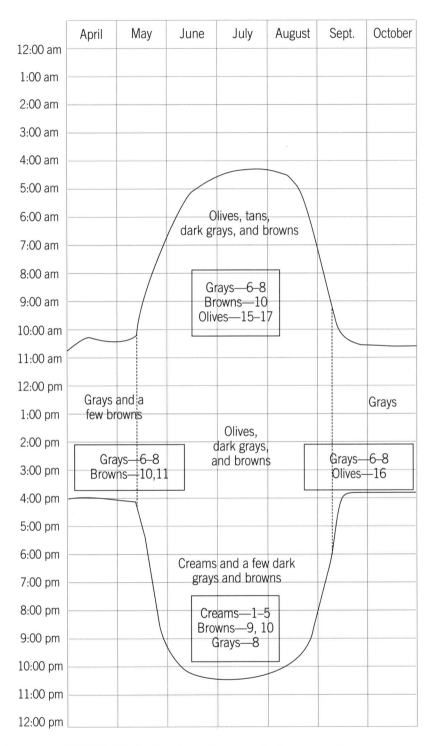

TABLE 10.2: Special patterns and when to use them.
(Numbers refer to special pattern numbers in this chapter.)

(at least for me) is difficult. So it's up to you to select the right pattern. Will it be a conventional tie, a special fly, or a restricted pattern? The choice is yours.

WET FLIES

Ah! My first few years of fly-fishing bring back fond memories. Even after 50 years, I still remember those early years on my hometown stream. My favorite pattern was a snelled wet March Brown. That pattern caught trout—and plenty of them. It ensured that I'd fly-fish the rest of my life.

What has happened to wet flies in the past few years? Most of the fly-fishers who use these underwater patterns prefer something like the Pheasant Tail, Tan Caddis, Glo Bug, or Prince Nymph, and usually with a beadhead. Seldom do I see anglers using the old-fashioned patterns that worked so well for so many years. Look at that old snelled wet fly, the dark March Brown: That pattern caught trout

TABLE 10.3: Special Patterns for Duns—East and Midwest

Hook Size	6	8	10	12	14	16	18	20	22	24	26
1. Creamish white		X		X	X	X					X
2. Yellowish cream			X	X	X						
3. Pale yellow with olive reflections				X	X	X	X				
4. Pale yellow-orange				X	X						
5. Yellow-tan	X	X	X								
6. Gray-olive			X	X	X	X	X	X	X	X	
7. Medium gray				X	X						
8. Dark gray		X	X	X	X	X	X				
9. Tan				X	X						
10. Tannish brown					X	X					
11. Reddish tan					X						
12. Chocolate brown						X					
13. Dark brown						X				X	
14. Brownish black				X	X		X				
15. Light olive									X	X	
16. Medium olive					X	X	X	X	X	X	
17. Dark olive					X						

TABLE 10.4: Special Patterns for Duns—West

Hook Size	6	8	10	12	14	16	18	20	22	24	26
1. Creamish white					X	X					
2. Yellowish cream				X	X	X					
3. Pale yellow with olive reflections						X	X				
4. Pale yellow-orange				X	X	X					
5. Yellow-tan	X	X									
6. Light gray with olive reflections				X			X	X	X	X	
7. Medium gray				X	X	X					
8. Dark gray				X	X	X	X				
9. Tan				X	X	X					
10. Tannish brown				X	X	X	X				
11. Reddish brown						X	X				
12. Chocolate brown								X			
13. Dark brown				X	X			X			
14. Brownish black									X	X	
15. Light olive					X	X		X	X	X	
16. Medium olive					X						
17. Dark olive				X							

for me for more than two decades. If you're fortunate enough to find a fly-fisher who still uses these downwing wet flies, you'll probably find a successful angler. Why do these old patterns still work? They copy one of the most important food source for trout—the emerger.

I use the same colors for the wet fly as I do for the dry fly. However, I use materials that help the pattern sink. Instead of a body of dubbed poly, I use opossum or angora. For the tail and legs, I use hen hackle.

SPECIAL PATTERNS

If you're tired of the confusing mess of tying patterns to match each hatch and then, when a hatch occurs, trying to find the right pattern in your fly box—why not try

Hook Size	6	8	10	12	14	16	18	20	22	24	26
18. Light gray					X	X					
19. Medium gray				X	X						
20. Dark gray						X	X				
21. White					X	X					
22. Cream											
23. Cream-pink					X	X					
24. Yellow-orange				X	X						
25. Tannish brown								X	X	X	
26. Brown							X	X			
27. Reddish brown					X	X	X				
28. Maroon				X							
29. Dark brownish black									X	X	X
30. Dark olive								X	X		
31. Dark olive-black					X	X					

matching some of the hatches with special patterns? In tables 10.3 to 10.6 I've listed the colors and the sizes you'll need. You might add some more sizes so you're prepared for the unexpected.

Special Patterns—Duns

The four basic colors of the bodies of duns that you'll encounter in your matching-the-hatch trips are cream, gray, brown, and olive. The 17 color combinations that follow will match just about any hatch. Here are the materials you'll need for tying any of these parachute dry flies:

Hook: Dry-fly hook, such as a Mustad 94833

Body: Poly of the recommended color

Post: Deer or elk hair or calf body hair of the recommended color

Tail: Hackle fibers of the suggested color

Hackle: Rooster hackle a size larger than what you'd use on a Catskill pattern

TABLE 10.6: Special Patterns for Spinners—East and Midwest

Hook Size	6	8	10	12	14	16	18	20	22	24	26
18. Light gray						X					
19. Medium gray					X	X					
20. Dark gray			X	X							
21. White		X	X	X	X					X	X
22. Cream					X	X	X	X			
23. Cream-pink				X							
24. Yellow-orange				X	X						
25. Tannish brown	X	X	X			X	X				
26. Brown				X	X	X					
27. Reddish brown			X	X	X	X					
28. Maroon			X	X	X						
29. Dark brownish black				X		X	X		X	X	
30. Dark olive						X		X			
31. Dark olive-black				X	X	X					

Creams

1. CREAMISH WHITE
Thread: Cream
Tail: White
Wing: Creamish yellow
Body: Cream poly
Hackle: Cream

2. YELLOWISH CREAM
Thread: Pale yellow
Tail: Cream
Wing: Creamish yellow
Body: Yellowish cream poly
Hackle: Pale yellow cream

3. PALE YELLOW WITH OLIVE REFLECTIONS
Thread: Pale yellow
Tail: Pale yellow
Wing: Pale gray
Body: Pale yellow poly with slight olive reflections
Hackle: Pale yellow

4. PALE ORANGE
Thread: Pale yellow
Tail: Pale yellow
Wing: Pale yellow
Body: Pale orange poly
Hackle: Pale yellow

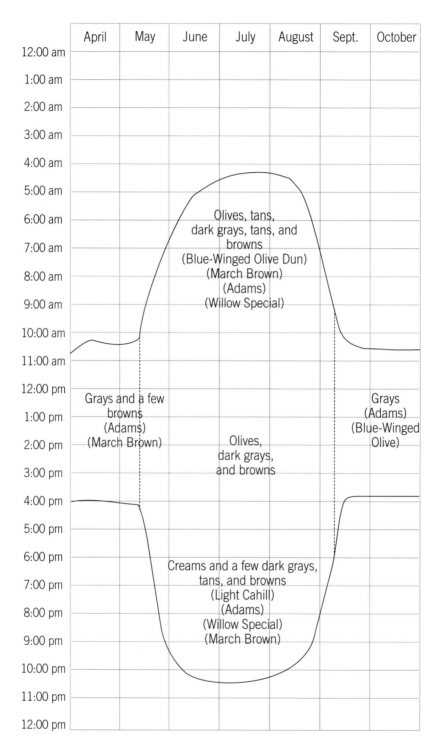

TABLE 10.7: Restricted patterns to match the hatches

TABLE 10.8: Restricted Patterns to Match Most of the Hatches

Pattern	Wing	Tail	Body	Hackle
1. Adams	Grizzly hackle tips	Brown and grizzly hackle fibers	Medium gray poly	Grizzly and brown, mixed
2. March Brown	Yellow-brown-dyed mallard flank feather	Dark brown	Tannish brown poly, dubbed	Grizzly and brown, mixed
3. Blue-Winged Olive Dun	Dark gray hen hackle	Olive-gray hackle barbules	Medium olive poly, dubbed	Olive-gray hackle
4. Light Cahill	Pale-yellow-dyed mallard flank feather	Cream hackle barbules	Cream poly	Cream
5. Willow Special	Dark gray hen hackle	Dark gray	Dark brown poly	Grizzly

5. YELLOW-TAN
Thread: Tan
Tail: Brown
Wing: Pale gray
Body: Yellow-tan poly
Hackle: Tan

Grays
6. LIGHT GRAY WITH OLIVE REFLECTIONS
Thread: Gray
Tail: Olive-tan
Wing: Light gray
Body: Light olive-gray
Hackle: Olive-tan

7. MEDIUM GRAY
Thread: Medium gray
Tail: Medium dun
Wing: Medium gray
Body: Medium gray
Hackle: Medium dun

8. DARK GRAY
Thread: Light gray
Tail: Dark dun
Wing: Dark gray (or light gray)
Body: Dark gray
Hackle: Dark gray

Browns
9. TAN
Thread: Tan
Tail: Tan
Wing: Pale gray (or light gray)
Body: Tan
Hackle: Tan

10. TANNISH BROWN
Thread: Light brown
Tail: Brown
Wing: Pale gray (or light gray)
Body: Light brown poly
Hackle: Tannish brown

Pattern	Thread	Body	Tail	Wing
1. Cream Spinner	Cream	Cream	Cream	White
2. Tan Spinner	Tan	Tan	Tan	White
3. Rusty Spinner	Medium brown	Medium brown	Medium	White
4. Red Quill Spinner	Reddish brown	Reddish brown	Brown	White
5. Dark Brown Spinner	Dark reddish brown	Dark reddish brown	Dark brown	White
6. Dark Olive Spinner	Dark olive	Dark olive	Dark olive	Pale gray

11. REDDISH TAN
Thread: Reddish tan
Tail: Reddish tan
Wing: Pale gray
Body: Reddish tan poly
Hackle: Reddish tan

12. CHOCOLATE BROWN
Thread: Dark brown
Tail: Brown
Wing: Medium gray (or light gray)
Body: Chocolate-brown poly
Hackle: Dark brown

13. DARK BROWN
Thread: Dark brown
Tail: Dark brown
Wing: Dark gray (or light gray)
Body: Very dark brown poly
Hackle: Dark brown

14. BROWNISH BLACK
Thread: Black
Tail: Blackish brown
Wing: Dark gray
Body: Brownish black poly
Hackle: Very dark brown

Olives
15. LIGHT OLIVE
Thread: Light olive
Tail: Pale olive-gray
Wing: Pale gray
Body: Light olive poly
Hackle: Pale olive-gray

16. MEDIUM OLIVE
Thread: Medium olive
Tail: Medium olive-gray
Wing: Dark gray (or light gray)
Body: Medium olive poly
Hackle: Medium gray

17. DARK OLIVE
Thread: Dark olive
Tail: Dark olive-gray
Wing: Dark gray (or light gray)
Body: Dark olive poly
Hackle: Dark olive gray

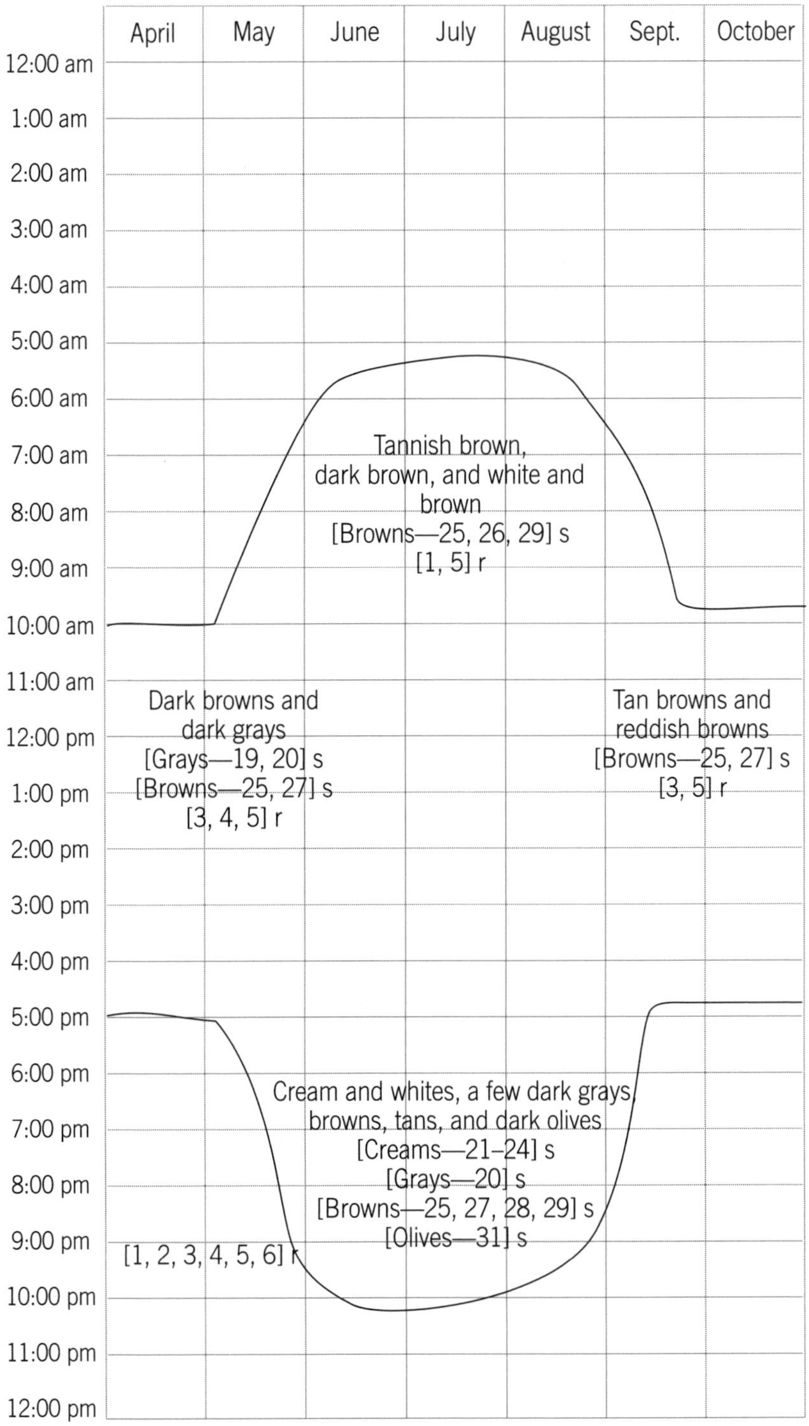

April
May
June
July
August
Sept.
October
12:00 am
1:00 am
2:00 am
3:00 am
4:00 am
5:00 am
6:00 am
7:00 am
8:00 am
9:00 am
10:00 am
11:00 am
12:00 pm
1:00 pm
2:00 pm
3:00 pm
4:00 pm
5:00 pm
6:00 pm
7:00 pm
8:00 pm
9:00 pm
10:00 pm
11:00 pm
12:00 pm
Tannish brown, dark brown, and white and brown [Browns—25, 26, 29] s [1, 5] r
Dark browns and dark grays [Grays—19, 20] s [Browns—25, 27] s [3, 4, 5] r
Tan browns and reddish browns [Browns—25, 27] s [3, 5] r
Cream and whites, a few dark grays, browns, tans, and dark olives [Creams—21–24] s [Grays—20] s [Browns—25, 27, 28, 29] s [Olives—31] s
[1, 2, 3, 4, 5, 6] r

TABLE 10.10: Special (s) and restricted (r) patterns for spinners

Special Patterns—Spinners

As I noted in chapter 9, there were four basic colors for spinners; you'll find them in the patterns that follow. All of these patterns use the following materials:

Hook: Dry-fly hook similar to a Mustad 94833
Tail: Hackle fibers in recommended colors
Wing: White poly yarn, tied spent
Body: Poly dubbing of recommended color

Grays

18. Light Gray
Wing: White poly yarn, tied spent
Tail: Tannish gray
Body: Light gray poly

19. Medium Gray
Wing: White poly yarn, tied spent
Tail: Dark dun
Body: Medium gray poly

20. Dark Gray
Wing: White poly yarn, tied spent
Tail: Dark dun
Body: Dark gray poly

Creams

21. White
Wing: White poly yarn, tied spent
Tail: White
Body: White poly

22. Cream
Wing: White poly yarn, tied spent
Tail: Cream
Body: Cream poly

23. Cream-Pink
Wing: White poly yarn, tied spent
Tail: Pale yellow poly
Body: Pale cream poly with a pink cast

24. Yellow-Orange
Wing: White poly yarn, tied spent
Tail: Pale yellow
Body: Pale yellow poly with an orange cast

Browns

25. Tannish Brown
Wing: White poly yarn, tied spent
Tail: Brown
Body: Tannish brown poly

26. Brown
Wing: White poly yarn, tied spent
Tail: Brown
Body: Medium brown poly

27. Reddish Brown
Wing: White poly yarn, tied spent
Tail: Dark brown
Body: Dark reddish brown

28. Maroon
Wing: White poly yarn, tied spent
Tail: Dark brown
Body: Dark maroon poly

29. Dark Brownish Black
Wing: White poly yarn, tied spent
Tail: Very dark brown (blackish brown)
Body: Dark brownish black poly

Olives
30. MEDIUM OLIVE
Wing: White poly yarn, tied spent
Tail: Dark olive-gray
Body: Medium olive

31. DARK OLIVE-BLACK
Wing: White poly yarn, tied spent
Tail: Dark olive-black
Body: Dark olive-black poly (1 part
    olive mixed with 10 parts black)

RESTRICTED PATTERNS

Patterns. Patterns. Patterns. We're confronted with thousands of possible choices, whether we want to match the hatch or not. In his classic book *The Fisherman's Handbook of Trout Patterns,* Donald DuBois listed more than 6,000 flies—and that was published in 1956. Think how many new patterns have come on the market since then! Look at his listings for just Quill Gordon and Hendrickson patterns: DuBois noted 28 patterns that copy the Hendrickson and 34 for the quill Gordon. For just two mayflies, there were at least 62 patterns. Given the recent explosion in the use of synthetics, that number now has to be well over 100. What can you do? Maybe you can carry a compartmented fly box, like I do, that holds thousands of patterns. Or you can try limiting the number of patterns by using just a few that match several hatches. That's what the five restricted patterns (table 10.8) do. You'll see recommendations in chapters 5 through 9.

Ask many people what pattern they use most often and many of them will say the Adams. That's probably one of the best choices you can make. Why? Look at table 10.7, which lists the predominant colors of the mayflies at various times of the day and year. At any time of the year—and at any time of the day—you're apt to see gray mayflies. In spring the Adams matches hatches like the blue quill and quill Gordon; on summer mornings it again copies blue quills. On late-spring evenings and again in fall, the Adams is a good selection to copy the slate drake.

The Light Cahill is one of the best possible choices if you plan to fish on a late-spring or summer evening. This is the time of the cream and pale yellow mayflies.

The Blue-Winged Olive Dun is a good choice if you plan to fish late-spring or early-summer mornings. This is the time that many of the blue-winged olives appear. Trico female duns also have a light olive body.

Use the Willow Special on summer mornings—especially if you plan to fish western rivers. That's when some of the dark brown duns appear.

Tie the Blue-Winged Olive and Adams patterns in sizes 12 through 20 and you'll match the vast majority of hatches. Tie the Light Cahill and March Brown in sizes 8 through 20 and the Willow Special in sizes 12 through 16.

Suggestive Patterns: The Laid Back Hex

A refined version of the Stimulator pattern works well, especially for the larger hatches. It's called the Laid Back Hex. Rusty Gates—a well-known fly-fisher and fly-shop owner on Michigan's AuSable River—first tied this pattern 20 years ago (see chapter 8). Use olive, brown, cream, yellow, and gray body colors. Here's how to tie the Laid Back Hex.

Hook: Mustad 94831, sizes 6–16

Thread: The same color as the body (in this case, yellow). In addition, cut off a 5-inch piece of tying thread that you'll use at the bend of the hook.

Tail: Two long pheasant tail fibers and a dozen shorter deer hair fibers

Wing: Deer hair, tied downwing

Body: Rusty uses sparkle rug yarn or Uni-Yarn; you can use poly yarn in yellow, cream, olive, brown, or gray. On top will be the deer hair brought from the tail and tied in at the wing.

Hackle: Brown and grizzly tied in halfway up the shank and palmered to the wing; cut it off on the bottom.

1. Tie in the pheasant tails. Make certain they're almost as long as the shank of the hook.
2. Tie in a bunch of about a dozen deer hair fibers at the bend of the hook. The fibers should be very short. Don't cut off the butts—you'll use them later. Leave a piece of yellow tying thread at the bend of the hook.
3. Wind the appropriate-colored body material halfway to the eye.
4. Tie in a brown and grizzly hackle and palmer to the wing. Leave enough room for the wing and hackle.
5. Bring the butt section of the deer hair up and over the body and tie in just behind the eye. Clip off the excess. Bring the loose piece of yellow tying thread to the bend of the hook and rib the deer hair to the eye.
6. Tie in, downwing-style, two dozen deer hair fibers and clip off the butts to form a small head like a Muddler Minnow's.

Rusty cuts off the hackle on the top and the bottom of the pattern to make it float more flush with the surface; this suggests an emerging nymph.

It worked for me in Labrador. Try this same pattern for some of the more common and larger hatches, especially when trout become highly selective.

CONVENTIONAL PATTERNS
Patterns for Spring
When I think of spring and the great afternoon hatches I think of gray and tan patterns. Common patterns like the Hendrickson, Black Quill, and Quill Gordon immediately come to mind. On western coastal waters this is the time of the western March brown hatch. Don't overlook the two smallest hatches, the blue quill and the blue-winged olive. You'll find hatches of these two in all regions of the United States. You'll find patterns for all of these hatches listed later in this chapter.

Patterns for Summer Mornings
Two colors reign supreme on summer mornings—olive and dark gray. Look at the common hatches on those mornings. In late May through June and early July, anglers are confronted with plenty of blue-winged olive duns. These hatches range in size from 12 to 18, and just about all can be copied with a medium to dark olive body (special patterns 16 and 17).

Summer mornings host many blue quill species (*Paraleptophlebia*) across the United States. The spring blue quill emerger (*P. adoptiva*) is often the most important of the season. Why? It appears in early to mid-April when cool weather is still a common occurrence. Cool temperatures delay the dun from taking flight quickly, giving trout a chance to feed on the dun. On any lousy drizzly or cool summer morning, one of the dozen or more blue quill species that appear will likely dawdle on the surface. I've hit blue quill hatches early in July and August and found dozens of trout rising to the hatch.

So the two most important colors to copy duns on summer morning are olive and dark gray (and to some extent brown in the West). Chapter 2 looks at some of the colors of spinners found on summer mornings.

Patterns for Summer Evenings—Light
If you see a light-colored mayfly, the dun has probably emerged on a late-spring or summer evening. Furthermore, the spinner will also fall in the evening. So if you plan to fish in the evening from May through early September, then be prepared with plenty of cream and yellow patterns to match emerging duns and falling spinners.

Spinners of cream mayflies are often lighter in color than are the duns. There are, however, many exceptions, including the March brown. Look also at the green drake and cream Cahill: Both spinners are white.

Most of the hex (*Hexagenia rigida, H. munda, H. limbata*) hatches appear in the evening in summer. Most of these are also creamish tan to pale yellow in abdomen color. These plus the yellow drake (*Ephemera varia*) and brown drake (*E. simulans*) have unusual markings on their bodies, often in the form of brown dashes or triangles.

How can you copy these large mayflies with striped bodies? Here's a simple way to do it. Take a 6-inch piece of pale yellow (or the color you're using to match the hatch) poly yarn and add a piece of brown thread (heavy tying thread or sewing thread). Place one end of both of them in the vise and the other end (again, of both thread and poly) in a hackle pliers. Give a flick with your fingers on the hackle pliers so the two materials spin around themselves about 20 to 30 times. Take off the hackle pliers and bring one end of the material toward the piece in the vise. Place a bodkin where you want the poly to twist. The materials will curl up and form a lifelike large mayfly body, complete with markings.

Now take the body (pinch the two ends so it doesn't unwind), extend it out over the bend of the hook rib with yellow tying thread up to the wing, and cut off the excess. This forms an excellent buoyant body that copies many of the drakes.

Patterns for Summer Evenings—Dark

There are half a dozen important yellow-brown, dark brown, or dark gray mayflies that appear on summer evenings These include the hex (*Hexagenia atrocaudata),* slate drake, brown drake, dark blue quill, and dark brown dun. Of these the slate drake and brown drake are most important. Two dark gray mayflies (dark blue quill and slate drake) seem to appear earlier than the others. If you know the water doesn't hold one of these, opt for a cream-colored pattern if you're fishing on a summer evening.

Patterns for Fall

We revert back to grays for the fall. As in spring, many of these hatches appear in the morning or afternoon. I have, however, seen slate drakes appear as late as 6 PM in mid-September.

Recipes for the Conventional Patterns

In the pages that follow you'll find patterns that match specific hatches, grouped by the time of year they emerge and the chapter in which they were discussed. You'll find not only patterns for the duns and spinners, but also recommended imitations for the nymphs. The same colors that predominate among duns and spinners are viable for the nymphs: brown (many shades), black, gray, and dark olive.

Chapter 5: Early Spring
East and Midwest

Little Blue-Winged Olive Dun
Copies *Baetis tricaudatus* and other *Baetis* species
Thread: Dark gray
Tail: Medium to dark gray hackle fibers
Body: Gray muskrat or medium gray poly, dubbed; for the Little Blue-Winged Olive use olive-gray poly
Wings: On smaller sizes (20) use dark gray mallard quills; on larger sizes use dark gray hackle tips
Hackle: Blue dun
Shuck (optional): Brownish black Z-lon
Hook: Sizes 18–20

Rusty Spinner
Thread: Dark brown
Tail: Dark grayish brown hackle fibers
Body: Grayish brown poly, dubbed and ribbed with fine tan thread
Wings: Pale gray poly yarn, tied spent
Hook: Sizes 18–20

Nymph
Thread: Dark olive
Tail: Dark-olive-dyed wood duck fibers
Body: Dark olive-brown opossum
Wings: Dark gray mallard quill section
Hackle: Dark-olive-dyed cree or ginger variant hackle
Hook: Size 18

Blue Quill
Copies all *Paraleptophlebia* species
Thread: Dark gray
Tail: Medium to dark gray hackle fibers
Body: Eyed peacock herl, stripped, or dark gray poly, dubbed
Wings: Dark gray hackle tips
Hackle: Light to medium blue dun

Shuck (optional): Dark brownish black Z-lon
Hook: Sizes 18–20

DARK BROWN SPINNER
Thread: Dark brown
Tail: Dark brown hackle fibers
Body: Dark brown poly, dubbed
Wings: Pale gray poly yarn, tied spent
Hook: Sizes 18–20

NYMPH
Thread: Dark brown
Tail: Dark-brown-dyed mallard flank feather
Body: Dark brown angora, dubbed
Wings: One dark gray mallard quill, tied down
Hackle: Dark gray
Hook: Sizes 16–18

QUILL GORDON
Copies species like *Epeorus pleuralis, Ameletus ludens,* and some *Rhithrogena* species
Thread: Dark gray
Tail: Dark gray hackle fibers
Body: Eyed peacock herl, stripped and lacquered
Wings: Wood duck or imitation wood duck, divided; or dark gray hackle tips
Hackle: Dark gray hackle
Shuck (optional): Black Z-lon
Hook: Size 14

RED QUILL SPINNER
Thread: Brown
Tail: Bronze dun hackle fibers
Body: Dark tannish brown poly, dubbed and ribbed finely with tan thread
Wings: Pale gray poly yarn, tied spent
Hook: Sizes 14–16

NYMPH

Thread: Dark brown
Tail: Dark-amber-dyed fibers from a mallard flank feather
Body: Dark brown fur or angora, mixed with a bit of lighter brown or amber
Wings: Mottled brown turkey, tied down over thorax
Hackle: Cree or ginger variant hackle (dark and amber mixed)
Hook: Size 14

HENDRICKSON AND RED QUILL

The Red Quill copies the male and the Hendrickson the female of *Ephemerella subvaria* and several closely related subspecies. In addition the Red Quill effectively imitates many spinners like *Ephemerella subvaria, Epeorus pleuralis,* and the male spinner of *Ephemerella invaria* and *E. rotunda.*

Thread: Brown
Tail: Medium gray hackle fibers
Body: Red Quill—reddish brown hackle fiber stripped of its barbules and wound from the bed of the hook to the wings. Hendrickson—tan poly, dubbed.
Wings: Wood duck, divided. Optional on the Hendrickson are gray hackle tips.
Hackle: Medium gray hackle
Shuck (optional): Brownish black Z-lon
Hook: Sizes 14–16

RED QUILL SPINNER

Thread: Brown
Tail: Bronze dun hackle fibers
Body: Dark tannish brown poly, dubbed and ribbed finely with tan thread
Wings: Pale gray poly yarn, tied spent
Hook: Sizes 14–16

NYMPH

Thread: Dark brown
Tail: Brown-dyed fibers from a mallard flank feather
Body: Dark brown angora, mixed with a bit of amber
Wings: Mottled-brown turkey, tied down over thorax
Hackle: Cree hackle
Hook: Sizes 12–14

WESTERN MARCH BROWN
Copies species like *Rhithrogena morrisoni* and *R. hageni*
Thread: Brown
Tail: Medium brown
Body: Medium brown poly, dubbed
Wings: Medium gray hackle wings
Hackle: Dark brown hackle
Hook: Size 14

DARK TAN SPINNER
Thread: Tan
Tail: Dark brown hackle fibers
Body: Dark brown poly, dubbed
Wings: Pale gray poly
Hook: Size 14

NYMPH
Thread: Dark brown
Tail: Imitation wood duck fibers
Body: Dark brown rabbit fur with brown hackle rib, clipped at the bottom
Wings: Dark brown turkey
Hackle: Very dark cree hackle
Hook: Size 14

LITTLE BLUE-WINGED OLIVE DUN
Copies *Baetis bicaudatus, B. tricaudatus, B. intermedius,* and others
Thread: Dark gray
Tail: Medium to dark gray hackle fibers
Body: Gray muskrat or medium gray poly with a slight olive cast, dubbed (the body of *Baetis bicaudatus* is more olive than the others)
Wings: On smaller sizes (20) use dark gray mallard quills; on larger sizes use dark gray hackle tips
Shuck (optional): Dark olive-brown Z-lon
Hackle: Blue dun
Hook: Sizes 18–20

Optional pattern tied with vernille:

Thread: Dark olive

Tail: None

Body: Fine medium olive vernille extending 1/8 inch back past the bend of the hook. Tie in the body by ribbing.

Wings: Gray turkey

Hackle: Gray

Hook: Sizes 18–20

Rusty Spinner

Thread: Dark brown

Tail: Dark grayish brown hackle fibers

Body: Grayish brown poly, dubbed and ribbed with fine tan thread

Wings: Pale gray poly yarn, tied spent

Hook: Sizes 18–20

Baetis Nymph

Thread: Dark olive

Tail: Dark-olive-dyed wood duck fibers

Body: Dark olive-brown opossum

Wings: Dark gray mallard quill section

Hackle: Dark-olive-dyed cree

Hook: Sizes 18–20

Chapter 6: Summer Mornings
East and Midwest

Blue-Winged Olive Dun

Copies many *Drunella* (*Ephemerella*) and *Dannella* (*Ephemerella*) species like *cornuta, longicornus, attenuata, cornutella, lata, simplex, walkeri,* and others

Thread: Olive

Tail: Grayish olive hackle fibers

Body: Light to medium olive poly, dubbed

Wings: Dark gray hackle tips

Hackle: Medium creamish olive

Shuck (optional): Dark olive-black Z-lon

Hook: Sizes 14–20

DARK OLIVE SPINNER
Thread: Dark olive or black
Tail: Moose mane (dark brown)
Body: Dark olive poly (almost black, with an olive cast)
Wings: Pale gray poly yarn, tied spent
Hook: Sizes 14–20

NYMPH
Thread: Olive
Tail: Wood duck
Body: Dark brown angora, tied over, dubbed in olive opossum
Wings: Brown turkey
Hackle: Olive-dyed ginger variant
Hook: Sizes 14–18

CHOCOLATE DUN
Copies species like *Ephemerella needhami* (male dun only) and *Eurylophella*
  (Ephemerella) bicolor
Thread: Brown
Tail: Medium gray
Body: Chocolate-brown poly, finely ribbed with lighter brown thread
Wings: Dark gray hackle tips
Shuck (optional): Dark brown
Hackle: Tan hackle
Hook: Size 16

CHOCOLATE SPINNER
Thread: Dark brown
Tail: Tannish gray hackle fibers
Body: Dark rusty brown poly, dubbed
Wings: Pale gray poly yarn, tied spent
Hook: Size 16

NYMPH
Thread: Brown
Tail: Light brown mallard flank feather fibers
Body: Light brown poly nymph dubbing
Wings: Dark gray mallard quill

Hackle: Brown hackle
Hook: Size 16

Olive Sulphur

Copies *Ephemerella needhami*
Thread: Olive
Body: Female—medium olive poly, dubbed. Male—dark brown poly, dubbed.
Wings: Cream hen hackle tips
Hackle: Cream
Shuck (optional): Dark olive-brown
Hook: Size 16

Olive Sulphur Spinner (female)

Thread: Dark olive
Tail: Cream
Body: Dark olive poly, dubbed
Wings: White poly yarn, tied spent

Olive Sulphur Nymph

Thread: Grayish brown
Tail: Brown pheasant tail fibers
Body: Brown (ground color) fur
Wings: Dark gray mallard quill section, tied down over thorax
Hackle: Cree hackle
Hook: Sizes 14–18

Dark Green Drake

Copies species like *Litobrancha recurvata*
Thread: Dark gray
Tail: Dark brown moose mane
Body: Dark slate poly, dubbed and ribbed with yellow thread
Wings: Dark-green-dyed mallard flank, heavily barred
Hackle: Rear—tannish brown hackle. Front—dark brown hackle.
Shuck (optional): Tannish brown Z-lon
Hook: Sizes 8–10

BROWN DRAKE SPINNER

Thread: Brown
Tail: Brown hackle fibers
Body: Reddish brown poly, dubbed and ribbed with yellow thread
Wings: Pale gray poly yarn, tied spent
Hackle: Dark brown
Hook: Sizes 8–10

NYMPH

Thread: Light brown
Tail: Three dark bronze hackles, trimmed and tied in
Body: Tan angora or opossum with a grayish cast
Wings: Dark brown turkey
Hackle: Dark cree
Hook: Sizes 8–10

TRICO DUN

Copies all *Tricorythodes* species
Thread: Pale olive
Tail: Cream hackle fibers
Body: Female—pale olive-green poly, dubbed. Male—dark brown poly.
Wings: Pale gray hackle tips
Hackle: Cream hackle
Shuck (optional): Olive-brown Z-lon
Hook: Sizes 20–24

TRICO SPINNER

Thread: Dark brown
Tail: Female—short cream hackle fibers. Male—long dark brown moose mane.
Body: Female—rear one-third is cream poly, dubbed, and front two-thirds is
    dark brown poly, dubbed. Male—dark brown poly, dubbed, and ribbed with
    a fine light tan thread.
Wings: White poly yarn, tied spent
Hook: Sizes 20–24

Nymph

Thread: Black
Tail: Dark brown hackle fibers
Body: Dark brownish black fur
Wings: Dark gray mallard quill section
Hackle: Dark reddish brown
Hook: Size 22

West

Dark Red Quill

Copies species like *Cinygmula par*
Thread: Brown
Tail: Medium dun hackle fibers
Body: Dark reddish brown hackle stem, stripped
Wings: Dark mallard quills, dark gray calf tail, or hackle tips
Hackle: Bronze dun
Shuck (optional): Dark gray Z-lon
Hook: Size 16

Red Quill Spinner

Thread: Brown
Tail: Pale dun hackle fibers
Body: Reddish brown hackle stem
Wings: Pale tan poly, tied spent
Hackle: Brown
Hook: Sizes 16–18

Red Quill Nymph

Thread: Dark brown
Tail: Amber-dyed mallard flank
Body: Dark grayish brown Furry Foam over amber angora
Wings: Dark mallard quill
Hackle: Dark grouse or partridge
Hook: Size 16

QUILL GORDON

Copies western species like *Epeorus longimanus* and
   many *Rhithrogena* species like *R. futilis*

Thread: Gray

Tail: Medium dun hackle

Body: Pale to medium gray poly or muskrat fur, dubbed

Wings: Dark mallard quills, dark gray calf tail, or dark gray hackle tips

Hackle: Pale tannish gray

Shuck (optional): Dark brown Z-lon

Hook: Size 14

QUILL GORDON SPINNER

Thread: Tan

Tail: Moose mane

Body: Pale yellowish brown poly or dark gray peacock herl, stripped

Wings: Pale tan poly

Hackle: Ginger with a turn of brown

Hook: Size 14

QUILL GORDON NYMPH

Thread: Dark brown

Tail: Amber-dyed mallard flank

Body: Dark brown Furry Foam over top

Wings: Dark mallard quill

Hackle: Dark grouse or partridge

Hook: Size 14

SPECKLE-WINGED DUN

Copies *Callibaetis americanus* and other closely related species

Thread: Tan

Tail: Cream-ginger hackle fibers

Body: Medium gray poly

Wings: Dark gray mallard flank

Hackle: Pale bronze dun

Shuck (optional): Dark brown Z-lon

Hook: Sizes 14–16

SPECKLE-WINGED SPINNER
Thread: Gray
Tail: Cream-ginger hackle fibers
Body: Pale gray poly
Wings: Mallard flank feather
Hackle: Pale bronze dun
Hook: Sizes 14–16

SPECKLE-WINGED NYMPH
Thread: Brown
Tail: Pheasant tail fibers
Body: Medium brown angora
Wings: Dark mallard quill
Hackle: Dark brown grouse
Hook: Size 14

WESTERN GREEN DRAKE
Copies species like *Drunella grandis*
Thread: Dark olive
Tail: Moose mane
Body: Olive black poly, ribbed with pale yellow thread
Wings: Dark-gray-dyed impala
Hackle: Grayish black
Shuck (optional): Dark olive-brown Z-lon
Hook: Sizes 10–12

GREAT RED SPINNER
Thread: Black
Tail: Moose mane
Body: Olive-black poly, ribbed with pale yellow thread
Wings: White poly, tied spent
Hackle: Brownish black
Hook: Sizes 10–12

GREEN DRAKE NYMPH
Thread: Dark brown
Tail: Amber-dyed mallard flank feather

Body: Dark olive angora
Wings: Mottled-brown turkey
Hackle: Olive-brown
Hook: Size 12

PALE BROWN DUN
Copies species like *Cinygmula reticulata*
Thread: Tan
Tail: Ginger-cream hackle fibers
Body: Pale brown poly
Wings: Yellow mallard flank
Shuck (optional): Dark brown Z-lon
Hackle: Ginger-cream
Hook: Sizes 12–14

DARK RUSTY SPINNER
Thread: Brown
Tail: Dark brown hackle fibers
Body: Dark brown poly
Wings: Pale yellow poly
Hackle: Dark brown
Hook: Sizes 12–14

PALE BROWN DUN
Copies *Rhithrogena hageni*
Thread: Olive
Tail: Cream hackle fibers
Body: Tannish olive poly
Wings: Gray mallard quills or dark gray hackle tips
Hackle: Cream-ginger
Shuck (optional): Light olive-brown Z-lon
Hook: Size 12

DARK TAN SPINNER
Thread: Tan
Tail: Gray hackle fibers
Body: Pale olive-tan poly

Wings: Pale gray poly
Hackle: Cream mixed with dark tan
Hook: Size 12

PALE BROWN NYMPH

Thread: Dark brown
Tail: Wood duck (few fibers)
Body: Greenish brown rabbit with claret hackle
Wings: Dark brown turkey
Hackle: Dark brown
Hook: Size 12

DARK RED QUILL

Copies species like *Rhithrogena undulata*
Thread: Dark reddish brown
Tail: Gray
Body: Dark reddish brown hackle stem
Wings: Dark gray hen hackle
Hackle: Dark brown
Shuck (optional): Dark brown Z-lon
Hook: Sizes 12–14

RED QUILL SPINNER

Thread: Dark brown
Tail: Dark brown hackle fibers
Body: Dark reddish brown poly
Wings: White poly yarn
Hackle: Dark brown
Hook: Sizes 12–14

DARK BROWN NYMPH

Thread: Dark brown
Tail: Wood duck (few fibers)
Body: Dark brown rabbit
Wings: Dark brown turkey
Hackle: Dark brown
Hook: Size 12

DARK BROWN DUN

Copies species like *Ameletus veloxi*
Thread: Dark brown
Tail: Dark brown hackle fibers
Body: Dark brown poly
Wings: Teal flank feather
Hackle: Dark brown
Shuck (optional): Dark brown Z-lon
Hook: Sizes 12–14

DARK BROWN SPINNER

Thread: Dark brown
Tail: Dark brown hackle fibers
Body: Dark brown poly
Wings: Yellow-dyed teal flank feather
Hackle: Dark brown
Hook: Sizes 12–14

DARK BROWN NYMPH

Thread: Dark brown
Tail: Wood duck (few fibers)
Body: Dark olive-brown rabbit with claret hackle
Wings: Dark brown turkey
Hackle: Dark brown
Hook: Size 12

BLACK QUILL

Copies *Choroterpes* species
Thread: Dark brown
Tail: Dark bronze dun hackle fibers
Body: Eyed peacock herl, stripped
Wings: Dark gray hackle tips
Hackle: Dark brown hackle with a turn or two of tan hackle in the rear
Hook: Size 14

EARLY BROWN SPINNER

Thread: Dark brown
Tail: Dark brown hackle fibers
Body: Dark reddish brown poly ribbed with pale yellow thread
Wings: Pale tan poly
Hackle: Dark brown hackle
Hook: Size 14

BLACK QUILL NYMPH

Thread: Dark brown
Tail: Dark brown hackle fibers
Body: Chocolate-brown angora, loosely dubbed
Wings: Dark mallard section
Hackle: Dark brown hackle
Hook: Sizes 12–14

BLUE DUN

Copies species like *Thraulodes bicornuta*
Thread: Dark gray-brown
Tail: Medium gray hackle fibers
Body: Dark gray poly
Wings: Dark gray hackle tips
Hackle: Medium gray or dun
Shuck (optional): Dark brown Z-lon
Hook: Size 14

BLUE DUN SPINNER

Thread: Dark brown
Tail: Dark brown hackle fibers
Body: Dark brown poly, dubbed
Wings: Pale gray poly yarn, tied spent
Hook: Size 14

Chapter 7: Summer Evenings—The Creams
East and Midwest

LIGHT CAHILL

Copies diverse species like *Stenonema ithaca, Stenacron interpunctatum, Heptagenia marginalis,* and many others

Thread: Cream or tan

Tail: Cream hackle fibers

Body: Cream poly, fox fur, or angora, dubbed (for the female of *S. interpunctatum,* the body should be creamish orange)

Wings: Pale-yellow-dyed mallard flank feather, divided

Hackle: Cream hackle

Shuck (optional): Dark brownish black Z-lon

Hook: Size 14

LIGHT CAHILL SPINNER

Thread: Cream or tan

Tail: Cream hackle fibers

Body: Cream poly, fox fur, or angora, dubbed (for the female of *S. interpunctatum,* the body should be creamish orange)

Wings: Pale yellow poly yarn, tied spent

Shuck (optional): Dark brownish black Z-lon

Hook: Size 14

NYMPH

Thread: Brown

Tail: Brown-dyed fibers from a mallard flank feather

Body: Dark brown angora yarn on top with a pale amber belly, dubbed

Wings: Dark brown turkey

Hackle: Dark cree

Hook: Size 12

SULPHUR DUN

Copies *Ephemerella rotunda, E. invaria, E. septentrionalis,* and, to a lesser degree, *E. dorothea*

Thread: Yellow

Tail: Cream hackle fibers

Body: Usually pale yellow poly with an orange (and sometimes olive-orange) cast (in *E. septentrionalis* and *E. dorothea,* the body has more yellow than orange)

Wings: Pale gray hackle tips

Hackle: Cream hackle

Shuck (optional): Medium to dark brown Z-lon

Hook: Sizes 16–18

SULPHUR SPINNER

Thread: Tan

Tail: Tan deer hair

Body: Female with eggs—yellowish tan poly. Female without eggs—tan poly. Male—bright red hackle stem, stripped and wound around the hook.

Wings: Pale gray poly yarn, tied spent (also tie some upright)

Hook: Sizes 16–18

SULPHUR NYMPH

Thread: Grayish brown

Tail: Brown pheasant tail fibers

Body: Brown (ground color) fur

Wings: Dark gray mallard quill section, tied down over thorax

Hackle: Cree hackle

Hook: Sizes 14–18

MARCH BROWN

Copies *Stenonema vicarium* (now combined with *S. fuscum*)

Thread: Yellow

Tail: Dark brown hackle fibers

Body: Tan poly, dubbed and ribbed with dark brown thread

Wings: Yellowish-brown-dyed mallard flank feather, divided

Hackle: One cream and one dark brown, mixed

Shuck (optional): Dark brown Z-lon

Hook: Size 12

GREAT RED SPINNER

Thread: Dark brown

Tail: Dark brown hackle fibers

Body: Dark reddish brown poly, dubbed
Wings: Pale gray poly yarn, tied spent
Hackle: Dark brown with a turn or two of pale ginger, mixed
Hook: Size 12

NYMPH

Thread: Brown
Tail: Brown-dyed fibers from a mallard flank feather
Body: Brown angora yarn, tied on top over cream. Tie in brown at the tail, and dub in cream so that the top (tergites) of the body is brown and the belly (sternites) is cream.
Wings: Dark brown turkey, tied down over thorax
Hackle: Dark cree
Hook: Size 12

GRAY FOX

Copies *Stenonema ithaca* and lighter *S. vicarium* naturals
Thread: Cream
Tail: Tan deer hair
Body: Cream poly, dubbed
Wings: Pale-yellowish-tan-dyed mallard flank feather, divided
Hackle: Cree hackle or one brown and one cream, mixed
Shuck (optional): Dark brown Z-lon
Hook: Sizes 12–14

GINGER QUILL SPINNER

Thread: Brown
Tail: Dark brown hackle fibers
Body: Tan-dyed eyed peacock herl, stripped, or grayish brown poly, ribbed with brown thread
Wings: Gray hackle tips (conventional); or pale gray poly, tied spent
Hackle: Dark ginger (conventional); or none with poly wings
Hook: Sizes 12–14

NYMPH

Thread: Brown
Tail: Brown-dyed fibers from a mallard flank feather

Body: Brown angora yarn, tied on top over cream. Tie in brown at the tail, and dub in cream so that the top (tergites) of the body is brown and the belly (sternites) is cream.
Wings: Dark brown turkey, tied down over thorax
Hackle: Dark cree
Hook: Size 12

PALE EVENING DUN

Copies species like *Ephemerella dorothea* and *E. septentrionalis;* many *Heptagenia* species like *H. walshi; Leucrocuta* species like *L. aphrodite;* and others
Thread: Pale yellow
Tail: Cream hackle fibers
Body: Pale yellowish cream poly, dubbed
Wings: Pale yellow hackle tips
Hackle: Cream
Shuck (optional): Dark olive-brown Z-lon
Hook: Sizes 16–20

PALE EVENING SPINNER

Thread: Cream
Tail: Cream hackle fibers
Body: Pale yellowish cream poly, dubbed
Wings: Pale gray poly yarn, tied spent
Hook: Sizes 16–20

NYMPH

Thread: Brown
Tail: Dark brown pheasant tail fibers
Body: Dark tan opossum dubbing
Wings: Gray mallard quill section
Hackle: Cree
Hook: Sizes 16–18

PINK CAHILL

Copies the female *Epeorus vitreus;* the male dun is copied with a Light Cahill, size 14 or 16
Thread: Cream

Tail: Gray hackle fibers
Body: Female—pinkish cream poly, dubbed. Male—pale yellow poly, dubbed.
Wings: Pale-yellow-dyed mallard flank feather
Hackle: Cream-ginger hackle
Shuck (optional): Dark brownish black Z-lon
Hook: Sizes 14–16

SALMON SPINNER

Thread: Pink
Tail: Cream-ginger hackle fibers
Body: Pinkish red poly, dubbed
Wings: Pale gray poly yarn, tied spent
Hook: Sizes 14–16

NYMPH

Thread: Tan
Tail: Dark brown fibers from a pheasant tail
Body: Dub amber on the entire shank, tie in a strand of dark brown yarn at the bend of the hook, bring it up and over, and tie it in where you tie in the wings
Wings: Brown turkey section
Hackle: Several turns of ginger hackle
Hook: Size 14

YELLOW DRAKE

Copies *Ephemera varia*, *Hexagenia rigida*, and *H. munda*
Thread: Yellow
Tail: Tan deer hair; dark gray deer hair (*H. rigida*)
Body: Pale yellow poly, dubbed
Wings: Pale-yellow-dyed deer hair, divided; olive-green-dyed deer hair (*H. rigida*)
Hackle: Pale yellow with a turn or two of grizzly in front
Shuck (optional): Pale tannish gray Z-lon
Hook: Size 12 for *Ephemera varia* and 6–8 for *H. rigida*

YELLOW DRAKE SPINNER

Thread: Yellow
Tail: Dark brown deer hair

Body: Pale yellow poly, dubbed
Wings: Gray poly yarn, tied spent
Hook: Size 12 for *Ephemera varia* and 6–8 for *H. rigida*

Nymph
Thread: Tan
Tail: Pale gray hackle, trimmed
Body: Amber-colored angora or opossum
Wings: Medium to light brown turkey
Hackle: Ginger
Hook: Sizes 10–12

Green Drake
Copies *Ephemera guttulata*
Thread: Cream
Tail: Moose mane
Body: Cream poly, dubbed
Wings: Yellowish-green-dyed mallard flank, divided
Hackle: Rear—cream hackle. Front—dark brown hackle.
Shuck (optional): Pale grayish Z-lon
Hook: Sizes 8–10

Coffin Fly
Thread: White
Tail: Light tan deer hair
Body: White poly, dubbed
Wings: Grayish yellow poly yarn, tied spent
Hook: Sizes 8–10

Green Drake Nymph
Thread: Tan
Tail: Three medium brown hackles, trimmed
Body: Pale tan angora
Wings: Dark brown turkey, tied down and over thorax
Hackle: Cree
Hook: Sizes 8–12

BIG YELLOW DRAKE

Copies *Hexagenia rigida* and *H. munda*
Thread: Yellow
Tail: Tan deer hair
Body: Pale yellow-tan poly, dubbed
Wings: Pale-yellow-dyed mallard flank feather or tan elk hair, tied in a post
Hackle: Pale yellow with a turn or two of grizzly
Shuck (optional): Pale tannish gray Z-lon
Hook: Sizes 8–10

BIG YELLOW DRAKE SPINNER

Thread: Yellow
Tail: Dark brown deer hair
Body: Pale yellow-tan poly, dubbed
Wings: Gray poly yarn, tied spent
Hook: Sizes 8–10

NYMPH

Thread: Tan
Tail: Pale gray hackle, trimmed
Body: Tannish gray angora or opossum
Wings: Medium to light brown turkey
Hackle: Ginger
Hook: Sizes 10–12

CREAM CAHILL

Copies species like *Stenonema pulchellum* and *S. modestum*
Thread: Cream
Tail: Cream hackle fibers
Body: Very pale cream (almost white) poly, dubbed
Wings: Pale-yellow-dyed mallard flank feather, divided
Hackle: Cream
Shuck (optional): Brownish black Z-lon
Hook: Sizes 14–16

CREAM CAHILL SPINNER

Thread: White
Tail: Pale cream hackle fibers

Body: White poly, dubbed
Wings: Pale poly yarn, tied spent
Hook: Sizes 14–16

CREAM CAHILL NYMPH

Thread: Olive-brown
Tail: Light brown hackle fibers
Body: Dub pale creamish gray on the hook, then tie pale brownish olive yarn in at the bend and bring it over the top to the wing case and tie in
Wings: Dark brown turkey
Hackle: Dark olive-brown
Hook: Sizes 14 and 16

WHITE MAYFLY (DUN AND SPINNER)

Since the female dun never changes to a spinner, I've listed one pattern for both phases. It copies *Ephoron leukon, E. album,* and other similar species.
Thread: White
Tail: White hackle fibers
Body: Female dun—creamish white poly, dubbed. Male spinner—a couple of turns of dark reddish brown poly at the rear, then white poly for the rest of the body, dubbed.
Wings: Pale gray hackle tips
Hackle: Cream (a turn or two of dark brown for the male spinner)
Shuck (optional): Pale tannish gray Z-lon
Hook: Sizes 14–16

NYMPH

Thread: Gray
Tail: Tannish gray hackle fibers
Body: Pale gray angora or opossum, dubbed heavily
Wings: Pale gray mallard quill sections
Hackle: Cream-ginger
Hook: Sizes 14–16

West

PALE EVENING DUN

Copies species like *Heptagenia elegantula*

Thread: Pale yellow
Tail: Cream hackle fibers
Body: Pale yellowish cream poly, dubbed
Wings: Pale yellow hackle tips
Hackle: Cream
Shuck (optional): Dark brown Z-lon
Hook: Sizes 16–20

PALE EVENING SPINNER
Thread: Cream
Tail: Cream hackle fibers
Body: Pale yellowish cream poly, dubbed
Wings: Pale gray poly yarn, tied spent
Hook: Sizes 16–20

PALE EVENING NYMPH
Thread: Dark brown
Tail: Brown-dyed mallard flank fibers
Body: Dark brown angora, loosely dubbed
Wings: Dark mallard section
Hackle: Grouse
Hook: Size 14

PALE MORNING DUN
Copies species like *Ephemerella inermis, E. infrequens,* and *E. lacustris*
Thread: Cream
Tail: Cream hackle fibers
Body: Varies from a bright olive to a creamish yellow. Use poly and dub.
Wings: Pale gray hackle tips
Shuck (optional): Dark brown Z-lon
Hackle: Cream
Hook: Sizes 16–18

PALE MORNING SPINNER
Thread: Orange
Tail: Tan
Body: Tan

Wings: Pale gray poly yarn
Hook: Sizes 16–18

PALE MORNING NYMPH
Thread: Dark brown
Tail: Ginger-dyed mallard flank fibers
Body: The belly is amber angora or nymph dubbing, with a darker brown back
Wings: Brown turkey
Hackle: Cree
Hook: Sizes 16–18

LIGHT CAHILL
Copies species like *Cinygma dimicki*
Thread: Yellow
Tail: Ginger hackle fibers
Body: Pale creamish yellow poly
Wings: Wood duck (or imitation) flank feather
Hackle: Ginger-cream
Shuck (optional): Dark brown Z-lon
Hook: Size 12

LIGHT CAHILL SPINNER
Thread: Yellow
Tail: Ginger hackle fibers
Body: Yellowish cream poly
Wings: Pale gray poly
Hackle: Yellowish cream
Hook: Size 12

PINK LADY
Copies species like *Epeorus albertae*
Thread: Cream
Tail: Cream-ginger hackle fibers
Body: Grayish cream poly
Wings: Gray mallard quills or dark gray hackle tips
Shuck (optional): Dark brown Z-lon

Hackle: Cream or badger
Hook: Size 12

SALMON SPINNER
Thread: Cream
Tail: Dark brown moose mane
Body: Female—pinkish red poly. Male—cream-gray poly.
Wings: Pale gray poly
Hackle: Pale blue dun
Hook: Size 12

PINK LADY NYMPH
Thread: Brown
Tail: Brown mallard flank
Body: Medium brown Furry Foam over tan angora
Wings: Light mottled turkey
Hackle: Sandy dun
Hook: Size 12

GRAY FOX
Copies many species like *Heptagenia solitaria*
Thread: Tan
Tail: Bronze dun hackle fibers
Body: Yellowish tan poly
Wings: Pale gray hackle tips
Hackle: Bronze dun
Shuck (optional): Dark brown Z-lon
Hook: Size 12

GINGER QUILL SPINNER
Thread: Tan
Tail: Ginger hackle fibers
Body: Tan-dyed eyed peacock herl, stripped
Wings: Pale gray poly
Hackle: Ginger
Hook: Size 12

GRAY FOX NYMPH
Thread: Brown
Tail: Brown mallard flank
Body: Dark brown Furry Foam over pale yellow
Wings: Dark mottled turkey
Hackle: Grouse or partridge
Hook: Size 14

Chapter 8: Summer Evenings—Dark Grays and Browns
East, Midwest, and West

SLATE DRAKE
Copies all *Isonychia* species
Thread: Black
Tail: Dark gray hackle fibers
Body: Peacock herl (not from eye), stripped; or dark gray poly or muskrat, dubbed
Wings: Dark gray hackle tips
Hackle: One cream hackle tied in behind and one dark brown hackle tied in front
Shuck (optional): Black Z-lon
Hook: Sizes 12–14

WHITE-GLOVED HOWDY
Thread: Dark brown or maroon
Tail: Medium gray hackle fibers
Body: Dark mahogany poly, dubbed
Wings: Pale gray poly yarn
Hook: Sizes 12–14

SLATE DRAKE NYMPH
Thread: Dark brown
Tail: Three dark brown hackle with one side cut off
Body: Dark brown angora or opossum
Wings: Dark gray mallard quill section, tied down over thorax
Hackle: Pale-olive-dyed cree hackle
Hook: Sizes 10–12

BROWN DRAKE

Copies *Ephemera simulans*
Thread: Dark brown
Tail: Moose mane
Body: Yellowish brown poly, dubbed
Wings: Yellowish-brown-dyed mallard flank feather, divided
Hackle: Rear—cream. Front—dark brown.
Shuck (optional): Tannish gray Z-lon
Hook: Sizes 10–12

BROWN DRAKE SPINNER

Thread: Dark brown
Tail: Brown hackle fibers
Body: Yellowish brown poly, dubbed
Wings: Gray poly yarn, tied spent
Hook: Sizes 10–12

BROWN DRAKE NYMPH

Thread: Brown
Tail: Three light brown hackles, trimmed and tied in
Body: Tan angora or opossum
Wings: Brown turkey, tied down and over thorax
Hackle: Dark cree
Hook: Sizes 10–12

BIG SLATE DRAKE

Copies *Hexagenia atrocaudata*
Thread: Dark gray
Tail: Dark brown deer
Body: Dark gray poly
Wings: Dark gray mallard or turkey
Hackle: Dark brown
Shuck (optional): Tan Z-lon
Hook: Size 8

RUSTY BROWN SPINNER

Thread: Yellow
Tail: Dark brown deer hair

Body: Tannish yellow poly, ribbed finely with brown thread
Wings: Pale gray poly yarn, tied spent
Hook: Size 8

HEX NYMPH

Thread: Brown
Tail: Three light brown hackles, trimmed and tied in
Body: Pale tan angora or opossum
Wings: Brown turkey, tied down and over thorax
Hackle: Dark cree
Hook: Sizes 10–12

HEX OR MICHIGAN CADDIS

Copies *Hexagenia limbata*
Thread: Tan
Tail: Brown
Body: Pale yellowish tan poly
Wings: Smoky gray teal flank feather
Hackle: Cream-ginger and a turn or two of brown
Shuck (optional): Tan Z-lon
Hook: Size 6

HEX SPINNER

Thread: Yellow
Tail: Tan deer hair
Body: Pale creamish tan poly
Wings: Gray poly yarn, tied spent
Hook: Size 6

HEX NYMPH

Thread: Brown
Tail: Three light brown hackles, trimmed and tied in
Body: Tan angora or opossum
Wings: Brown turkey, tied down and over thorax
Hackle: Dark cree
Hook: Sizes 10–12

Dark Brown Dun—Male
Olive Sulphur—Female

Copies species like the male of *Ephemerella needhami*

Thread: Dark brown
Tail: Cream
Body: Dark brown poly (female is bright olive-green)
Wings: Pale gray hackle tips
Hackle: Pale yellow
Shuck (optional): Dark brown Z-lon
Hook: Sizes 14–16

Dark Brown Spinner

Thread: Dark brown
Tail: Dark brown hackle
Body: Dark brown poly (female is bright olive-green)
Wings: White poly yarn, tied spent
Hook: Sizes 14–16

Nymph

Thread: Brown
Tail: Three light brown hackles, trimmed and tied in
Body: Dark olive-brown opossum
Wings: Brown turkey, tied down and over thorax
Hackle: Dark cree
Hook: Sizes 14–16

Dark Blue Quill

Copies species like *Serratella deficiens*

Thread: Black
Tail: Dark dun
Body: Grayish black poly
Wings: Dark gray hackle tips
Hackle: Dark gray
Shuck (optional): Dark brownish black Z-lon
Hook: Size 16

Dark Blue Quill Spinner

Thread: Black
Tail: Dark brown moose mane

Body: Grayish black poly
Wings: Gray poly yarn, tied spent
Hook: Size 16

NYMPH
Thread: Brown
Tail: Three light brown hackles, trimmed and tied in
Body: Brownish black opossum
Wings: Brown turkey, tied down and over thorax
Hackle: Dark brown
Hook: Size 16

Chapter 9: Fall Grays

See previous listings.

TYING THE PATTERNS

Catskill tie, parachute, comparadun—which is my favorite way to tie patterns that match the hatches? I'm convinced that the lower the profile of the fly, the more effective it is—at least on most occasions. With many of my high-riding Catskill-type dry flies, I've resorted to cutting off the bottom hackle during a hatch. That often does the trick, and I begin to catch more trout. It first happened to me on the Arkansas River near Buena Vista in Colorado. Phil Camera, Don Puterbaugh, and I fished while a hatch of pale morning duns appeared on the surface. We had little success with a conventional , high-riding PMD tie. Finally Don grabbed my pattern and cut off the hackle on the bottom. I immediately began to catch trout.

The comparadun pattern is highly effective. This pattern has no conventional hackle, but is buoyed on the surface by its semicircular deer hair wing. I'll never forget a day on north-central Pennsylvania's Pine Creek in late May more than 20 years ago. Dirk Blakeslee cast to a dozen or more trout rising to a March brown hatch. I too cast to the same pod of trout. Dirk used a March Brown Comparadun while I used a conventional March Brown that matched every part of the natural. While I caught one trout on that high-riding pattern during the hatch, Dirk caught five. Finally I asked him for one of his comparaduns, and I began catching more trout as well.

These two incidents taught me an important lesson: I feel certain that when trout are feeding on a hatch, they prefer to take an artificial that rides lower in the surface than one riding higher.

Which Pattern to Use and When to Use It

I've given you plenty of choice for the hatches. You can match the hatch with a conventional pattern; use one of the 31 special patterns; or try some of the well-known restricted patterns like the Adams to match many hatches. You have similar choices with the spinner patterns. You can see your choices for the times of day and the seasons in tables 10.2, 10.7, and 10.10.

What will you do? How will you copy the hatches? If you've followed the thinking in this book, you might want to try the special patterns and see how effective they are for you. No matter what kind of patterns you're happiest with, however, you should find them here.

11. SPECIAL CONSIDERATIONS ——————

Why aren't hatches found on all streams? Why do you find a hatch on one stream or river and not another that's just a few miles away? Conditions are just not right for the mayfly to appear. I've talked to many anglers who have attempted to transfer mayflies from one stream or river to another. Few have had any success. Let me share an experience that happened to me almost 30 years ago.

In the many years that I've fished the hatches, I've seen my share of weird events. I'll never, never forget that trip to central Pennsylvania's Little Juniata River on June 1, 1973. That evening Jack Conyngham, Dick Mills, and I fished a stretch of this recovering river just half a mile below Spruce Creek. Around 8 PM green drakes began appearing on the surface by the hundreds. Now, up to this date, in previous years, I had never seen more than a handful of these large mayflies on the Little Juniata. The drakes appeared in an unusual manner that evening—upside down. Every one of these duns appeared on the surface with its abdomen facing upward, flapping furiously to right itself. I didn't see one drake take flight, and not one trout rose to this unexpected hatch—not one.

For years that convoluted hatch bothered me. Why did these green drakes emerge upside down? Why hadn't this river had the hatch in prior years? Then, a few years later, it came to me in a split second—green drakes have a two-year life cycle. This means that fertilized eggs deposited in 2002 will become adults in 2004. Spruce Creek, a major tributary to the Little Juniata River, has a tremendous hatch of green drakes. In 1972 Hurricane Agnes devastated central Pennsylvania. That storm deposited more than 15 inches of rain on the Little Juniata River and its major tributary, Spruce Creek. Both were in flood stage for more than a week. I surmise that one-year-old green drake nymphs were dislodged from their burrows in Spruce Creek and transported by the floodwaters a couple of miles downriver into the foreign waters of the Little Juniata River.

When these nymphs, hatched from eggs in 1971—dislodged on June 25, 1972—finally emerged in 1973, they did so in strange environs. And because these waters were not exactly what the species needed or because they'd been moved, the green drake duns were so disoriented that they emerged upside down.

Remember this incident before you transport mayflies from one stream to another. If conditions are right, the mayfly will probably appear on a particular stream all on its own. In 1986, for instance, the green drake returned to the Little Juniata River

On the Deschutes River in Oregon the pale morning dun appears in late May.

in unbelievable numbers. Something had apparently changed in the makeup of the river, allowing it to harbor the mayfly in heavy numbers. (The river has since lost the hatch because of an unknown source of pollution.)

There are other considerations you should think of when you're fishing the hatches. One of the most important is weather; others include predicting when a mayfly will appear, multiple hatches, color variation, and differing hatch intensities. We'll examine all of these.

WEATHER

Weather affects the hatches and spinner falls tremendously. Show me an overcast, drizzly, cool day during the fishing season and I'll show you a little blue-winged olive hatch. When the weather turns bad, hatches tend to linger on the surface. The greatest fishing day I have ever experienced occurred when a normally fast-escaping BWO hatch remained on the surface of Penns Creek in central Pennsylvania. The hatch continued for more than five hours that July 4 morning and afternoon. I conservatively estimate that in that period of time I saw more than 200 trout rise to these mayflies. The air temperature that day never rose above 59 degrees, and a slight drizzle fell for most of the day.

Cool evenings often affect spinners, too. Just ask Bryan Meck what happened the evening he went to fish the hex hatch on Michigan's AuSable River. As you'll recall from chapter 8, the night before he fished he hit a spectacular spinner fall. But the next evening—with temperatures in the high 40s and low 50s—the spinner never appeared. I've seen the same thing happen time and time again with the brown drake. I've watched the males gather high in the sky near the stream, undulating—and then it began raining, and the spinners disappeared back into the trees to wait for another evening.

Temperatures affect the timing of the hatches also. Show me a hot July or August morning and I'll predict a hurried trico spinner fall. Conversely, on a cool, overcast day in those same two months, the trico hatch and spinner fall will often be prolonged. When the tricos appear in September and October—in cooler weather—they often don't appear until 10 or 11 AM. In the heat of summer the hatch appears on the surface around 7 AM or even earlier. I've encountered late-October trico hatches where I've seen the spinners on the water as late as 3 PM.

Weather affects the early-spring hatches considerably. Duns normally appear on the surface at 2 PM, but on warm April mornings I've encountered Hendricksons as early as 9 AM.

Cold weather, drizzle, and overcast conditions can extend a hatch by several hours. Sulphurs, pale morning duns, and little blue-winged olives all appear for a longer time when the weather is less than desirable.

How important is fishing on inclement days? In *Great Rivers—Great Hatches* I devoted an entire chapter to fishing on those lousy days.

INTENSITY OF THE HATCH

I've quit on rare occasions in the middle of a hatch. Trout rose everywhere—to my right, to my left, and directly in front of me. Why did I quit? There were too many duns or spinners on the surface. It's happened several times during the green drake hatch and coffin fly spinner fall on Penns Creek in central Pennsylvania, and during a pale morning dun hatch on the Kootenai in northwestern Montana. Just about every square inch of water surface contained a floating coffin fly on Penns Creek. Yes, some trout rose, but how in the devil did any angler fishing that evening have a chance competing against all those naturals? The same thing occurred on the Kootenai in the middle of a cool, overcast, rainy day: Pale morning duns covered the surface for hours.

And then there were days like those on the Lackawaxen and Delaware Rivers in the Northeast when Hendrickson duns covered the surface but not one trout rose. Why? Was it the cool spring temperatures? Were trout feeding on the nymphs under the surface?

What can you do to compete with all those naturals on the surface? I have two possible answers. First, try sinking your pattern under the surface. Whether it's a pattern copying a dun emerging or a spinner falling—sink it. It's worked for me several times when the hatch or fall seemed too heavy. I sank a Green Drake dry fly on Penns Creek one evening after an hour of trying to coax trout to take my pattern. I landed a 20-inch brown trout with that sunken pattern. On the Driftwood Branch of the Sinnemahoning in north-central Pennsylvania, the only way any of the four anglers I fished with caught trout one evening was by tugging the Green Drake under the surface.

Penns Creek holds great blue-winged olives.

What if sinking the pattern doesn't work? Try using a different pattern or a smaller size of the same pattern. I can remember a trico hatch on the South Platte River below Elevenmile Reservoir in Colorado. Trout fed within a few feet of me on this heavily fished water. No Trico pattern I used worked for me. Finally, in a fit of frustration, I tied on a size 20 Patriot—yes, a Patriot. I landed three trout that morning on that attractor pattern.

If the hatch is heavily fished, try downsizing—use a smaller pattern to match the hatch. I do this with trico spinners on occasion. If the natural on the surface is a size 24—and your eyes are good enough—try using a size 26 pattern.

I've often enticed trout to strike when I've moved the pattern slowly. In Labrador the green drake often moves violently attempting to escape from the surface. When I gently twitched a Laid Back Hex pattern, trout struck the fly violently (see chapter 7).

MULTIPLE HATCHES AND SPINNER FALLS

You've already read about multiple-hatch days in "A Mixed Bag on a Summer Day" in chapter 6. If you fish long enough, especially on some of the more fertile rivers and streams, you'll encounter more than one mayfly hatch appearing at one time. I've seen this occur on the Beaverkill and Delaware Rivers in New York; on Big Fishing Creek, Penns Creek, and the Little Juniata River in central Pennsylvania; on the AuSable in Michigan; on the Metolius River in Oregon; and of course on Henry's Fork in Idaho.

The first time I encountered more than one dun on the surface at one time, I was oblivious to it. I kept fishing my Western Green Drake pattern on Henry's Fork while trout switched to the smaller pale morning dun. I've seen this happen many times since: Even if there's a large mayfly on the surface, trout often prefer a smaller one emerging at the same time. Countless times I've seen green drakes appear at the same time as sulphurs in the East—and trout prefer the latter. When a multiple hatch occurs, how do you determine which insect the trout are taking? Take some time out and watch what the trout are doing. In the midst of a green drake/sulphur hatch I noticed that the majority of trout were taking the sulphur—but there were some trout feeding on the larger mayfly, the green drake. I had a Green Drake tied on my tippet, so before I switched to a smaller Sulphur I cast to a few trout feeding on the larger mayfly. I caught a few of those trout, then switched to the Sulphur pattern—and caught trout on that fly, too.

The same frustrating event can occur with spinner falls. I can't recall all the evenings I've prepared for one particular spinner—but more than one fell to the surface. Be prepared for such an event and switch patterns quickly if you get a lot of refusals.

DURATION OF THE HATCH

When a hatch lasts for some time, trout tend to become highly selective—especially if the hatch or spinner fall is heavily fished. The trico is the prototypical example of a hatch and spinner fall that lasts for a long time. In many areas the trico emerges from July though much of October. That's almost a full four months that this hatch appears—daily. In the Southwest the hatch can appear throughout much of the year.

A long-duration hatch can bring a lot of fishing pressure. Trout are confronted daily with a host of anglers presenting Trico patterns. The South Platte River below Elevenmile Reservoir and the Grand River in Ontario are good examples.

NO HATCH APPEARS

Let's face it: On many of the fishing trips you make, you'll see few hatches. Unless you fish water like Henry's Fork in Idaho, you'll often see only a few mayflies, stoneflies, or caddisflies. Yes, fertile waters like the Delaware and Beaverkill, Big Fishing Creek, and the AuSable in Michigan have hatches almost on a daily basis. For the vast majority of streams and rivers, however, that's not the case.

Many times you can't set your schedule around the hatches—so you appear on the stream when no hatch appears. I once fished with an angler who cast only over rising trout. One evening he cast his fly only a few times over a single, solitary rising trout. What a waste of fishing time!

	March	April	May	June	July	August	Sept.	October	Nov.
1	Little Blue-Winged Olive		Sulphur		Trico	Trico	Little Blue-Winged Olive		
2		Blue Quill		March Brown	Yellow Drake	Whitefly			
3		Quill Gordon		Light Cahill	Light Cahill	Hex		Slate Drake	
4		Hendrickson		Slate Drake	Blue Quill	Hex		Whitefly	
5		Great Olive Dun		Green Drake			Blue Quill	Blue Quill	
6		Black Quill		Dark Green Drake			Cream Cahill		
7	Speckle-Winged Dun			Blue-Winged Olive					
8	Dark Quill Gordon			Blue Quill					
9				Olive Dun					
10									
11				Olive Sulphur					
12				Sulphur-3					
13									
14									
15				Pink Lady					
16				Brown Drake					
17				Hex					
18				Yellow Drake					
19				Cream Cahill					
20									
21									
22									
23									
24									
25									

TABLE 11.1: Number of mayflies that can emerge at any given day in the East and Midwest

	March	April	May	June	July	August	Sept.	October	Nov.
1	Western March Brown					Gray Drake		Blue Quill	
2		Little Blue-Winged Olive				Trico / Blue Quill		Little Blue-Winged Olive	
3			Speckle-Winged Dun			Gray Fox		White Fly	
4		Blue Quill	Pale Morning Dun					Trico	
5			Red Quill			Little Blue-Winged Olive		Light Cahill	
6				Western Green Drake		White Fly			
7				Blue-Winged Olive					
8				Little Blue-Winged Olive					
9				Pink Lady					
10				Pale Brown Dun					
11									
12				Quill Gordon					
13									
14					Dark Brown Dun				
15					Pale Evening Dun				
16					Light Cahill				
17					Brown Drake				
18					Blue Quill				
19					Dark Brown Dun				
20					Trico				
21									
22									
23									
24									
25									

TABLE 11.2: Number and common names of mayflies that can emerge at any given day in the West

When no hatch appears, it's time to improvise. Until a few year ago I used only dry flies. I hated using wet flies. Besides, I wasn't a very good wet-fly angler. With the advent of the tandem, however, I've begun using wet flies on almost every fishing trip. Using a dry fly as the strike indicator with a wet fly placed behind it has proved extremely effective for me—especially on hatchless days. I proposed in *How to Catch More Trout* that fly-fishers compile a list of wet-fly patterns that seem to work, and use these flies on days when no hatch appears. Do you already have a list of flies that seem to work for you? Keep updating it as you find new, more effective flies.

EMERGENCE DATES

Emergences in the East and Midwest can be predicted fairly accurately. I feel comfortable that the green drake will appear annually on Spruce Creek in Pennsylvania on May 26; on the Delaware River on May 29; and on Penns Creek in central Pennsylvania around May 30.

In the East the Hendrickson appears in New York, New Jersey, and Pennsylvania around April 22. In Michigan that same hatch appears in early May.

When I wrote *Meeting and Fishing the Hatches* in 1977 I included an emergence date map. This map gives approximate dates of mayflies for various parts of the

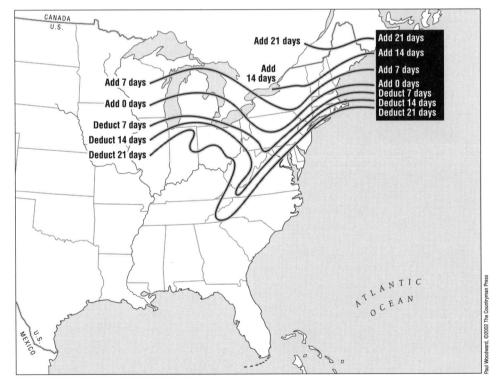

TABLE 11.3: Emergence dates for eastern and midwestern hatches

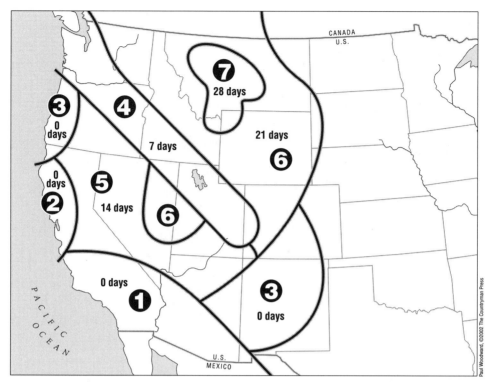

Paul Woodward, ©2002 The Countryman Press

TABLE 11.4: Emergence dates for western hatches

East and Midwest based on the annual degree days (table 11.3). That chart has worked well for me for more than 24 years. I have included that map and one for the West (table 11.4). Both are based on total degree days. The western version, however, is much less accurate because of local weather conditions and elevation.

Look at Zone 1 in table 11.4. The Southwest presents an entirely different problem: Some summer hatches appear throughout the winter. I've seen less-than-spectacular trico spinner falls on New Year's morning on the Salt River near Phoenix, Arizona. I've fished some spectacular trico spinner falls in the middle of February on the upper Verde River near Cottonwood, Arizona. Little blue-winged olives appear almost daily on these waters throughout the winter. On southwestern streams and rivers you're apt to see little blue-winged olives and tricos emerging daily throughout much of the winter (see chapter 9).

In Zones 2 and 3 hatches like the western March brown appear in late February or early March. In Zone 4 add seven days to the emergence date. Remember that this is only a rough tool—it's not accurate in any way.

Yes, predicting a hatch in the West from one river to another is difficult at best. I've seen western green drakes on Oregon's Metolius River on May 25. I've seen that same hatch on Idaho's Henry's Fork on June 25—one month later. I've fished the

Colorado's South Platte River below Elevenmile Reservoir. Tricos are heavy here.

salmon fly (a stonefly) on the Deschutes River in Oregon near the end of May, then hit that same hatch on the Yellowstone River near Gardiner, Montana, in early July—more than a month later.

The hatch dates listed in all of the emergence charts are just good estimates. I've witnessed some great hatches well after the hatch should have ended for the year. I talked earlier about the quill Gordon, which normally hatches in mid-April. On occasion I've seen a few of these mayflies on the water until mid-May. Several years ago I fished a small mountain stream in north-central Pennsylvania, Sixmile Run, and found a heavy quill Gordon hatch in mid-June. Yes, mid-June! Trout rose to the heavy hatch. Furthermore, at 7:30 PM trout rose to the spent-winged adult, the red quill spinner.

On another occasion I discussed in chapter 5, John Randolph and Jay Nichols of *Fly Fisherman* magazine fished a stream near Harrisburg, Pennsylvania, Clarks Creek, hitting a fantastic great olive spinner fall (*Siphloplecton basale*). John said trout rose for every spinner that fell; he caught more trout on that spinner imitation than he had on any other trip. Talk about a memorable day! You'll note in the charts that I list this large mayfly's average emergence date as April 15. John and Jay were fishing a month after that date.

COLOR VARIATIONS

A word of caution on matching the hatches—especially when you match the dun: Body colors can vary tremendously. One of the most varied mayflies in the United States is the pale morning dun. I collected olive-bodied ones from the Kootenai River in northwestern Montana and the Metolius River in central Oregon. I've seen reddish brown bodies on the duns in the Box Canyon section of Henry's Fork. Those on the Bitterroot are pale yellow. On still other waters I've seen tan-colored duns. I sent a mayfly in each of these colors to a noted entomologist when I prepared the manuscript for *Meeting and Fishing the Hatches.* All four mayflies came back identified as pale morning duns *(Ephemerella inermis).* Evidently this species—more than any other—varies tremendously in color from one location to another.

But it's not the only mayfly to do so. In the East and Midwest you have the March brown. On some waters like the Delaware River in New York and Pine Creek in Pennsylvania you'll see mayflies that are much lighter than the same species on the Lackawanna River and Elk Creek in Pennsylvania. I sent both mayflies—one lighter and one definitely darker—to an entomologist; both, I was told, were March browns. Sulphurs, green drakes, and western green drakes too vary considerably from one stream to another. That's just a partial list. In your trips to fish the hatches you'll se many more.

Some hatches, like the slate drake and the western green drake, even change color after they're out of the water for a while. Paul Weamer tells me that when slate drakes emerge on the Delaware River, they have a definite olive sheen to their dark gray bodies. They lose that olive sheen after a short while out of the water. The western green drake also changes color—from bright olive to a darker shade.

TABLE 11.5: Species Where Male and Female Often Differ Dramatically in Color

Common Name	Scientific Name	General Coloration of the Female	General Coloration of the Male
Green drake	*Hexagenia rigida*	Pale yellow	Pale brown
Olive sulphur	*Ephemerella needhami*	Olive-green	Dark brown
Pink lady	*Epeorus vitreus*	Pale pinkish cream	Cream
Light Cahill	*Stenacron interpunctatum*	Orange-cream	Cream
Hendrickson	*Ephemerella subvaria*	Tannish	Light red
Sulphur	*Ephemerella rotunda*	Creamish yellow with olive reflections	Tan

Often the male and female of the same species vary tremendously in color. Table 11.5 lists some common species that feature this gender difference.

No Mating Swarms—Parthenogenesis

For years I've tried to find a male dark quill Gordon (*Ameletus ludens*) dun. In the 10 years that I've seen the hatch, I've never found one. I searched for a male little blue-winged olive dun (*Baetis bicaudatus*) for a year before I found one. What causes this phenomenon? Entomologists now think that several mayflies can produce viable eggs without fertilization—scientists call this parthenogenesis.

I've encountered dark quill Gordons hatching on many April fishing trips. This mayfly often emerges near shore and rests on a rock nearby rather than flying to a tree. Why? Look at its wings. They're relatively small for the size of the mayfly. Since there is little or no mating for these mayflies, wings are not needed for a mating flight.

These are just a few of the special considerations you should note when you attempt to fish the hatches.

12. A FINAL HATCH————————

I discussed my first trip to Montana in 1976 in chapter 7. But it's important to review what I said. The very first publisher to whom I sent my initial manuscript, *Meeting and Fishing the Hatches*, accepted the book proposal on one condition: I had to include information on the western hatches. I had to hurry, too—the publisher gave me a couple of months to finish the project. I planned to take a tour of western rivers to complete that manuscript in the summer of 1976. That first trip to Montana and Wyoming was fraught with trepidation. I had no guide, no local contacts, and planned to fish more than two dozen rivers across two states. Thank God for people like Charlie Brooks. This excellent writer took me under his wing and gave me a list of rivers to fish. He truly saved the day for me. At the end of each day I'd call Charlie and review where I had fished and how well I had done.

As I noted, I first chose to fish the Bitterroot River near Victor, Montana. I had fished the hatches for more than 20 years in the East and had noted the dominant colors of mayflies at different times of the day and of the fishing season. I suspected that the same phenomenon occurred in the West. I prepared for that first morning with plenty of gray and olive patterns, including some large Western Green Drake patterns. As I sat mesmerized by the high snow-fed waters, I saw a few mayflies emerge. They were huge, and trout fed all over the run in front of me. Maybe a dozen heavy fish chased the duns in the high water. I had the match—the Western Green Drake in a size 12 took just about every rising trout that first morning. No problem to this western fishing—it was simple.

Then it happened. Just as the green drake hatch concluded another, much smaller mayfly appeared on the Bitterroot. It was *Ephemerella infrequens*, a yellow mayfly imitated by a size 18 pattern. What was this doing, emerging at this time? Now I was confused. There went my theory on light mayflies appearing in the evening. But in the weeks to follow on all of those western waters I saw only pale morning duns (mainly *E. inermis* but also *E. infrequens*) appear in the morning—no other light mayfly. And I encountered not only PMDs that had yellow bodies but also many that were olive, tan, or reddish brown.

I learned a lot on that inaugural trip to the western rivers, especially about colors of mayflies and when they appeared. What I've experienced in the past 30 years has corroborated my earlier thinking. What have you learned from this book? If you've read all of the chapters you should have noted the following:

Early Spring

- Gray patterns like the Adams, Blue Quill, and Quill Gordon will match many of the early hatches you encounter whether you're fishing in the East, Midwest, or West. Carry some tan and light brown patterns for the Hendrickson and western March brown hatches. Look for the hatches to appear from 11 AM to 5 PM.

Midspring

- In mid-May a transition occurs in the East and Midwest. March browns come off the water in the afternoon. As the season advances and evenings get warmer, these large mayflies often appear just at dusk. When sulphurs first appear, they often do so the first couple of days in the afternoon. Another May emerger in some of its territory is the pale morning dun. It can appear in the morning, afternoon, or evening. Be prepared for the PMD with tan, olive, reddish brown, and pale yellow patterns.

Late Spring and Summer

- A notable change takes place in the East around the end of May; in the Midwest in early June; and in the West near the end of June. First, gray, brown, and olive mayflies now appear in the morning and, to a lesser degree, the afternoon. Second, if any cream mayflies appear, they most often do so in the evening (except pale morning duns and hatches in cool tailwaters). Most hatches appear at the most comfortable time of the day—morning and evening (again, watch out for exceptions on tailwaters).

- Mornings now hold some good gray-, olive-, and brown-bodied hatches like the blue-winged olive dun, blue quill, and, later, the trico. In the West it's the time of the brown to dark brown *Rhithrogena*, blue-winged olive duns, blue quills, western green drakes, and little blue-winged olive duns.

- Evenings hold the great cream and yellow hatches like the green drake, light Cahill, cream Cahill, and white fly.

- Evenings also hold a few dark brown and gray mayflies that can produce spectacular matching-the-hatch opportunities. Brown drakes, some hex hatches (which can be classified as cream or yellow), and slate drakes are some of the darker evening mayflies that create feeding frenzies from late May through early August.

Late Summer and Early Fall

• By early September gray patterns again reign supreme: little blue-winged olives, blue quills, and slate drakes in the East and Midwest, and blue quills and little blue-winged olive duns in the West. Look for most of these to appear about the same time the hatches appear in early spring—in the afternoon.

There you have it. You can predict the colors of most of the hatches based on time of year and time of day. Can it be any easier than that—*The Hatches Made Simple*?

APPENDIX:
MAYFLY IDENTIFICATION

L et me start by saying I leave definitive mayfly identification to the experts—the entomologists who specialize in this. Whenever I have a question about a mayfly species, I capture some duns (including several males), takes photos of them, and then place them in a plastic bottle with plenty of holes in it. I also place a sprig or two of vegetation in the bottle to give the mayflies moisture, and keep the jar out of direct sunlight. If I'm in the West collecting species, I often put a glass of water next to the jar to give the mayflies more moisture. I keep checking the bottle to see when the dun has transformed into a spinner. I take photos of the dun and spinner, and then I place one of the male spinners in a 70 percent alcohol solution and ship it to an entomologist friend, who does the final identification. In a couple of weeks I receive a positive identification on the mayfly. I then have photos of the dun and spinner stages.

Still, with the proper keys, basic mayfly identification isn't that difficult. Many anglers on the stream want to know what a specific hatch is—and with hundreds of possibilities, on-stream identification is risky at best. However, the following chart should help you make quick identifications. Remember, no matter what the mayfly is, if you have a pattern that matches the color and size the trout are feeding on, you'll probably catch fish.

How do you use the chart? Here's an example. You're fishing in late April in the early afternoon and you see a lot of mayflies emerging from the water. You grab one and examine it. It's dark gray with three tails and is small (a size 18 fly would copy it). Now look at the chart below. Look under "Early Season" (you found the hatch in late April); then "Three Tails"; then "Dark." Three species are listed there—the Hendrickson, black quill, and blue quill. None is boldfaced, since all three emerge during the day and not the evening. The Hendrickson and black quill are copied with a size 14 hook. The only small three-tailed mayfly appearing at that time of the year is the blue quill. So the mayfly you saw emerging is probably the blue quill. Or let's look at a hatch appearing in the West—again in April—on Oak Creek in Arizona. This is again a small mayfly appearing in the middle of the day, and it has two tails. A glance at the chart will reveal two possibilities—both little blue-winged olive duns.

That's how easy the chart is to use. Just remember the time the hatch appears (time of day and time of year); how many tails the mayfly has; whether it's large (hook size 14 or larger) or small (size 16 or smaller); and whether the general coloration is light or dark. Those mayflies that are near a size 14 or 16 are included in both sizes. Those that appear light to one person and dark to another are included in both. *Note: The features listed below are from the dun of the species. The spinner or mating adult is often totally different in coloration.*

TABLE A.1: Mayfly Dun Identification Chart, East and Midwest

Early Season (March 1–May 10)

Two Tails

Dark
> (S*) Little blue-winged olive dun—*Baetis tricaudatus.* Note that other *Baetis* species appear in the early season. The dun and spinner move their abdomens from side to side.
> (L*) Quill Gordon—*Epeorus pleuralis.* Can appear as late as late June.
> (L) Dark quill Gordon—*Ameletus ludens.* Usually find duns on rocks next to the stream.
> (L) Speckle-winged dun—*Callibaetis skokianus.* Slow-water or lake species; wings are speckled.
> (L) Great olive dun—*Siphloplecton basale.* Large gray mayfly that appears in April and May.

Three Tails

Dark
> (L) Hendrickson—*Ephemerella subvaria.* Belly of the male (reddish) and female (tan) differ in color.
> (L) Black quill—*Leptophlebia cupida.* Middle tail is somewhat shorter than the outer two.
> (S) Blue quill—*Paraleptophlebia adoptiva.* Body is thin and dark gray.

Midseason (May 11–June 30)

Two Tails

Light
> (L) **Light Cahill**—*Stenacron interpunctatum canadense.* Often appears most heavily around 7 PM.
> (L) **Light Cahill**—*Epeorus vitreus.* The male is yellow and the female has a pink body.
> (L) **Light Cahill**—*Stenonema ithaca.*
> (L) **Pink lady**—*Epeorus vitreus.* Female.
> (L) **Cream Cahill**—*Stenonema modestum.* Spinner is chalky white.
> (L) March brown (gray fox)—*Stenonema vicarium.*
> (L) **Green drake**—*Hexagenia rigida.* Wings of the dun are often olive.

Dark
> (L) Quill Gordon—*Epeorus pleuralis.* I've seen this mayfly appear in fishable numbers into June.
> (L) Dark green drake—*Litobrancha recurvata.* Usually appears around 2 pm. Has a middle vestigal (just a trace) tail.
> (L) Gray drake—*Siphlonurus quebecensis* and *S. mirus.* Male spinner (S. mirus) has black rear wing. Very common in early June in northwestern Pennsylvania.
> (L) **Michigan caddis**—*Hexagenia limbata.* Belly is cream or pale yellow.

*(S = Small—16+) (L = Large—14 and lower)   **Bold** *(emerge at evening or dark)*

Three Tails

Light

(L) **Golden drake**—*Anthopotamus distinctus.* Weak veins in wings. Middle tail is shorter.

(L) **Sulphur**—*Ephemerella rotunda* and *E. invaria.*

(L) **Pale evening dun**—*Ephemerella septentrionalis.* Looks like E. dorothea but is slighly larger.

(S) **Pale evening dun**—*Ephemerella dorothea.*

Dark

(S) Blue quill—*Paraleptophlebia mollis* and *P. guttata.* Emerge much of the summer.

(L) **Green drake**—*Ephemera guttulata.* Dark on top and cream on the bottom.

(L) **Brown drake**—*Ephemera simulans.* Brown to dark tan mayfly.

(L) Blue-winged olive dun—*Drunella cornuta.*

(L & S) Blue-winged olive dun—*Drunella cornutella.* A size smaller than D. cornuta, it appears in early to mid-June and continues into July.

(L & S) Blue-winged olive dun—*Drunella lata.* Appears three weeks later than D. cornutella.

(L) **Slate drake**—*Isonychia* bicolor. Front legs are dark brown; rear two pairs are cream.

(S) **Dark blue quill**—*Seratella deficiens.* Very dark, almost black, three-tailed mayfly.

(S) Little blue-winged olive dun—*Danella simplex.* Very small three-tailed mayfly.

(L) Chocolate dun—*Eurylophella* bicolor. Legs are cream.

(S) **Olive sulphur**—*Ephemerella needhami.* Legs, tail, and wings are cream. Body of female dun is medium olive; body of male dun is dark brown.

(L) **Yellow drake**—*Ephemera varia.* Front legs are black and cream.

Late Season (July 1–October 30)

Two Tails

Light

(L & S) **Cream Cahill**—*Stenonema modestum.*

(L) **White fly**—*Ephoron leukon.* Male.

(L) **Green drake**—*Hexagenia rigida.*

(L) **Michigan caddis**—*Hexagenia limbata.* Belly is cream.

Dark

(L) **Dark slate drake**—*Hexagenia atrocaudata.* Male spinners undulate about 30 feet in the air around 7 pm. Duns emerge well after dark.

(S) Little blue-winged olive dun—*Baetis tricaudatus.* Very common throughout the United States, it appears in spring and fall.

Three Tails

Light

(L) **White fly**—*Ephoron leukon.* Female.

(L) **Yellow drake**—*Ephemera* var.

(S) Trico—*Tricorythodes allectus.* Female.

(S) **Little white mayfly**—*Caenis* spp. Size 26 or smaller.

Dark

(S) Trico—*Tricorythodes allectus.* Male.

(L) **Slate drake**—*Isonychia* bicolor.

(L) Blue Quill—*Paraleptophlebia guttata.*

TABLE A.2: Mayfly Dun Identification Chart, West

Early Season (March 1–May 10)

Two Tails

Dark

- (S) Little blue-winged olive dun—*Baetis tricaudatus.* Note that other Baetis species appear in the early season. The dun and spinner move their abdomen from side to side.
- (S) Little blue-winged olive dun—*Baetis intercalaris.* Looks like Baetis tricaudatus.
- (L) Western March brown—*Rhithrogena morrisoni.* Appears for more than three months on some western rivers.
- (L) Speckle-winged dun—*Callibaetis americanus.* Wings are heavily speckled.

Three Tails

- (S) Blue quill—*Paraleptophlebia memorialis.*

Midseason (May 11–June 30)

Two Tails

Light

- (L) **Pale evening dun**—*Heptagenia elegantula.*
- (L) **Gray fox**—*Heptagenia solitaria.* A fairly large light mayfly that often emerges late in the season.
- (L) **Pink lady**—*Epeorus albertae.*

Dark

- (S) Little blue-winged olive dun—*Baetis bicaudatus.* Brighter olive than most.
- (S) Dark brown dun—*Diphetor hageni.* A small dark brown Baetis.
- (L) Speckle-winged dun—*Callibaetis americanus.* Wings are heavily speckled.
- (L) Quill Gordon—*Rhithrogena futilis.*
- (L) Pale brown dun—*Cinygmula reticulata.*
- (L) Gray drake—*Siphlonurus occidentalis.* A large gray mayfly that has a distinctly ribbed body.
- (L) Pale brown dun—*Rhithrogenia hageni.*
- (L) Dark red quill—*Rhithrogena undulata.*

Three Tails

Light

- (S) Pale morning dun—*Ephemerella infrequens.*
- (S) Pale morning dun—*Ephemerella inermis.* Body color of this mayfly varies considerably from stream to stream.

Dark

- (L) **Brown drake**—*Ephemera simulans.*
- (L) Western green drake—*Drunella grandis.* Variable color from dark olive to olive-black.
- (S) Blue quill—*Paraleptophlebia heteronea.*
- (S) Blue quill—*Paraleptophlebia memorialis.*
- (S) Blue quill—*Paraleptophlebia viciva.*
- (L) Blue-winged olive dun—*Drunella flavilinea.* Morning and evening emerger; morning seems heavier.

Late Season (July 1–September 30)

Three Tails

Light

- (S) Trico—*Tricorythodes minutus* and *T. fictus.* Can be light or dark.
- (L) **White fly**—*Ephoron album.* The male spinner has two tails and the female dun has three.

Dark
- (L) **Brown drake**—*Ephemera simulans*.
- (M, L) Western green drake—*Drunella grandis*.
- (S) Blue quill—*Paraleptophlebia bicornuta*.
- (S) Blue quill—*Paraleptophlebia memorialis*.
- (S) Blue quill—*Paraleptophlebia viciva*.
- (L) **Blue-winged olive dun**—*Drunella flavilinea*. Morning and evening emerger; morning seems heavier.

Two Tails

Light
- (L) **Pale evening dun**—*Heptagenia elegantula*.
- (L) **Gray fox**—*Heptagenia solitaria*.
- (L) **Pink lady**—*Epeorus albertae*.
- (L) **White fly**—*Ephoron album*. The male spinner has two tails and the female dun has three.

Dark
- (S) Little blue-winged olive dun—*Baetis bicaudatus*. Brighter olive than most.
- (S) Dark brown dun—*Diphetor hageni*.
- (L) Speckle-winged dun—*Callibaetis americanus*. Wings are heavily speckled.
- (L) Quill Gordon—*Rhithrogena futilis*.
- (L) Pale brown dun—*Cinygmula reticulata*.
- (L) Gray drake—*Siphlonurus occidentalis*.
- (L) Pale brown dun—*Rhithrogenia hageni*.
- (L) Dark red quill—*Rhithrogena undulata*.

---

*(S = Small—16+)   (L = Large—14 and lower)   **Bold** (emerge at evening or dark)

NOTES ABOUT THE HATCH IDENTIFICATION CHARTS

Season

I've divided hatches into early, mid-, and late season. Some—like the blue quill (*Paraleptophlebia guttata*) and the yellow drake (*Ephemera varia*)—emerge in two of the time frames. Just about every common hatch you'll ever encounter is listed in this hatch chart.

Number of Tails

Since tails are so important in helping you identify a mayfly, I've listed the number of tails found on each of the major hatches in table A.3. All mayflies have either two or three tails. Some (like *Hexagenia* and *Litobrancha*) have what is called a *vestigial* tail. These mayflies have just two tails, but if you look closely you'll see a hint of a middle tail (the length of this vestigial tail often differs by sex). Other species can be quickly identified because they have tails of unequal length; usually the middle tail is shorter than the outer two. Look for male mayflies when you check for the shorter middle tail. The middle tail of the black quill (*Leptophlebia cupida*) is only half the length of the outer two. With the golden drake (*Anthopotamus distinctus*), the middle tail is also shorter.

A simple way of determining which mayfly you're matching is to count the number of tails. This works with most species—except the white fly. When the white fly emerges, the male changes from a dun to a spinner, usually in a few minutes. The female, however, never molts and remains and breeds as a dun. The male spinner has two tails and the female dun three.

Light and Dark

Light and *dark* refer to the coloration of the back of the body. For example, look at the green drake. If you examine the belly or abdomen of this mayfly, you'll see cream. But look at the back and you see a darker insect.

A close look at the chart will reveal several bits of information. First, the chart verifies our hypothesis that cream mayflies appear in the evening. You'll also see that gray and brown mayflies appear in spring and again in fall.

Variation in Color

Dave McMullen owns and operates the Six Springs Fly Shop in Spruce Creek, Pennsylvania. He's one of the finest fly-casters I've ever seen. Show him a narrow opening between two trees and he'll land a dry fly delicately on the surface without getting hung up on a single branch. Dave also operates a trout hatchery in Spruce Creek and has made some keen observations there. Recently he showed me one of his findings. Dave netted three trout from a hatchery pool and placed them in a white bucket. Within minutes these trout had turned much lighter in color. He then returned the three to the hatchery pool; for almost five minutes we could tell which three they were because they were much lighter than the other trout.

What does this prove? Many life-forms are capable of changing color to some extent. Call it protective coloration or whatever you want, it happens. What about the coloration of nymphs? Have you heard someone say that nymphs in one area or on one stream are lighter or darker than in another area or stream? Do you think many aquatic insects have this same capability?

Night or Day Emergers

Those mayflies listed in bold usually emerge at night and those in regular type usually appear during the day. Of course, times vary with temperature and weather. I've seen Hendrickson hatches appear as early as 9 AM on hot April days and as late as 6 PM on others. You'll see sulphurs mentioned in this book many times. For the first couple of days that the sulphur appears, it often does so in the afternoon. After a few days the hatch usually changes to evening, appearing just before dusk.

Add a drizzly, overcast day and all kinds of things can happen. I've seen sulphurs and pale morning duns emerge all day long on inclement days. Green drakes,

TABLE A.3: Number of Tails

Common Name	Scientific Name —Genus	Two Tails	Three Tails	Comments
Hex	*Hexagenia*	X		Look carefully and you'll see just a stump or hint of a middle tail. The female middle tail is somewhat longer than the male.
Dark green drake	*Litobrancha*	X		Look carefully and you'll see just a hint of a third (middle) tail.
March brown Light Cahill Cream Cahill	*Stenonema* *Stenacron*	X		
Quill Gordon Pink lady	*Epeorus*	X		
Light Cahill	*Cinygma*	X		
Dark brown dun Western March brown	*Rhithrogena*	X		
Pale evening dun	*Heptagenia*	X		
Pale evening dun	*Leucrocuta*	X		
Dark olive dun	*Siphloplecton*	X		
Little blue-winged olive dun	*Baetis*	X		
Blue dun	*Pseudocloeon*	X		
Little blue-winged olive dun	*Plauditis*	X		
Dark brown dun	*Diphetor*	X		
Speckle-winged dun	*Callibaetis*	X		
Pale brown dun	*Cinygmula*	X		
Dark brown dun Dark quill Gordon	*Ameletus*	X		
White fly—male	*Ephoron*	X		
Slate drake	*Isonychia*	X		
Gray drake	*Siphlonurus*	X		A middle tail is just a stub. Two tails on the spinner are twice as long as the body.
Blue quill	*Paraleptophlebia*		X	
Green drake Yellow drake Brown drake	*Ephemera*		X	

Table continues on next page

TABLE A.3: Continued

Common Name	Scientific Name —Genus	Two Tails	Three Tails	Comments
Sulphur	*Ephemerella*		X	
Pale morning dun				
Hendrickson				
Olive sulphur				
Blue-winged olive dun	*Drunella*		X	
Blue-winged olive dun	*Attenella*		X	
Chocolate dun	*Eurylophella*		X	
Dark blue quill	*Seratella*		X	
Little blue-winged olive	*Danella*		X	
White fly—female	*Ephoron*		X	Short stubby tails
Trico	*Tricorythodes*		X	
Little white fly	*Caenis*		X	
Golden drake	*Anthopotamus*		X	Middle tail is somewhat shorter
Blackquill	*Leptophlebia*		X	Middle tail is shorter

too, will often appear earlier on overcast days and on streams with a heavy canopy. (See "A Mixed Bag on a Summer Day" in chapter 6.)

Large and Small

You'll see an *S* or an *L* in front of each mayfly in the chart. Hatches that can be matched with a size 14 or larger hook (14–6) have an *L* in front of them. Those matches with a size 16 or smaller hook (16–26) have an *S*. Size varies tremendously.

Other Features

To further help you identify some of the mayflies, I've added comments that might set one mayfly off from another. If male and female duns have different colors, I mention them in this column. Many of the features in this column refer to coloration of the mayfly. Look at the notation for the speckle-winged dun (*Callibaetis* spp.)—"wings are heavily speckled." If you look closely at the wings of the dun or spinner, you'll see that they're heavily speckled or marked. This an important identifying feature of this mayfly.

GLOSSARY

Chapter 2

Spent-winged spinner—When a spinner dies or is dying, it often lies on the surface with its wings spread out.

Spinner fall—When a number of adult mayflies (usually females) fall onto the surface while they lay eggs or shortly afterward.

Weighted spinner—Usually a pattern that has weight added to the body when it is tied to make it sink beneath the surface.

Chapter 3

Conventional downwing patterns—Recipes found at the end of this chapter that copy specific caddisflies and stoneflies.

Downwing—Usually refers to a caddisfly or stonefly because of the way these insects fold their wings when at rest.

Henryville—A caddis pattern that has a body that is palmered (ribbed) with a hackle.

Pupa—A resting stage for caddisflies.

Special downwing patterns—Twelve downwing patterns that will copy just about any caddisfly or stonefly that you encounter.

Stonefly—An aquatic insect that usually spends its larval or nymphal stage attached to a rock.

Twisted Caddis—A different way to tie a caddis pattern using spun poly yarn.

Chapter 4

Burrowers—Mayflies that, as nymphs, live underneath the bottom of the stream. Burrowing mayflies are large.

Caddisfly—A member of the order Trichoptera and an important source of food for trout. Members of this order of insects look somewhat like moths and spend their larval life underwater.

Chironomid—Another name for midge.

Clingers—Mayfly nymphs that spend most of their underwater lives on the underside of rocks and boulders in the stream.

Concentrated—A hatch where the duns emerge in good numbers usually for half an hour to two hours.

Diptera—One of the true flies, like the midge.

Downwing—Any insect that has its wings folded down over its back when at rest. Downwings include caddisflies and stoneflies.

Dun—The nonmating stage of the mayfly when it first emerges from the water. Duns usually have cloudy wings. Scientists call this a **subimago**.

Emerger—That part of the emergence process when a mayfly changes from a nymph to an air-breathing dun. This change usually takes place at or just under the surface and is the most vulnerable stage of the life cycle.

Ephemeral—Something that lasts only a short time.

Exoskeleton—A thick protective outer covering found on mayfly and stonefly nymphs and many other insects.

Family—A group of genera that have several physical features in common.

Generation—When a mayfly appears two times a year, it has two generations. Some mayflies appear more than two times a year and thus have multiple generations.

Genus—A group of similar species. Some important mayfly genera (plural) are *Ephemerella, Ephemera,* and *Stenonema.*

Hatch—A number of insects appearing on the surface at one time. A hatch usually signals a feeding frenzy for trout.

Hatch chart—A emergence chart showing when many of the major mayflies, caddisflies, and stoneflies will appear on the surface.

Larva—The immature or underwater stage of the mayfly, caddisfly, or stonefly. Immature stonefly and mayfly larvae are often called nymphs.

Matching the hatch—Using a fly that copies a hatch on the water.

Mayfly—An insect in the order Ephemeroptera and an important source of food for trout. The word *ephemeral,* "short lived," indicates that a mayfly adult lives out of the water for just a couple of days.

Midge or chironomid—A member of the order Diptera or true flies. Although most of these are small (usually copied on a size 20 hook or smaller), they are an important source of food for trout.

Multiple hatches—When two or more hatches appear on the surface at the same time.

Nymph—The immature or underwater stage of the mayfly and stonefly.

Order—A group of families with some similar features.

Parthenogenesis—Mayflies that lay eggs that are not fertilized by a male.

Pupa—A resting stage in an insect's life cycle. The caddisfly has a larval or resting stage; the mayfly and stonefly don't.

Species—Similar insects (in this example) that are capable of breeding.

Spinner—The mating stage of the mayfly. Swarms of female spinners often fall on the surface at one time, creating a "spinner fall." Scientists call this stage the imago.

Sporadic—A hatch in which duns emerge over an extended period of time and not many appear at any one time. Often the spinner of this hatch is more important than the dun.

Stonefly—Member of the order Plecoptera, meaning "ancient." As the name suggests, the underwater nymphs of this order spend most of their time on rocks and stones. When they're ready to emerge, most swim to an exposed rock or to shore.

Subspecies—Sometimes some insects are very closely related to others, yet there are enough differences to add a subspecies. If the mayfly is a subspecies, it has three names rather than two (see *Stenacron*).

Superhatches—Those heavily fished hatches that appear on many streams. One example is the hex hatch on Michigan's AuSable River.

Swimmers—Mayfly nymphs that are not attached to a rock and do not burrow underneath, but swim freely.

Terrestrial—Landborne insects that are blown onto or wander onto the surface of a stream or river. Terrestrials include beetles, ants, grasshoppers, caterpillars, crickets, and others.

Vestigial—A hint of a middle tail. Usually very short and often observable only with difficulty.

CHAPTER 11

Color variation—Differences in color among members of the same species.

Duration of the hatch—How long the insects continue to emerge.

Emergence dates—Approximate date and time that a hatch will occur.

Intensity of the hatch—How many insects appear on the surface at any given time.

Mating swarms—Usually a large group of males. The female spinners enter this swarm and are mated.

Multiple hatch—When two or more species of mayflies, caddisflies, or stoneflies are on the surface at one time.

Parthenogenesis—Used to describe the reproductive process when a female is capable of laying eggs without fertilization by a male.

FOR MORE INFORMATION

Caucci, Al, and Bob Nastasi. *Hatches II.* New York: Lyons Press, 1995.

McCafferty, W. Patrick. *Aquatic Entomology.* Jones & Bartlett, 1983.

Schwiebert, Ernest. *Nymphs: A Complete Guide to Naturals and Imitations.* New York: Lyons Press, 2001.

INDEX

Y

Books from The Countryman Press
and Backcountry Guides

We offer many more books on hiking, bicycling, canoeing and kayaking, travel, nature, and country living. Our books are available at bookstores and outdoor stores everywhere. For more information or a free catalog, please call 1-800-245-4151, or write to us at The Countryman Press, P.O. Box 748, Woodstock, Vermont 05091. You can find us on the Internet at www.countrymanpress.com